ACKNOWLEDGEMENTS

I am greatly indebted to many people who assisted me with the preparation of this book, and who also encouraged and inspired me. My first thanks must go to the small group of friends whose collective enthusiasm saw this project – and simultaneously the Ulster-Scots Language Society – begin and flourish. Jack McKinney, Ernie Scott, Isobel McCulloch, John McIntyre, John Erskine, Ian Adamson, Will McAvoy, Elspeth Barnes, and many more, have supported, contributed to, read and criticised this work, and most importantly, tolerated the unavoidable compromises I have had to make.

James Fenton, author of *The Hamely Tongue*, deserves a special mention. His native skill in, and understanding of, the spoken language so far outstrips my own that I was genuinely intimidated at the prospect of receiving his response to an early draft. His patient and detailed critique has had a significant effect on the final product. In his own pioneering work, Jim may have discovered how lonely a task it can be to approach the Ulster-Scots tongue in a serious, scholarly and sympathetic way. His friendly help and tolerance was born of a shared respect for the subject, and it has been a major support for me.

To Professor Michael Montgomery, Honorary President of the Forum for Research on the Languages of Scotland and Ulster, I owe another special debt – not only for contributing a foreword, but also for a significant input into the book itself. As an American linguist who has published extensively on the links between Ulster-Scots and southern U.S. speech; as the editor of a Dictionary of Smokey Mountain English (and a participating observer in several Ulster-English and Ulster-Scots dictionary projects); as a regular contributor to *Ullans*; as the co-author with Professor R J Gregg of the chapter on 'The Scots Language in Ulster' in the *History of Scots* (ed. Charles Jones, Edinburgh University Press, 1997); and, most of all, as a distinguished grammarian, he has been a 'silent' collaborator on this project. I use the term 'collaborator' advisedly, for such was the extent of his help. Each year, on his recent annual academic visits to Ulster, Michael has devoted weeks to working – section by section – on already heavily annotated drafts which he had prepared after lengthy hours back home in the USA. His heavy investment of time and expertise to keep me on the 'straight and narrow' is sincerely appreciated. Where I have strayed from the path I have only myself to blame.

Finally, when the draft was in what I had hoped would be its final form, Professor A J Aitken suggested that he would like to see it. Some weeks later I received the first batch of detailed notes, corrections and observations – for me to "make a kirk or a mill o". Naturally, I have attempted to use his suggestions to make both. Professor Aitken is Honorary Preses of the Scots Language Society, a former editor of the multi-volume *Dictionary of the Older Scottish Tongue,* and Honorary Professor of Edinburgh University. His legendary reputation as one of the greatest living lexicographers and the academic father of Scots-language scholarship in the present generation was fully justified when he nurtured the *Concise Ulster Dictionary* (Oxford University Press, 1996) as Editorial Consultant. My own involvement with the *Concise Ulster Dictionary* and subsequent friendship with Jack Aitken have been two of the most rewarding experiences of my academic career. For his generosity and practical help I am deeply grateful.

FOREWORD

A remarkable development in modern-day Western Europe is the revival of many regional cultures and languages. At one level the European Community has sought to consolidate governmental functions and to eliminate traditional national borders. At another, through its Bureau of Lesser Used Languages, the EC has recognised more than forty minority languages and has argued that they deserve preservation, cultivation, and a rightful place in the mosaic of a United Europe. As a result, many of the historic languages of Western Europe have been documented for the first time, even rediscovered by their own speakers, within the last decade.

One of these reawakening languages is Ulster-Scots. Like others, it has a history going back several centuries. Like others, it has been primarily a spoken language used in the home and associated with rural life, factors which have caused it gradually to lose status at the expense of English and have caused its many thousands of speakers often to be unaware of its distinctiveness. Like others, it has rarely been acknowledged in schools or by the media and has been little documented and described outside the rather technical works of linguists (and their work has dealt with only some aspects of the pronunciation and vocabulary of Ulster-Scots).

This book, which provides the first grammatical sketch of Ulster-Scots and which documents much of its history, is a long-needed volume that gives Ulster-Scots its proper place and assists efforts to recognize, revive, and cultivate it. It will be welcomed by linguistic scholars, the Ulster-Scots community of speakers, and indeed all with an interest in the languages and historic cultures of Ireland. As the most detailed and accessible account of the variety of Scots spoken in Ulster for four hundred years, it gives specialists and non-specialists alike a richer, fuller, and more accurate understanding of the linguistic diversity of the island.

This volume is a scholarly triumph both in what it achieves and in what it makes possible for others to achieve. Philip Robinson has invested a tremendous amount of historical and literary research in it, drawing on a wide range of documents and publications from the past four hundred years that he found in manuscript libraries, dusty microfilms, and local archives. Many of these are either unpublished or were previously unknown to scholars, relegated to obscurity because of the continuing decline in status by Ulster-Scots since the early seventeenth century. The marginalization of Ulster-Scots for social and political reasons has led many modern-day linguists who did not know its history (and did not have access to a book like the present one) to consider it a variety of Hiberno-English rather than Scots (as it is more properly classified), and it has led many Ulster-Scots to consider their native speech to be "bad English," as schools have often – and erroneously – asserted that it was.

Thus, although the author goes to considerable lengths to stress the preliminary nature of his account and although he does not address the matter directly, his work provides by far the best basis for establishing how closely Ulster-Scots is related to other language varieties in Ireland and elsewhere. It will be used by scholars in the British Isles wishing to compare Ulster-Scots to Scots and English and to assess its influences from and on English and Irish Gaelic in Ireland. It will be mined by scholars in North America and elsewhere to determine the influence of Ulster-Scots on colonial varieties of English. It is grammatical patterns which are most crucial in such efforts; they are "deeper" in a language's structure and less likely to change than sounds and vocabulary terms. The latter are the smaller and more superficial units of language traditionally studied by linguists. Though it is largely a sketch of contemporary Ulster-Scots and some of its features likely have changed in the past two centuries, this grammatical sketch features numerous forms and patterns that American scholars can relate to their own varieties across the Atlantic, especially those in the southern United States. As a treatment that is necessarily broad rather than deep, it should inspire linguists to undertake much research of their own.

The book in many ways opens the door to further study and exploration on topics such as regional variation and historical change in Ulster-Scots. It is to be hoped that its appearance will prompt Ulster-Scots speakers from different parts of the historic province to compare their usage, to become collectors, to recall and record terms from their experience, to study their native speech on a more formal basis, and perhaps even to become trained linguists themselves.

This volume often draws illustrative examples from the Rhyming Weavers, rural poets of the late-18th and early-19th century, but it is primarily an account of modern-day spoken Ulster-Scots. Most of the author's material comes from patient, careful observation and reflection. One must appreciate the challenges he has faced in composing a grammar without having such things to draw on as a consensus on how to spell the language, a single standard variety to restrict himself to, or information on how current and widespread many of the patterns he discusses are. He weighs these considerations carefully and finds it necessary in some cases to introduce special notations and conventions that are explained and justified early in the book. Still, the author is aware that some speakers of Ulster-Scots will disagree with some details of his presentation. This may reflect variation in the language or, just as likely, differences of opinion about how a spoken language should be rendered into written form. Debate about such matters is healthy and is encouraged by the author. It must be remembered that this book is not a "grammar" in the sense that it is complete or that it seeks to dictate how Ulster-Scots should be used. It is not a guide to "correct" Ulster-Scots but a partial description of the language as it is, and as it has been. As the process of reviving Ulster-Scots makes progress, this grammar seeks a role – and it will surely have a major one – in the development of a generally accepted written form of the language.

The book is admirable for its accessibility. Any chapter or section can be read without reviewing earlier material except that readers will want to study chapter one on the spelling and pronunciation of Ulster-Scots before proceeding. This will greatly facilitate the reading of the hundreds of examples in the text (surely one of the book's most attractive features) and in particular the reading of them aloud, a process which will bring familiar sounds to many readers who may never before have seen a word of Ulster-Scots in print. Also, the terminology used in the book makes it greatly accessible to the non-scholar. Much of this will be familiar to readers from their school days, but all of it is in any case explained by the author as new topics are introduced.

For linguists, one important result of works like this one on Ulster-Scots is the necessity to revise traditional accounts of European languages, as more becomes known of the history of various minority languages. Modern-day textbooks and language histories are written largely from the perspectives of national capitals and the "standard" varieties that have become synonymous with national languages like English. Heretofore, linguistic surveys of the British Isles have rarely acknowledged the existence of Ulster-Scots. With the publication of this volume (along with James Fenton's *The Hamely Tongue*), this will change. And speakers of Ulster-Scots themselves will have a reference work to which they can turn for information on their own language. They and many in the scholarly community will truly be indebted to Philip Robinson.

Professor Michael B Montgomery
Department of English
University of South Carolina

CONTENTS

INTRODUCTION

This book has been written for two reasons. In the first place, the grammar of the Ulster-Scots language stands in need of popular exposition. And, secondly, there is an urgent need for a reference text for those who wish to study, learn or teach Ulster-Scots.

Ulster-Scots, as it is spoken today, is a language capable of expressing the full range of emotions and topics. However, it is difficult for outsiders to hear it in its full, 'braid' form and equally difficult for speakers to express it in written form. It deserves recognition as a language subject in its own right, from which base it is hoped that proper studies may be developed of its linguistic origins, its development, its place within the Ulster-Scots community, its literature, its contribution to the linguistic diversity of Ulster, and its influence both upon and from English and Gaelic.

0.1 The Ulster-Scots language today

Ulster-Scots or 'Ullans' is a close relative of the language called Scots. The Scots language in Scotland is sometimes called 'Lallans', from 'Lowland Scots'. The 1787 Belfast edition of Robert Burns's *Poems* (his first edition was published in Kilmarnock in 1786) had a glossary which defined the word *Lallans* as 'the Lowland Scotch tongue'. Ulster-Scots, however, is usually known to its native speakers as 'Scotch' or 'Braid Scotch'. Despite the existence of a rich literary tradition extending back for centuries, Ulster-Scots is today a highly stigmatised language which many speakers are reluctant to use either in public situations or in 'educated' company. The absence of any recognition of the language in formal education has virtually obliterated the literary tradition, and nowadays very few native speakers are also competent in the written language. Furthermore, native speakers increasingly abandon the spoken language as they pursue education and careers. Popular awareness of its eroded status and of the differences with Lowland Scots often elicits the description 'broken Scotch'.

Ulster-Scots is a west Germanic language which is derived from, and has its closest linguistic parallels with, Lowland Scots or Lallans. Indeed, Ulster-Scots has been described as a 'variant' of Scots, and as such has been accommodated within the coverage of the *Scottish National Dictionary* programme. However, many Scots language academics have observed that Ulster-Scots differs from its sister tongue: Ulster-Scots has its own range of dialects, along with its own distinctive literary tradition, vocabulary, and grammar; all of which differ in some respects from Lallans. In simple terms, the relationship between Ulster-Scots and Lallans could be compared to the relative positions of Irish and Scottish Gaelic.

The Scots language itself, at times indistinguishable in literary form from Ulster-

Scots, is derived from Old Northumbrian or northern forms of Anglo-Saxon. The Anglian dialects north of the Humber had become differentiated from the Anglo-Saxon dialects of other parts of southern Britain by the Viking period beginning in the late 8th century. These differences were accentuated by Old Norse influence when at its height in the Danelaw of north Britain. Following the stabilisation of the Scottish Border in the 13th century, Scots became a distinctive, national language of government and literature, spreading from a core area between the Tweed and the Forth, before establishing itself finally in Ulster during the early 1600s.

It has been estimated, in the absence of census data, that around 100,000 people in the Ulster-Scots areas are capable of speaking both Ulster-English and Ulster-Scots.[1] Many more people might claim some knowledge of the language, or wish to identify with the language and culture, but perhaps as few as 15,000 people are monoglot ('one language') speakers who use Ulster-Scots all the time regardless of social context. The number of people with literary competence in the language is now very small and, furthermore, those that do read and write Ullans tend not to be the monoglot speakers. The vernacular language has been retreating for some years to the advantage of Ulster-English (that is, what are called the Mid-Ulster dialects of Hiberno-English) and, of course, it has been subject to erosion by the spread of urban speech and of 'Standard English'. Thirty years ago the late Brendan Adams, Dialect Archivist at the Ulster Folk Museum, estimated that there were then about 170,000 Ulster-Scots speakers in those areas where 'Ulster-Scots has survived as the rural speech'.[2] Adams also claimed that virtually all speakers of Ulster-Scots were 'bi-dialectal, using the regional form of Standard English as an alternative ... according to their audience'.

The 'core areas' of Ulster-Scots survival were mapped by Professor R J Gregg in the

---

[1]This estimate by the Ulster-Scots Language Society [*Ullans*, Vol. 2 (1994), p. 56] represents less than 30% of the total population in the Ulster-Scots speaking areas (see Figure 1). As a proportion, this seems conservative compared to the findings of recent surveys conducted in Scotland by the General Register Office. Professor A J Aitken has provided the following extract from his entry on *Scots* in the forthcoming *Encyclopedia of European Languages*:

> "The general Register Office for Scotland did commission several surveys into the viability of such a [language census] question, one outcome of which was that about 30% of respondents said they could speak Scots. In 1995, a separate investigation had arrived at a much higher proportion, 255 of the 450 persons interviewed, or 57%, who claimed to speak Scots. These surveys, of course, report only respondents' self-estimates, without addressing the question of what degree of Scottishness of usage constitutes 'speaking Scots'. This question will, however, be targeted in a project under way at the University of Aberdeen."

Dr Steve Murdoch, of the University of Aberdeen, wrote (partly in defence of Ulster-Scots) to the Spring 1997 issue of *Causeway*, concerning some of his findings:

> "...the British Government has published its own figure for the first time on the number of people believed to be Scots speaking – 1.5 million. My own findings give about 2.1 million. An unprecedented government/official definition of the Scots language is stated, and the strongest Scots speaking areas are identified ... there is a continuum of speech type in the Scottish population ranging from clearly English to clearly Scots. Many people's speech can be clearly assigned by researchers as predominantly stemming from one or other of the two languages. ... At one point in their survey the civil servants were confronted with monoglot Scots speakers that had to have English translated into Scots for them and their answers translated from Scots to English for the interviewers."

[2]G B Adams, 'A Brief History of Ulster-Scots'. Unpublished Typescript, Ulster Dialect Archive, Ulster Folk and Transport Museum.

1960s and his findings published in 1972.[3] His work confirms that north, mid and south-east Antrim, north-east Londonderry, north-east Down, and east Donegal represent the heartland of the language (see figure 1). Elsewhere in Ulster the vernacular tongue, although markedly influenced by Scots, is arguably closer to the English dialects of north-west England than to the Scots of west and south-west Scotland.

The Ulster-Scots Language Society was formed in 1992 to 'encourage an interest in traditional Ulster-Scots literature, whether it be prose, poetry or drama; to support the use of the Ulster-Scots tongue in present-day speech and education; and to encourage the Ulster-Scots tradition in music, dance, song, ballads and story-telling.' According to its published aims the Society wishes to 're-establish the dignity of Ulster-Scots as a language with an important part to play in our cultural heritage'. It publishes the magazine *Ullans*, and the news letter *Kintra Sennicht*.

Recognising the parallel situation of Frisian as another language once stigmatised as 'vulgar dialect' in the Netherlands but now recognised as a historical tongue, the USLS decided in 1993 to establish an Ulster-Scots Academy, on the model of the Frisian Academy. It is under the auspices of the Ulster-Scots Academy that this grammar has been published, following the publication in 1995 of James Fenton's dictionary of Ulster-Scots in County Antrim – *The Hamely Tongue* (Ulster-Scots Academic Press). Over the last 50 years, since its foundation, the Frisian Academy has published grammars, translated classics, compiled dictionaries of Old and Modern Frisian, produced teaching resources and a Frisian Bible, and supported an energetic programme of scientific and popular publications, including newspapers, magazines and children's materials. Increasingly, Frisian is used in public and school life, although its lower status in relation to Dutch was reflected in a recent survey which revealed that still only about 12% of native Frisian speakers in Friesland can read and write in Frisian. Frisian is, however, now used alongside Dutch in most Friesland primary schools. The future development of the Scots language in Scotland and Ulster may well follow a similar pattern, now that both tongues have been given international recognition through their adoption by the European Bureau of Lesser-Used Languages.

0.2 The history of Ulster-Scots: background, origins and development

For 1000 years, almost since the watershed between the prehistoric and historic eras, Germanic, Celtic and Romance languages have interfaced around the land fringe of the Irish Sea Basin. Ulster-Scots is one of the direct descendants of the west Germanic element as far as north-east Ireland is concerned.

The earliest uses of west and north Germanic languages among the people of east Ulster are obscure. At the end of the prehistoric period, during the 4th and 5th centuries, the inhabitants of east Ulster (the Ulaid) had been a linguistic and ethnic confederacy, but were wholly Gaelic speaking by the 7th century. Some late 19th century historians asserted that Frisians had settled not only on the east coast of Scotland in the 4th and 5th centuries (the firth of Forth was known as the 'Frisian Sea'), but that

---

[3]R J Gregg, 'The Scotch-Irish Dialect Boundaries in Ulster', in M F Wakelin, ed., *Patterns in the Folk Speech of the British Isles* (London, 1972), 109–39.

they had also travelled around the north of Scotland and established settlements near Dumfries (supposedly the 'Fort of the Frisians') in south west Scotland. However, this interpretation is now rejected by Celtic scholars, and along with it the assumption that they had settled at the same time on the Co Down coast (for example at Ballyferris). There is some evidence that the Anglian and Northumbrian (Old English or 'Anglo-Saxon') Early Christian settlements of the 9th and 10th centuries around Whithorn in south-west Scotland were in contact with the Ulaid, but we cannot be sure of any significant or lasting effect.

The earliest conclusive evidence for the extensive use of forms of a Germanic language by people living in east Ulster comes during the period following the Viking raids of the 8th century. During the period between 850 and 1200 AD an extensive body of personal name, place name, archaeological and documentary evidence confirms an Old Norse linguistic presence. Of course, this Germanic influence interfaced with Gaelic (and probably intermixed with it). However, a tenuous Germanic linguistic presence remained in parts of east Ulster up to the time of the Norman settlements of the Middle Ages, when influences from Latin, Norman-French and northern Middle English (including Older Scots) were introduced.

The end of the 14th century witnessed a late-medieval Gaelicisation of the ruling class, and the re-establishment of Gaelic as the vernacular tongue in many parts of east Ulster. Throughout this period, however, the local forms of Middle English continued to be the vernacular language in reduced areas of south-east Antrim and east Down. So it is that Ulster-Scots in east Ulster may trace some of its earliest Germanic linguistic precedents to Old Norse in the 8th to 10th centuries, rather than to Old English or Anglian of the 6th to 7th centuries, as is the case with Lallans in Scotland.

From the late 1500s, vanguard 'plantations' of immigrants from western Scotland to north Antrim, and from northern England to Down, heralded an enormous movement of lowland Scots across east and north Ulster during the 17th century. These settlers brought their language with them, and Ulster-Scots, as spoken today, is dominated by the Scots forms introduced during this Plantation period. At that time in Scotland, Scots was taught as a written language, quite distinct from English, and used for legal and business purposes. Consequently, a considerable body of Ulster-Scots documentary material survives from the early decades of the 1600s.

From about 1650 onwards in Ulster, Scots written forms were generally discarded in favour of English and the language survived only in spoken form until the literary revival of the late 18th century. During this period and throughout the first decades of the 19th century scores of Ulster-Scots vernacular poets – some of them preceding Robert Burns – published volumes of their works. This later written language, however, was 'intentional', or selfconscious Scots, and differed considerably in its orthography from the unselfconscious Scots forms of the 17th century.

The language survives today largely as a spoken tongue, widely perceived as 'ignorant dialect' even by many Ulster-Scots themselves. It remains the preserve of 'performances' in recitations, local drama, poetry, song, etc for many bilingual speakers, and it is notoriously difficult for professionals and academics to elicit. Most Ulster-Scots today have some difficulty with the 'braid Scotch' literature of the 18th century, partly because of the erosion of vocabulary, and partly because of loss of contact with the poetic tradition. However, most can manage easily the written dialogue of the 'kail-yard' novels which became a literary fashion from about 1850 and which continued until the 1950s.

0.3   Ulster-Scots: vocabulary, grammar and syntax

Despite a history of long-standing and widespread use, almost nothing exists in print to describe the structure of the Ulster-Scots language. It has been allowed to become one of the most stigmatised and culturally marginalised lesser-used languages of Europe. The only aspects of Ulster-Scots which have been subject to scholarly attention until recent times are its vocabulary and, to a lesser extent, its pronunciation. Linguistic studies making mention of Ulster-Scots have been conducted almost exclusively by academics with an English language specialism and from an English language perspective.[4] Indeed, with very few exceptions, these scholars have not been themselves speakers of Ulster-Scots and their consequent 'dialectal' approach to Ulster-Scots may have increased, rather than decreased, its marginalisation. Even within the field of lexical studies, for example, the available dictionaries have considerable limitations. With the exception of James Fenton's *The Hamely Tongue*,[5] dictionaries of Scots and Ulster-Scots are restricted in their value in that they fail to provide the total vocabulary of the modern language (including words and meanings shared with English). Furthermore, as they provide only the English meanings for non-standard English or 'dialect' Ulster words (and none of the reverse English-to-Ulster-Scots meanings), we have no way of discovering how an Ulster-Scots speaker would express a particular English word. For example, we cannot look up 'material' and discover that the Ulster-Scots equivalent is *stuff*. Indeed we cannot even look up the word *stuff* in any of the Scots or Ulster 'dialect' dictionaries since the word (with this sense) happens to be shared with English. In contrast, we may look up 'material' in an English-Norse dictionary to find *stoff*, or even in an English-Dutch dictionary to find *stof*.

All languages differ from each other in grammar and syntax just as they do in vocabulary. Unfortunately for the reputation of Ulster-Scots as a language in its own right, most of its creative writers (that is, those writers who have deliberately attempted to write in Ulster-Scots) have tended to concentrate on including pronunciation-spellings or distinctive 'dialect' words in their work, at the expense of using distinctive grammatical or syntactic features. This is particularly true of the Ulster-Scots poets who, since the 1700s, have consciously written verse with a fuller Ulster-Scots vocabulary than later writers, while at the same time preferring English rules of

---

[4]In Scotland, numerous scholarly studies of detailed aspects of Scots grammar have been published in recent decades. These have appeared mostly in academic rather than popular publications, and comprehensive overviews of Scots grammar are less numerous. Indeed, most books dealing with Scots grammar were published before 1930;

J Murray, *The Dialect of the Southern Counties of Scotland* (London, 1873).

J Wilson, *Lowland Scotch as Spoken in the Lower Strathearn District of Perthshire* (Oxford, 1915).

W Grant and J M Dixon, *Manual of Modern Scots* (Cambridge, 1921).

W Grant, ed. 'Introduction' Vol I, *The Scottish National Dictionary* (Edinburgh, 1929).

T A Robertson and J J Graham, *Grammar and Usage of the Shetland Dialect* (Lerwick, 1991).

D Purves, *Grammar and Usage of Scots* (Forthcoming).

[5]James Fenton, *The Hamley Tongue: a personal record of Ulster-Scots in County Antrim* (Ulster-Scots Academic Press, 1995).

grammar and sentence construction. So it is that <u>written</u> Ulster-Scots differs significantly from the <u>spoken</u>, vernacular language which has its own peculiar grammar. Ulster-Scots grammar, therefore, cannot be studied from the written texts alone, for the grammatical evidence in the corpus of literature is scant. An intimate knowledge of the spoken tongue is also required.

The vocabulary, or the range of words used by the speakers of a language, can provide only a partial view of that language. No-one can properly learn a language by reference to a dictionary alone. *Syntax* – or the rules of combining, structuring and modifying words into meaningful sentences – is the essence of any language. If Ulster-Scots speakers were to employ only Standard English syntax when articulating 'dialect' words, then we would not be describing a 'language'. However, it is important to note the relationship between Ulster-Scots and English both in vocabulary and in grammar. Some words are shared by both languages and so are some grammatical rules. More importantly, however, it is also true that not all the words and not all the grammatical rules of every-day English are used in Ulster-Scots.

The point that Ulster-Scots speakers employ their own distinctive range of words but without a <u>full</u> English vocabulary is not often appreciated. 'Partly-corrected' Ulster-Scots, that is, Ulster-Scots modified by Standard English, is a fact of life as each generation witnesses the erosion of its distinctive vocabulary by Standard English. 'Meat' (full Ulster-Scots form *mait* or *mate*) was, in the recent past, preferred to the alternative English word 'food'; 'over' (full Ulster-Scots form *owre*) is often used instead of English 'too', as in 'the cost wasn't over dear'; 'corn' (full Ulster-Scots form *coarn*) is still preferred to 'oats'; 'maybe' (full Ulster-Scots form *aiblins*) is preferred to 'perhaps'; 'folk' (full Ulster-Scots form *fowk*) is preferred to 'people'; and 'sore head' (full Ulster-Scots form *sair heid*) is preferred to 'headache'. In trying to establish what is 'good' and what is 'bad' Ulster-Scots, it might be better to regard *sore head* as more acceptable Ulster-Scots than an artificial construction like *heidache*; *over* as better than 'too' spelt artificially as *tae*; *corn* as better than 'oats' spelt as *aits*; and similarly to regard *meat* as better than 'food' spelt as *fud* or *fuid*. Ulster-Scots speech is also characterised by understatement, so that *wairm* ('warm') tends to be used rather than *het* ('hot') and *cuil* 'cool' rather than *coul* ('cold'), for example in the frequently-heard observation *cuil day theday* (when 'cold day today' is meant). A scathing critique of some pretentious individual is not likely to be lengthy – probably no more than "*thon's a boy!*" ('he's a rare one').

It is inevitable that any 'grammar' of Ulster-Scots will focus on those features of the language which differ most from Standard English grammar. However, just as some 'non-standard English' words may be shared between Ulster-Scots and some English dialects, so too it is with grammar: some of the grammatical features which differ from those of Standard English, and which are noted in this book, may also be shared with English colloquial or dialectal speech, or even by speakers of some dialects of American English. It is well beyond the scope of this work to draw grammatical comparisons with dialects or languages other than Standard English. So, whenever 'English' is referred to hereafter, it can be taken to mean Standard (and usually, 'literary') English. When Ulster-Scots pronunciation is compared to 'English', this should, however, be taken to mean Standard English as spoken in Ulster. No claims are made that the grammatical features described here are unique to Ulster-Scots, for even the precise parallels with Scottish-Scots grammar are still relatively unknown.

Grammar and Syntax

Grammar and syntax, the main focus of this book, constitute the system of rules which speakers of any language use to produce, arrange and modify the words in their vocabulary in order to express themselves meaningfully. A *prescriptive* grammar book presents these rules in order to demonstrate how one ought to speak or write, and so provides a standard for the language. This grammar is not intended to be a prescriptive one, but rather it is a *descriptive* grammar, providing an externalised description of one speaker's perceptions of the language (although confirmed and substantiated in parts by others).

Unavoidably, this study is mostly introspective, for it is based on the author's own understanding of the Ulster-Scots tongue, an understanding formed by his upbringing, socially and geographically, just inside the periphery of the Ulster-Scots community in east Antrim. However, this 'native' understanding has been coloured by years of historical research involving familiarity with many early Ulster-Scots documents, and more recently, with a detailed exploration of 18th and 19th century Ulster-Scots literature.

0.4 Ulster-Scots: documentation and sources

On investigation, the range of published sources and documentary archives for Ulster-Scots is remarkably extensive and diverse. Writing in Ulster-Scots was sometimes produced unselfconsciously as part of the author's usual form of literacy. Otherwise, Ulster-Scots was selfconsciously (that is, deliberately) written to be different from the 'normal' literacy of the author.

'Unselfconscious' Ulster-Scots literature

Unselfconscious writings are of two sorts: those in which the writer has been schooled in Scots and writes Scots naturally (for Ulster this period lasted only a short time); and secondly those in which the every-day, schooled English literacy of the writer contains significant incidental elements of Ulster-Scots linguistic interest. Writings of this second type normally display considerable differences from contemporary Standard English although the writer has not deliberately introduced such features. The vast majority of this documentation is 'naive', for although the intention of the writer is to write in 'English', Ulster-Scots features are incorporated in spite of the 'education' of the author. The study of such a corpus involves a process of selective linguistic archaeology, and the documents must be carefully scrutinised and 'quarried' for Ulster-Scots linguistic information.

Early Medieval (Pre-Plantation) sources

Only a few scraps of 'Old Norse' runic writings survive from the Viking period in east Ulster, most notably a runic inscription on an abbot's grave slab at Nendrum, Co Down. However, numerous Old Norse elements survive in the place names of east Antrim and east Down, indicating the possibility of an Old Norse sub-structure to the Germanic linguistic tradition in east Ulster. Some of these place names, such as Olderfleet, Sketrick and Strangford, survive from our later medieval documentation.

From the early Christian period throughout the 'early Medieval' period the surviving documents in Ulster are mostly in Latin, with some bits and pieces in Medieval Norman-French, Gaelic, and Middle English. Sparse though it is, the documentation in Middle English provides Ulster-Scots with its next archaeological layer. The peculiarities of Ulster Middle English require specialist research, but it is apparent that the 'English' fragments among the 14th and 15th century correspondence of the Archbishops of Armagh, along with the records of medieval abbeys, manors and boroughs (such as Carrickfergus), contain some features which survive in later Ulster-Scots. Surveys, such as the Papal Taxation of 1306, reveal scores of Middle English townland place names in east Ulster that were subsequently Gaelicized in the 15th and 16th centuries.

With the influx of Lowland Scots in the late 1500s and early 1600s came not only our first substantial Ulster-Scots documentation but also the beginning of the corpus of Ulster-Scots literature.

The Plantation record

From the end of the Medieval period (about 1550) until about 1650, state and official writings were no longer written only in Latin or Middle English, but increasingly in more recognisable forms of Early Modern English. The quantity of other documentation from this period – in the form of letters, wills, legal agreements and surveys – is enormous. From the Ulster-Scots perspective it falls into two groups: the 'English' record of English settlers; and the 'Scots' record of Scottish settlers.

In the first group, the 'English' documentation of this period is of only passing interest, although it is clear that some Middle English forms and some contemporary English dialectal features which survive in Ulster-Scots can be illustrated from these records.

From this same period, however, we have a significant corpus of Scots writings in Ulster. Before this time Scots had become the state language of Scotland, and it was in the medium of Scots that literacy was taught in Scotland. Even some Ulster letters of the late 1500s (before the Plantation) were written in Scots. It is hardly surprising, therefore, that most of the Scots settlers had had their education in Scots, although they arrived after the Union of the Crowns under James VI of Scotland. James VI became James I of England and Scotland in 1603, an event which itself diminished the status of literary Scots.

So it is that the Ulster-based body of Older Scots writings from this period forms the first full Ulster-Scots literary corpus. The linguistic information from this corpus is not simply to be 'quarried' from among the English material but is, in essence, Ulster-Scots. This distinction, although important, is nevertheless one of degree, for these Ulster-Scots texts, like all Scots writings of the 16th and 17th centuries, were becoming increasingly Anglicized, with English and Scots forms often being used interchangeably. There can be no doubt that the King James Bible of 1611, in conjunction with a preference for English as the language used by Church and State, encouraged the perception of written Scots as 'inferior' to its closely related sibling tongue, English.

Second generation Scots settlers in Ulster were taught literacy not in Scots but in English, so that the period of full, written Scots (as a schooled literary language) was relatively short. Subsequent full Ulster-Scots writings are therefore the product of those whose literary skills had been schooled in English but who then made various attempts to articulate their spoken language, deliberately and consciously, in a 'Scotch' style.

Eighteenth and nineteenth century letters and minute books

Within the continuing unselfconscious written record of Ulster-Scots in the later years, the most productive documents (from a linguistic perspective) are the letters and other writings of those individuals whose 'education' had been least successful. These records were not intended by their writers to represent the Scots tongue, but the English written 'standards' of the day. The most interesting, from an Ulster-Scots perspective, are the informal, naive letters of the marginally literate. However, even those letters written by well-educated people can be surprisingly rich in Ulster-Scots grammatical features. American research on Ulster immigrant letters has already revealed much of linguistic interest. Some features of letter-writing follow very conservative formulas, such as the opening and closing sentences: the writers, presumably, copied the style and forms they read or heard themselves, and so 'archaic' literary forms could survive over a long period.

The same is true for official minutes and records of meetings. In the late 1500s, the official records of Carrickfergus Corporation still used a formula such as 'At a meeting houlden in le session-house de Knockfergus', revealing the persistence of Norman-French features in the written record centuries after they might be expected to have disappeared. Similarly, Presbyterian Kirk Session books frequently used Scots orthographic forms such as *qlk. (quhilk)* for 'which' well into the 18th century – many years after 'educated' scribes would have been taught these forms.

'Selfconscious' Ulster-Scots literature

The only 'full' Ulster-Scots written record that is a product of schooling in Scots literacy belongs to the 1550-1650 period. However, Scots communities for the next 300 years were aware that their spoken Scots was a different language from that of the written English which pervaded all contacts with the State, Church and College.

The renaissance of a literature in Scots, both in Scotland and Ulster, was wrought by people whose first <u>written</u> language was English. However, the works of Ramsay, Fergusson and Burns were widely read in Ulster as well as in Scotland, with early Belfast editions appearing almost simultaneously with those in Scotland. The Scots literary tradition of Scotland was integral to the Ulster-Scots literary tradition, while Ulster-Scots writers contributed significantly to this broader Scots renaissance in their own right.

Ulster-Scots poetry

Vernacular poetry, using mostly English syntax and sentence construction, was the literary medium for this renaissance which began about 1720. Ulster-Scots poets were publishing their 'Scotch' poems and songs contemporaneously with Ramsay, well before Robert Burns was born. For the next 150 years, embracing the 'Burns' period of the late 1700s and early 1800s, scores of Ulster-Scots poets published separate volumes of their works. Most of this corpus is inaccessible today to all but the most determined students, for only a handful of the tens of thousands of individual poems and songs in full Ulster-Scots have been republished in this century.

The literary language of this Ulster-Scots corpus differs significantly from the unselfconscious Ulster-Scots writings of the early 1600s. Most of the Older Scots orthographic forms had been abandoned (or forgotten), but the wealth of Ulster-Scots vocabulary was revealed for the first time. Many of the words used are clearly archaic yet they are not always to be found in the formal writings of the Plantation period because of the different nature of these two types of sources.

The kail-yard novels

From about 1830, popular taste in Scots literature began to turn from poetry to prose, largely as a consequence of the success of Sir Walter Scott's novels. In Ulster, as in Scotland, many stories and novels were written with English connecting prose, but with at least some, if not all, of the dialogue in Scots. Many were serialised in local newspapers such as the *Newtownards Chronicle* and the *Ballymena Observer*. However, only a fraction of the serialised novels in local newspapers were republished later in book form. Ulster-Scots novels were not generally written in full Ulster-Scots, but belong instead to a broader 'English' literary tradition. However, the Ulster-Scots linguistic content of these works should not be underestimated, nor should the extent of their more general historical and cultural significance.

Full prose Ulster-Scots books, newspaper stories and 'letters'

All full Ulster-Scots prose – even 'letters to the press' in Ulster-Scots – were consciously written as 'dialect', 'doric' or 'Scotch' by people who were very articulate in literary English. It was common for well-educated Ulster-Scots – including many of the newspaper editors, publishers and booksellers themselves – to adopt a 'country' pseudonym and contribute all sorts of features in full Ulster-Scots prose style, as if it "wes jist writ doon the road A spakes". In a sense, all this material is 'spoof', and it can be embarrassingly awful. It often had linguistic content of considerable interest to us in the late 18th and early 19th centuries, although by 1900 it had become generally stereotyped and linguistically degenerate. Whether for better or worse, this material is an important part of the full Ulster-Scots corpus.

Some writers of this genre such as W G Lyttle in Co Down and Archibald McIlroy in Co Antrim produced not only small newspaper features but also complete books in full Ulster-Scots prose. These works must be distinguished from the kail-yard novels, where only the dialogue is in Ulster-Scots, for this prose also belongs to the core corpus of full Ulster-Scots literature.

· · · · ·

Ulster-Scots literature, as a tradition in its own right, has survived some 400 years of schooling Ulster-Scots speakers exclusively in English language and literacy. The

only form of learning about writing in Ulster-Scots available to Ulster-Scots speakers has been the reading of Scots and Ulster-Scots writings outside of school. It is
hardly surprising, therefore, that the Ulster-Scots literary tradition has become less
competent and less self-confident, partly because of the erosion of the spoken language and partly because of the increasing ignorance of earlier works in Scots and
Ulster-Scots. In the absence of widely-available and widely-read Ulster-Scots and
Scots literature, the 'self-education' process for the Ulster-Scots community is no
longer adequate to ensure the continuity of this tradition.

Despite the richness of the Ulster-Scots literary tradition when it is uncovered, it cannot be used alone (or even predominantly) to reconstruct Ulster-Scots grammar. To
undertake the latter, a disproportionate emphasis must be placed on what students of
the language can observe of their own native speech. Normally it is the literature of
a language which authenticates grammar through the visible evidence of its written
record. Yet for Ulster-Scots this documentary evidence reveals a mixture of Scots
and English which, for reasons discussed above, must be sifted carefully. Students
must constantly set what can be discovered about the written structure of the
language against what they know of the spoken tongue. Generations of writers
attempting to write in Ulster-Scots have been unable to eradicate the influence of
their schooling in 'correct' English grammar.

The extent to which the description of Ulster-Scots grammar which follows is personal and inward-looking will inevitably make it unsatisfactory for those with a different experience and understanding of the language. Hopefully, however, it will
provide a beginning on which others may build. It has been written by an Ulster-Scot,
not by a linguist. It will prove worthwhile only if it enables other Ulster-Scots to
express themselves more confidently and more effectively in their native leid. It will
prove successful only if it acts as a catalyst for a more academic study of the Ulster-
Scots language.

0.5 Retrospect

The only type of Ulster-Scots literature which is reasonably well-known today is the
poetry of 200 years ago. However, these poems often seem like imitation Scots
because of the frequent use of words such as *sic* ('such'), *gif* ('if'), and *unco* ('very').
Although most people would instantly recognise these as Scots words, they are not
used in Ulster-Scots speech today. Many people assume that, therefore, they were
used only by Burns imitators as a literary device, and were not part of the poets'
everyday speech. Yet, these same weaver poets always protested that the language
they used was their own native tongue – and were often offended by suggestions
that it was artificial Scotch.

There is no doubt that the vocabulary – and presumably also the grammar – of
Ulster-Scots has gradually become less distinctive. As each generation passes,
slowly but surely, the proportion of uniquely Scots words that makes up Ulster-Scots
speech has been declining and contracting. The discovery of 'archaic' words in the
literary tradition can give some clue to the rate of decline in any one particular
area. Take, for example, the Ballycarry area of east Antrim. Today this district (the
home territory of the author) is on the edge of the Ulster-Scots speaking area, and
fewer and fewer people there speak the tongue of their ancestors. The Ordnance

Survey Memoirs for this parish (Templecorran) in the 1830s stated of the local population:

> "Their accent idioms and phraseology are strictly and disagreeably
> Scottish partaking only of the broad and coarse accent and dialect of
> the Southern Counties of Scotland."

A generation earlier, the most celebrated of all the Ulster-Scots poets (James Orr, the 'Bard of Ballycarry', 1777-1816), was using his Ulster-Scots tongue to dramatic effect. Orr displayed a confidence in his Scots tongue that characterised the renaissance of Scots vernacular writing in the Burns era. His poetry contains many words which would not be used in or around Ballycarry today. Nevertheless, although it can be demonstrated that these words were indeed part of his own local vocabulary, it is the repeated use of words such as *ilka, unco, gif* and *sic* by Orr (and also by almost all of his contemporary Ulster-Scots poets), that appear most 'artificial' to the modern eye. Some examples of the use of *gif* ('if') from Orr's work of 200 years ago give a good impression of how common this single feature was:

> *I ledge we'd fen gif fairly quat o*
> *we'd lieve, gif they wha bake cud brew thee*
> *Losh! 'twad be fine gif ilka youth ay*
> *gif thou'd withdraw for ae camping*
> *but, conscience! gif the auld delft nipple*
> *gif she wham ye court were like ane I'll no name*
> *gif Chanticliers ta'en frae the roost whare he craw't*
> *gif folk becam' obligin', atween an' day*
> *gif folk like you, think something o' me*
> *an' gif they notice us*
> *atween an May, gif bowls row right*
> *gif ye had pass'd his door, ye'd either heard*
> *gif that's na done, whate'er ilk loun.*

Orr, of course, was not alone among the Ulster-Scots poets in his regular use of *gif, unco, ilk, sic* etc. However, the question is, were these words part of Ballycarry speech in the late 1790s? Fortunately, we can go back yet another 200 years to find Ulster-Scots letters from the same district. Isobel Haldane, wife of Archibald Edmonstone at Ballycarry, wrote a number of letters in her only tongue – Scots – in the early 1600s. Like other contemporary Ulster-Scots documents, her letters reveal that words like *gif, unco, sic, ilka* etc were in regular use – and in a context where their use in speech must also be assumed. Some examples of Isobel Haldane's use of *gif circa* 1630 (at Ballycarry) include:

> *Ye will wrestle with it, ye say, giff I will*
> *And giff my outward actions hes nocht bein ansuerable*
> *It mycht be sa, bot to you, giff it was sa, it was far be my dessing*
> *Giff God hes nocht giffin me ane warldly wyse hairt*
> *Quhatever I be, giff it had bein Gods will I wald ye had the hairt to me*
> *I that man spend suld have keipit house to us all giff I war able*
> *and giff I wad nocht in everything doon as ye thocht fitt*
> *and giff myne be best*

and giff it was wrang
bot giff ye think your credit canocht stand without hingins.

The purpose of this book is not to describe the last remnants of a fast-disappearing tongue, but to attempt some sort of retrospective reconstruction which is based on both the literary record and the modern spoken forms. No 'lesser-used' language revival movement can re-introduce older words or grammatical forms without criticism – especially if these new forms are unknown to native speakers. With Ulster-Scots, it is not enough to show that such innovations are used in Scottish-Scots, or that they were used in Scots literature. In this book, 'archaic' forms (which are no longer in current use by native speakers) are identified as such in the text or in the glossary. Great care has been taken, nevertheless, to use only archaic forms that are well attested in the Ulster-Scots literary record.

It would be hard to imagine nowadays a notice in the *Belfast Newsletter* similar to one which appeared in that paper in 1756 – when a runaway apprentice from Newtownards in north Down was described as recognisable outside his home area because he "speaks the Scotch tongue". In 1777, the *Hibernian Magazine* said of Newtownards: "The language spoken here is a broad Scotch hardly to be understood by strangers." Similarly, the Ordnance Survey Memoirs of the 1830s describe the Scots tongue in other parts of County Antrim besides the Ballycarry district mentioned earlier in this section. In these cases the tone of the descriptions also reveals that prejudice against Ulster-Scots is nothing new:

Parish of Ballintoy (north Antrim)
      "They are all the descendants of the Scottish settlers of the 16th century, as may be inferred from their very broad Scotch dialect and accent."

Parish of Armoy (north Antrim)
      "They seem to be almost exclusively of Scottish extradition ... The inhabitants towards the more mountainous parts are very uncouth and ignorant."

Parish of Ahoghill (mid Antrim)
      "The inhabitants much resemble the Scots in their habits, customs and dialect. They are rather dogged, obstinate and blunt."

Parish of Grange of Shilvoden (Antrim)
      "The inhabitants display disagreeable Scottish manners."

Parish of Mallusk (east Antrim)
      "Their dialect, accent and customs are strictly Scottish, and among the old people are many homely and pretty old saws and proverbs. They are rather rough and blunt."

Parish of Carnmoney (east Antrim)
      "Their accent is peculiarly, and among old people disagreeably strong and broad. Their idioms and saws are strictly Scottish."

A single one of these references is couched in sympathetic terms:

Parish of Drumtullagh (north Antrim)
      "The Scotch language is spoken in great purity."

                              . . . . .
Not many years ago, gathering round the hearth of a home deep in the Ulster-Scots

countryside, a small group met to discuss how the Ulster-Scots language might be saved from extinction. There was talk of forming a Society, of asking for Government support, and so on. But, inevitably, the discussion turned to 'crack'.

"Hae ye ever heerd tell o the nummer four gettin caa'd fivver?"

"Na, no in Antrim oniehoo, its aye fower wi iz."

"Ach, the used fivver roon Greba, well."

Such exchanges about Ulster-Scots words are not unusual, but this one opened a debate on how the 'whole language' might be taught. 'How', for example, 'would you translate an ordinary English sentence into Ulster-Scots?' And so the collogue decided to tackle a simple sentence: "That floor needs cleaning today." The first stage was a word-for-word attempt:

"Thon flare needs cleaned theday."

But there were protests – 'we wudnae say that, it wud be mair like':

"Thon flare needs a guid clean theday."

Not to be outdone, another body added – 'ye wudnae say "needs" but. It shud be':

"Thon flare cud dae wi a guid clean theday."

Most agreed, and then tried to 'say' the Ulster-Scots version as if it was part of natural conversation. Written down it looked strange and unnatural. But how would such a sentence be constructed in the most natural Ulster-Scots speech? The suggestions were revealing:

"Dae wi a guid clean, thon flare, sae it cud."

"See thon flare, dae wi a guid clean theday sae she cud."

The need for an Ulster-Scots grammar was recognised, and the idea for this book was born.

—ooo0ooo—

ULSTER-SCOTS POETRY, 1720-1920

The following list represents the best-known collections of traditional Ulster-Scots poetry, mostly published between 1750 and 1900. The individual poets – 20 or so in this list – are cited throughout this book when literary examples are given, but referenced only by the poet's surname. The home location of each of these writers is superimposed on the map showing the Ulster-Scots speaking areas (figure 1).

Many of the books containing Ulster-Scots poetry also printed 'subscribers lists' – that is lists of personal names with the home towns or townlands of individuals who had pre-paid a subscription/order for the book. Over 8000 names are contained in these subscribers lists, the overwhelming majority of which were located in the same areas of Ulster as remain Ulster-Scots speaking today (apart from the numerous 'subscribers' listed for Belfast).

(Anon-Laggan)	'Scotch Poems' in *The Ulster Miscellany*, 1753
Beggs, Thomas	*Miscellaneous Pieces*, 1819
	Rathlin, 1820
	The Memento, 1828
	The Minstrel's Offering, 1834
	The Second Part of the Minstrel's Offering, 1836
	Poetical Works, 1869

Bleakley, William	*Moral and Religious Poems*, 1840
Boyle, Francis	*Miscellaneous Poems*, 1811
Campbell, James	*The Posthumous Works*, 1820
Carson, Joseph	*Poems*, 1831
Cleland, William	*Collection*, 1838
Colhoun, David	*Poems on Several Occasions*, 1810
Dickey, John	*Poems*, 1818
Dugall, George	*The Northern Cottage*, 1824
Gilmore, Robert	*Collection of Poems and Songs*, 1843
Given, Thomas	*Poems from College and Country*, 1900
Herbison, David	*The Fate of McQuillan*, 1841 *Midnight Musings*, 1848 *The Snow Wreath*, 1869 *Children of the Year*, 1876 *Select Works*, 1883
Huddleston, Robert	*Collection of Poems*, 1844 *Collection of Poems*, 1846
Kerr, Agnes	*Poems from Ahoghill*, c.1912
Leech, Sarah	*Poems*, 1828
Lynn, Adam	*Random rhymes frae Cullybackey*, 1911
McKenzie, Andrew	*Poems and Songs*, 1810
McKinley, John	*Poetic Sketches*, 1819
McWilliams, Hugh	*Poems and Songs*, 1816
Orr, James	*Poems on Various Subjects*, 1804 *Posthumous Works*, 1817
Porter, Hugh	*Poetical Attempts*, 1813
Savage-Armstrong, George	*Ballads of Down*, 1901
Starrat, William	Individual broadsheet poems published in Dublin, 1722-1734, eg: *"A Pastoral in Praise of Allan Ramsay By Willy Starrat"*, Dublin 1726 (published in most collected works of Allan Ramsay as "Epistle From Mr. William Starrat, Teacher of Mathematicks at Straban in Ireland", from an annotated version sent to Ramsay in 1722)

"An Elegy on the Much Lamented Death of Quarter-
master Brice Blare; Who died at Strabane", Dublin
1734 (Reprinted in *Ulster Journal of Archaeology*
Vol. XIII (1907) pp. 160-161)

Starrat was possibly the author of some of the
anonymous collection of 'Scotch Poems' published
from the Laggan area of east Donegal in *The Ulster
Miscellany*, Belfast 1753. See "Anon-Laggan"
(above)

Thomson, Samuel   *Poems*, 1793
                                   New Poems, 1799
                                   Simple Poems, 1806

The only significant collections of the works of these early poets that have been
reprinted in recent years (and once again made accessible to the public) are the following:

The Country Rhymes of Hugh Porter, The Bard of Moneyslane, c.1780, ed. Amber
Adams & J R R Adams, Vol. I *The Folk Poets of Ulster*, Pretani Press, 1992

The Country Rhymes of James Orr, The Bard of Ballycarry, 1770-1816, ed. Philip
Robinson Vol. II *The Folk Poets of Ulster*, Pretani Press, 1992

The Country Rhymes of Samuel Thomson, The Bard of Carngranny, 1766-1816, ed.
Ernest McA Scott & Philip Robinson, Vol. III *The Folk Poets of Ulster*, Pretani Press,
1992

Webs of Fancy: Poems of David Herbison, the Bard of Dunclug, ed. Ivan Herbison,
Dunclug Press, 1980

For a general account of these poets, with a select anthology, the standard work is
John Hewitt's *Rhyming Weavers and other country poets of Antrim and Down*,
Blackstaff Press, 1974.

**Note on Figure 1 (opposite): The Ulster-Scots speaking areas were mapped by
Prof R J Gregg in 1960-1963,[1] and the boundary for County Antrim confirmed
by James Fenton's *The Hamely Tongue*, 1995.
The Ulster-Scots cultural zone was mapped by P S Robinson in 1974,[2] and published in 1984, and represents the areas where (a) the majority of Protestants
are Presbyterian (rather than Anglican), and (b) the majority of people with
'non-Irish' surnames have Scottish rather than English surnames.**

[1]Gregg, R J, 'The Scotch-Irish Dialect Boundaries in Ulster' in M F Wakelin, ed. *Patterns in the Folk
Speech of the British Isles* (London, 1972).
[2]Robinson, P S, *The Plantation of Ulster: British Settlement in an Irish landscape, 1600–1670* (Dublin,
1984).

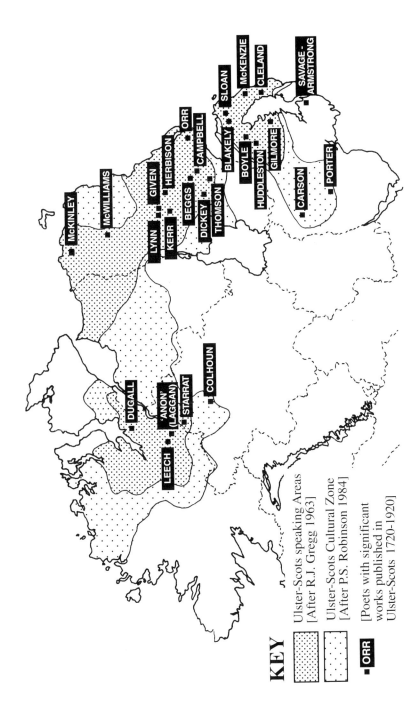

KEY

Ulster-Scots speaking Areas
[After R.J. Gregg 1963]

Ulster-Scots Cultural Zone
[After P.S. Robinson 1984]

■ ORR [Poets with significant
works published in
Ulster-Scots 1720-1920]

Figure 1: Map of Ulster-Scots Areas in Ulster, showing the distribution of the Ulster-Scots poets.

CHAPTER 1:
SPELLING AND PRONUNCIATION

Some spelling rules have become more widely used than others in modern Scots and Ulster-Scots, but not to the point of providing standard spellings. Nevertheless, few Scots writers today would think of spelling words such as 'head' and 'good' in any way other than *heid* and *guid*. It was not always so, however, even for such well-known conventions. From the early 1700s through the next two centuries, writers of Ulster-Scots prose often used spellings such as *'heed'* and *'gude'* for 'head' and 'good'. Other writers, especially those who were unaware of 'correct' English pronunciations, were content with 'English' spellings. Only in poetry, where for example 'head' might have been rhymed with a word like English 'greed', can we see what the intended pronunciation was.

On the surface, the vast range of spelling variations to be found in Ulster-Scots literature suggests an anarchic 'anything goes' approach. Indeed, for unusual words which writers had rarely, if ever, seen in print, the spellings are especially varied. Some spelling variations have reflected local pronunciation, but by no means all. In the 1960s, Brendan Adams distributed a questionnaire from the Ulster Dialect Archive at the Ulster Folk Museum, asking for words used to describe 'dusk'. The word *dailigon* or *dayligoin*, which derives from 'day-light gone, or going', was returned in more than 30 different spellings! Presumably none of these respondents had ever seen the word written down (although it certainly occurs in early Ulster-Scots literature). It is interesting to note that in the *Scottish National Dictionary* the word is given as *dayligaun* (meaning 'twilight'), with this spelling cited only from Scotland, while *dayligon, daylygoin, day-le-gone, dayligoin', daylagone, dailygin* and *day'l-agaun* are all cited in that dictionary from published Ulster-Scots sources.

Spelling variations in Ulster-Scots literature may also result from real differences in regional dialects of Ulster-Scots. *Abune* ('above'), for example, is pronounced *abain* in north Antrim and Londonderry. However in mid and east Antrim, and in most of county Down, *abin* is also found. In Donegal and mid Down we hear (and read) *abeen*. *Coup* ('tip over') is pronounced *cope* in north Antrim and east Donegal, but *cowp* in Down and east Antrim. Marked differences occur even within county Down. Around the middle of the Ards peninsula the word *owre* ('too') is always *iver* – unlike elsewhere in the Scots-speaking areas of the county. In the same locality the number 'four' is *fivver* rather than *fower*. Respecting such local variations and dialects is not always possible in a work such as this. Inevitably, individual speakers will discover unfamiliar words and spellings in this book. Not all the 'Ulster-Scots' forms used are (or were) found throughout every part of the Ulster-Scots speaking areas. Nowhere, however, will the reader encounter words or pronunciations that are not well attested either in a significant part of the spoken language or in the literary record. A distinction must be made between dialect differences within Ulster-Scots on the one hand and patchy survival of Scots forms on the other. It is not clear, for example, if the use of *iver* for *owre* in some areas is an ancient distinction, or the result of an erosion over the years from the 'Scots' form *owre* towards the Standard English 'over'[1].

However, despite the apparent chaos, some conventions have gradually emerged, and a modern revival of Scots and Ulster-Scots writing has reinforced a desire for standardisation. A consensus has also emerged among Scots and Ulster-Scots writers in favour of spelling rules which show clearly that Scots is distinct from English. For example, although apostrophes at the end of words such as *o', wi', ca', awa'* (for 'of', 'with', 'call', 'away') are universal in the traditional literature, modern Scots writers have eschewed them, particularly where the apostrophe marks only the omission of a letter from an English spelling.

Ulster-Scots writings included many distinctively Scots orthographic conventions in the early 1600s, but slowly these were eroded in favour of modern English conventions. 'English' spelling and sound rules have long been favoured by writers as a means of representing how words from the spoken Ulster-Scots language should be pronounced. Obviously this is one of the results of 400 years of schooling Ulster-Scots speakers to read and write only in English. Ulster-Scots has survived, in many people's eyes, as a spoken language only. The rich literary tradition in Ulster-Scots is largely unknown, particularly to the native speakers themselves. So it is that whatever conventions of spelling had been evolving in the 1700s and early 1800s were unfamiliar to later writers. Indeed, most native speakers of Ulster-Scots have never seen their own language in written form at all, and so when attempting to write, they usually adopt 'phonetic' spellings based on English vowel sounds.

Through time, local writers became more aware that words like 'door', 'foot', 'night', 'I', 'tea', 'heart', and so on are not pronounced *dure, fit, nicht, A, tay* and *hairt* elsewhere in the English-speaking world, and so English spellings have been modified to approximate the Ulster-Scots pronunciation. The folk poets of the 18th and early 19th centuries, however, never thought that any reader might interpret their spellings as indicating an 'English' rather than an 'Ulster-Scots' pronunciation. This is revealed in the rhymes of their poetry: (eg *tea* is used rather than *tay*, but rhymed with *stay*; *door* is used rather than *dorr* or *dure*, but rhymed with *moor*.) Other

---

[1]Prof. Aitken (letter to author, 18/3/97) believes that *ivver* and *fivver* must be regularly derived in some way:
"*fivver* thus must derive from Old English (OE) *fēower*, with diphthongal stress-shift and yod-absorption > *fōwer*, with the *ō* developing thereafter as in *guid* < OE *gōd, muin* < OE *mōna*, and the intervocalic -*w*- > the bilabial voiced fricative [β] > in some dialects, the voiced labio-dental fricative [v].
ivver, I have to conjecture, derives from a blend of OE *ofer* 'over', and OE *ufer(r)a* 'upper'. The latter would yield *uiver/ıvər/* quite regularly: *uferra* > ME *ōver* (by open syllable lengthening, late 13th century) > /y:ver/ (regular in Scots *circa* 1300), yields eventually the vowel of *guid* and *muin*. We have also to assume that in both cases the /y:/ was shortened by the Scottish Vowel-length Rule before the -*v* + syllabic liquid (which in other cases had a shortening effect in 16th century Scotland, eg in *nivver* 'never', *divvil* 'devil')."

examples of rhymes which indicate Ulster-Scots pronunciation from these poets include:

(Huddleston, 1846): *t'ugh* ('tough')/*shough* ('ditch')

(Orr, 1804):   *rough/leugh* ('laugh')/*cough/och!*
                          beuk ('book')/*leuk* ('look')
                          shoen ('shoes')/*done/soon/crown*
                          gied ('gave')/*bread*

(Porter, 1816):   *but/foot/hut/put/about/snoot*

The use of *'ch'* spellings for *'gh'* and *A* for *I* etc, are found much more commonly in the Ulster-Scots prose writings of the late 19th and early 20th century than in 18th century Ulster-Scots poetry.

In the following section of this chapter, the main spelling conventions used in this book are provided in summary form, for ease of reference. A fuller account of these spellings and their pronunciations, along with some others that may be encountered in Ulster-Scots writings, is provided in the later sections.

1.1 Summary of spelling conventions used

The following is a quick-reference list of the more distinctive conventions used for spelling consonants in Ulster-Scots, with English equivalents provided. These and other features are explained more fully later in this chapter.

(i)	*quh-*	corresponding to 'wh-' in words such as *quha* – 'who' (but only for pronouns and adverbs)
(ii)	*-ie*	representing final '-y' in words such as *daddie* – 'daddy' (almost always)
(iii)	*z*	corresponding to 'y' in words such as *bailzie* – 'bailiff' (but only for very few words)
(iv)	*z*	corresponding to 's' and 'ys' in words like *iz* ('us') and *sez* ('says')
(v)	*sch*	corresponding to 'sh' in words such as *schune* – 'shoes' (representing the Older Scots spelling of 'sh' as *sch*)
(vi)	*sh*	corresponding to 's' in words such as *shuin* – 'soon' (representing the Ulster-Scots pronunciation of 's' as [sh])
(vii)	*-(i)t*	corresponding to '-(e)d' in past tense verb forms such as *kilt* – 'killed'
(viii)	*-thè-* and *-dhè-*	representing loss of 'th' and 'dh' sound in the middle of words such as *ithèr* – 'other', and *shooldhèr* – 'shoulder' (to give pronunciations like [irr] and [shooler])
(ix)	*-dè-* and *-tè-*	representing the interdental 'dh' and 'tth' sound in words such as *shooldèr* – 'shoulder', *eftèr* – 'after', and *watèr* – 'water' (when pronounced [shooldher], [eftther] and [watther]).
(x)	*thà-*	representing an 'h-' sound at the start of words such as *thànks* – 'thanks' (but only for very few words)

(xi)	*hò-*	representing the loss of initial 'h' sound in words such as *hònest* and *hòspittle* – 'hospital' (but only for very few words)
(xii)	*thà-*	representing loss of initial 'th' sound in words such as *thàim-yins* – 'those' (applies only when these same words occur in certain contexts)
(xiii)	*-tt-*	representing a 'glottal stop' sound in words like *mettle* – 'metal', *bottle* – 'bottle', and *nettle* – 'nettle'
(xiv)	*-nnè-*	representing the interdental '-nthe-' sound in words such as *dannèr/dander*
(xv)	*-ng'r*	representing '-nger' in certain words such as *hung'r* – 'hunger'
(xvi)	*ch*	corresponding to 'gh' in certain words such as *nicht* – 'night'
(xvii)	*-nn*	corresponding to '-nd' in certain words such as *mynn* – 'mind'
(xviii)	*-un*	corresponding to '-nd' in certain words such as *laun* – 'land'
(xix)	*w*	corresponding to 'v' in certain words such as *beloweit* – 'beloved'
(xx)	*pp*	corresponding to 'pt' in certain words such as *kepp* – 'kept'
(xxi)	*-ul*	corresponding to '-ld' in certain words such as *houl* – 'hold'
(xxii)	*-ss*	corresponding to '-st' in certain words such as *less* – 'lest'.

For spelling vowels, the following are some of the most distinctive conventions used. These and other features are also explained more fully in subsequent sections of this chapter:

(i)	*a*	corresponding to 'e' in words such as *quhan* – 'when'
(ii)	*a*	corresponding to 'o' in words such as *stane* – 'stone'
(iii)	*ä*	representing 'i' in certain words such as *bäg* – 'big'
(iv)	*á*	representing a separately sounded 'a', or long 'aa' sound in words such as *roád* – 'road'
(v)	*-aa*	corresponding to '-all' in words such as *faa* – 'fall'
(vi)	*aa*	corresponding to 'al' in words such as *waak* – 'walk'
(vii)	*ae*	corresponding to 'o' in words such as *tae* – 'to'
(viii)	*ae*	corresponding to 'ee' in words such as *quaen* – 'queen'
(ix)	*-ae*	corresponding to '-a' in words such as *Americae* – 'America'
(x)	*ai*	corresponding to 'o' in words such as *baith* – 'both'
(xi)	*ai*	corresponding to 'ea' in words such as *hairt* – 'heart'
(xii)	*ai*	corresponding to 'a' in words such as *cairt* – 'cart'
(xiii)	*au*	corresponding to 'e' in words such as *quhaur* – 'where'
(xiv)	*-ay*	corresponding to '-ea' in words such as *tay* – 'tea'
(xv)	*e*	corresponding to 'ou' in words such as *yer* – 'your'
(xvi)	*e*	corresponding to 'a' in words such as *eftèr* – 'after'
(xvii)	*ee*	corresponding to 'ea' in words such as *heerd* – 'heard'
(xviii)	*ei*	corresponding to 'e' in words such as *reid* – 'red'

(xix)	*ei*	corresponding to 'ea' in words such as *heid* – 'head'
(xx)	*-ey*	corresponding to '-ea' in words such as *sey* – 'sea'
(xxi)	*o*	corresponding to 'a' in words such as *mon* – 'man'
(xxii)	*oo*	corresponding to 'ow' in words such as *coo* – 'cow'
(xxiii)	*oo*	corresponding to 'ou' in words such as *hoose* – 'house'
(xxiv)	*oa*	corresponding to 'o' in words such as *loast* – 'lost'
(xxv)	*ow*	corresponding to 'ol' in words such as *fowk* – 'folk'
(xxvi)	*u*	corresponding to 'e' in words such as *wur* – 'were'
(xxvii)	*u*	corresponding to 'ou' in words such as *wud* – 'would'
(xxviii)	*u*	corresponding to 'oo' in words such as *tuk* – 'took'
(xxix)	*ui*	corresponding to 'oo' in words such as *guid* – 'good'
(xxx)	*i*	corresponding to 'e' in words such as *niver* – 'never'
(xxxi)	*i*	corresponding to 'u' in words such as *rin* – 'run'
(xxxii)	*í*	representing the 'y' sound or the stressed 'i' in words such as *miníster* – 'minister', and *advertísement* – 'advertisement'
(xxxiii)	*y*	corresponding to 'i' in words such as *mynn* – 'mind'.

N.B. Throughout this book, the following conventions are used: Pronunciations are enclosed in square brackets thus: [thraycthor], and any alternative spellings or incorrect (ie non-existent) grammatical constructions are marked by an asterisk before the feature: *A gatnae onie mair. When an asterisk follows a particular word or feature, eg *fivver**, this has been inserted to indicate a rare, dialectal form within Ulster-Scots or (more usually), a 'dialectal' spelling which indicates a pronunciation that is not characteristic of the core Ulster-Scots speaking area in mid and north Antrim.

1.2 Older Scots spellings in Ulster-Scots before 1750

In the early 1600s, most Ulster-Scots were writing everything (letters, legal documents and so on – not just poetry or fiction) according to the 'rules' of Scots literacy in which they had been schooled. In other words, the great majority of Scottish settlers in Ulster, at the time of the Ulster Plantation, spoke – and if literate wrote – Scots. In 1624, an extra Clerk of the Council was appointed in Dublin to deal with official correspondence which "being written in the Scotch hand are either not read or understood". Until the early 1630s even the titled Plantation landlords were writing in Scots, as this was the way in which they too had been schooled. At that time (and of course, before then), Scots had some very distinctive spellings that were to give way almost completely to English 'rules' later in the 17th century. However, traces of the Older Scots system were still being used through the 18th century. For almost a century, between 1650 and 1750, the educated Ulster-Scots learned only English spelling rules, and Ulster-Scots had to survive as a spoken language. Second-generation Ulster-Scots landlords and their better educated tenants wrote their letters and reports in English after about 1640, even if they continued to speak Scots. At the same time, old session books of Presbyterian churches in Antrim and Down did contain entries that reveal that some old spellings and some Scots grammatical constructions were still being used many years later.

Thus, 18th and 19th century Ulster-Scots writers did not use many of the Older Scots spellings. Robert Burns and the 'Scotch poets' who preceded him in Ulster and

Scotland were deliberately reviving a written form for what was to them only a spoken language. For this they almost always used English grammar and spelling rules. They were largely unaware of, or had lost contact with, the earlier spelling conventions of the 17th century and before.

Consonants in Older Scots

quh- for 'wh-'

One of the most distinctive characteristics of Older Scots spelling is the *quh-* used in place of 'wh-'. We find in Ulster-Scots documents between 1550 and 1650 such spellings as the following:

> *quha* – wha (who)
> *quhairto* – whairto (whereto)
> *quhais* – whais (whose)
> *quhar/quhair* – whar/whair (where)
> *quhat* – what
> *quhatever* – whatever
> *quhan* – whan (when)
> *quhilk* – whilk (which)
> *quhyt* – white

and *quhairof, quhairin, quhairfoir, quharas, quhorbz* ('whereby'), etc.

This feature was so widely used then that Ulster-Scots scribes even took 'English' words (like 'which' rather than *whilk*, 'who' rather than *wha*, and so on) and used the '*quh-*' spelling to give: *quhich, quho, quhoum* ('whom') etc.

Sometimes the spelling was slightly different ('*qh-*' or '*qu-*') and abbreviations such as *qlk* ('which'), *qo* ('who'), *qn* ('when') and *qrof* ('whereof') are often found in old kirk session books. Sometimes this feature occurred in the middle of words as well as the beginning: *umquhille*, as in '*the umquhille Mr Crawford*', means 'the late' or 'former', and is probably from 'some while'. In earlier times, this *quh-* spelling reflected a [kwa] pronunciation (see section 1.5 below), and this is suggested by the apostrophe in the spelling used by Samuel Thomson, Bard of Carngranny (Antrim) in a poem of 1793:

> "*Had umqu'hile Spence a listener been*"

z for 'y'

One individual letter that was common to Older Scots and Middle English in the medieval period was called 'yogh', and was generally written: '$\mathfrak{z}$'. However, in Early and Middle Scots manuscripts, from the 14th century, the letters '$\mathfrak{z}$' and 'z' were indistinguishable as $\mathfrak{z}$, for example in *$\mathfrak{z}$outh* and *$\mathfrak{z}$ele* (=zeal). 16th century Scots printers took to printing 'z' for both, because there was no separate '$\mathfrak{z}$' fount. By 1600, most Scots writers were using the 'z' form of the letter as equivalent to 'y' in English. This rule was followed most frequently at the beginning of words such as *ze* ('you') and *zeir* ('year'). In both English and Scots at that time the letter 'y' could be understood to represent the old letter þ (called 'thorn' and which became 'th'). By the late 14th century, 'thorn' survived only as a letter indistinguishable from 'y'. As both languages, therefore, had *ye* for 'the' and *yat* for 'that', confusion is possible for the modern reader:

the (or, you)	-	*ye*
ye/you	-	*ze/zou*
their	-	*yair*
year	-	*zeir*
your	-	*zour*

A number of surnames retain the traces of 'yogh' letter and sound. Dalzell, although not normally pronounced 'Da-yell' in Ulster today, would often be so pronounced in Scotland. The Antrim name MacFadzean is of course pronounced [MacFadgeyin], and the surnames Bailey and Taylor are pronounced [bail-ye] and [tail-yer] in Ulster-Scots. The early spellings of these names were *Bailze* and *Tailzer*. Occasionally, a name like 'William' was written *Vilzame*. Mawhinney is pronounced [Mawhun-ye] in Co Down, and McFarlane as [McFarlyane] in parts of Co Antrim. For a fuller description of the 'yogh' sound, and its representation in Ulster-Scots, see section 1.6 below.

-*ie* for '-y'

Where 'y' is found at the end of a word in English spelling, this was (and is) avoided in Scots in favour of -*ie*. So, 'Aunty' becomes *Auntie*, 'Willy' becomes *Willie* or *Wullie*, and 'granny' becomes *grannie*. Of course, Scots words with no English equivalents such as *dominie* ('teacher') also follow this pattern. Surnames such as Montgomery were usually spelt *Montgomerie*.

many	-	*monie*
very	-	*verie*
any	-	*onie*
mostly	-	*maistlie*

The following sentence from an early 17th century Ulster document illustrates many of the Older Scots spelling features:

> *Ye quhilk soume of monies ye umquhile Claude Hamiltonne grantit ye zeir of god 1615.*

> 'The which sum of money the umquhile (late) Claude Hamilton granted the year of God 1615'.

sh for 's', and *sch* for '-sh-'

Some Ulster-Scots speakers have a tendency to pronounce 's' as [sh] and so we might sometimes hear *Miss* (an abbreviated form of 'mistress') pronounced [massh], although it would never be written in this way. 'Vessel', however, was written *veshel* in some of the early Ulster-Scots documents, 'sugar' was written as *shugger*, and 'soon' as *shune*. According to the *Concise Scots Dictionary*, the modern Scots word *sheuch* ('a drain, or open ditch with water lying in it') is derived from an Early Middle English word *sogh*, meaning a 'wet, swampy place'. In each of these cases, the *sh* spelling in modern Ulster-Scots contrasts with an 's' spelling in the English or Older Scots/Middle English equivalent.

On the other hand, where 'sh' is used in the English spelling of a word to represent the same sound, for example with 'she', 'ship', 'bishop' etc, '*sch*' was used regularly in Older Scots (*scho, schippe, bischop*, etc), as in other Germanic languages. The modern uses of *s*, *sh* and *sch* in Ulster-Scots are discussed further in section 1.5.

The development of the Older Scots forms *suld* 'should' and *sall* 'shall' is not parallel to that from *sogh* to *sheuch*. However, it should be noted that *shud* is current Ulster-Scots for 'should'. Although the forms *sall* and *I'se* ('I shall') appear in the Ulster-Scots literary record, 'shall' or *sall* are not used today at all.

Interchangeable letters 'v', 'u' and 'w'

In Older Scots, the letters '*w*', '*v*' and '*u*' were used interchangeably, but on occasion the substitution of '*w*' for 'v' reflected a contrast of pronunciation with English.

over	-	*ower* (modern Scots – *owre*)
give	-	*giwe* (modern Scots – *gie*)
have	-	*hawe* (modern Scots – *hae*)
dove	-	*dowe* (modern Scots – *doo*)
love	-	*lowe* (rare in modern Scots, except for in *belowit* – 'beloved')

The Ulster-Scots poets used words like *lo'ed* for 'loved', and *co'erd* for 'covered'. Before that, in the 1600s, *w* was often substituted for 'v' in words such as *adwise, craew* ('crave'), *Dawid, Gawan* ('Gavin'), *lewie* ('levy'), *wozd* ('void') and *elewint* ('eleventh'). Sometimes, *u* was also found in place of 'w' in words such as *ansuer, auin* ('own'), *duell, neuis, puer* ('power'), *sourd* ('sword'), *toune, tua* and *tuell*. *W* was substituted for 'u' in *perswade, trew, zow* ('you'), *dowble* and *grows* ('grouse'). *V* was used in place of *w* for *avay, vitt, vas, vater, ve* and *varrent*, etc. The interchangeable *v* and *w* raises the question of the Ulster-Scots adjective *brave* ('good' or 'pleasing'), which is synonymous with some meanings of the Scots adjective *braw*.

Note: Occasionally, *f* was substituted for 'v': *serf* ('serve'), *giffen* ('given'), etc. The *v* in *gavel* ('gable') and *ville-* ('bally-', 'town') is original, and not an alteration of the 'b' in the English and Gaelic equivalents.

Final *-it* for '-ed'

The Scots past tense verb ending in '*-it*' or '*-t*' (rather than '-ed' or '-d'), which is dealt with in section 7.4, is of course a historical form but it also reflects a pronunciation contrast with English.

1.3 Representation of vowel sounds in Ulster-Scots

Many pairs of English words, for example, 'meat' and 'meet', sound the same even if they have different meanings and different spellings. A common (and historic) pronunciation of 'meat' in Scotland and Ulster is [mate]. Similarly, 'eat', 'cheat', 'seat', 'beat', 'clean' and 'cheap' can be pronounced [ate], [chate], [sate], [bate], [clane] and [chape] in many parts of Ulster and Scotland.

The most consistent Scots spelling for this feature is -ai-. The *Concise Scots Dictionary* records the following equivalents, all of which have some currency in Ulster-Scots:

beard	-	*baird*
gleam	-	*glaim*
beagle	-	*baigle*
eat	-	*ait*
easy	-	*aisy*
cheat	-	*chait* (or *chate*)
east	-	*aist*
bleat	-	*blait*
feasible	-	*faisible*
cheap	-	*chaip* (or *chape*)
clear	-	*clair*
heathen	-	*haithen*
measles	-	*maisles*
mean	-	*main*
plead	-	*plaid*
seat	-	*sait/sate*
sheaf	-	*shaif*
tease	-	*taise*
treason	-	*traison*
treat	-	*trait*
weak	-	*waik*
sneak	-	*snaik*
beast	-	*baist/baste*
beat	-	*bait/bate*

Of course, not all words with an 'ea' spelling in English have this [ee] vowel sound in their Standard English pronunciation (like the metal 'lead'). Other words with an 'ea' spelling in English which do have the [ee] vowel sound (like 'fear') retain the same vowel sound and spelling in their Scots equivalents.

As a general rule, words such as 'meet' which have the same [ee] vowel sound in English, but have an 'ee' rather than an 'ea' spelling, do not have a vowel sound change in their Ulster-Scots equivalents. This means that words such as 'green', 'teen', 'meet', 'beet' and 'week' are spelt the same in Scots as in English, apart from several exceptions. 'Queer' is universally *quare* or *quair* throughout Ulster, but the other exceptions such as *fate* or *faet* and *maet* for 'feet' and 'meet' only represent unusual and occasional local anomalies. Where a word like 'meet' is pronounced [mate] locally, a *maet** spelling is adopted to maintain the clear and simple parallels reflected in the English synonyms, giving *mait* ('meat') and *maet* ('meet'); *waik* ('weak') and *waek* ('week'), etc.

It should be stressed that while *mait* for 'meat' is quite regular in Scots and Ulster-Scots, the '-ee-' to [ai] vowel sound change in *maet* for 'meet' is <u>not</u>. The latter represents a localised feature in the east Antrim dialect of Ulster-Scots (although also heard occasionally in Belfast and north Down). Many words such as 'green' and 'beef' do not occur as *graen or *baef, and those such as quaen or faet that can occur locally, even so, are used only occasionally, eg Get yer faet* aff the sait.

Mait, incidentally, refers to any type of food in Ulster-Scots, and not just flesch, while any form of butcher's meat is beef, eg Mawhunnyie's beef-cairt ('Mawhinney's butchers van').

N.B. Dialectal differences within Ulster-Scots can be quite marked, especially for some of the following features. Those examples which are rare in the core Ulster-Scots speaking area of mid and north Antrim, but frequent in the other areas (perhaps because of contact with Mid Ulster-English dialects, where similar pronunciations occur), are distinguished by an asterisk after the example eg 'clean' – clain*.

Ulster-Scots *ai* corresponding to English 'ea'

beard	-	*baird*
heart	-	*hairt* (rhymes with English 'pert')
read	-	*raid* (rhymes with English 'made')*
meat	-	*mait*
lead (verb)	-	*laid**
clean	-	*clain*
death	-	*daith*

Ulster-Scots *ae* corresponding to English 'ee'

queer	-	*quaer* (rhymes with English 'lair')
feet	-	*faet* (rhymes with English 'fate')*
queen	-	*quaen* (rhymes with English 'lane')*
beetle	-	*baettle* (rhymes with English 'fatal')*
sixteen	-	*saxtaen**
meet	-	*maet**
seen	-	*saen*

Ulster-Scots *ei* or *ee* corresponding to English 'ea'

lead (chemical)	-	*leid*
bread	-	*breid* (rhymes with English 'breed')
head	-	*heid*
dead	-	*deid*
heard	-	*heerd*
deaf	-	*deef*

Ulster-Scots *a*, *ay*, or *ey* corresponding to English 'ea'

seat	-	*sate* (or *sait*)
tea	-	*tay* (rhymes with English 'may')
sea	-	*sey**

Ulster-Scots *ui* corresponding to English 'oo'

One of the best-known conventions for representing Scots vowel sounds is the *-ui-* equivalent to English '-oo-'.

good	-	*guid* ([gid], [gud], [gyid] etc roughly rhymes with English 'hid', or in some areas with English 'mud')
blood	-	*bluid*
poor	-	*puir*
book	-	*buik*
moon	-	*muin*
school	-	*scuil*, or *schuil*
door	-	*duir**, or *dure**
floor	-	*fluir**, *flare* or *flure**

N.B. These 'conventions' of spelling disguise a great variety of pronunciations from region to region, which in turn can differ for each word in any one region. 'Floor' (*fluir*), for example, can be pronounced [floor], [flure], [flare] or [flower]. 'Book' (*buik*) is pronounced [buk] almost everywhere nowadays, but was often written as *beuk* [byuck] in the literature, while 'school' (*schuil*) is generally pronounced to sound like [skill]. *Meen* and *peer* are sometimes found as the spellings of 'moon' and 'poor'.

In some cases, slightly different spellings are preferred:

stood	-	*stud*
took	-	*tuk*
look	-	*luk* (also *leuk*)

The shortened vowel sounds suggested by *tuk* and *stud* are also reflected in the spelling conventions of *wud, cud, shud* etc, for '-ou-' in 'would', 'could', and 'should'.

Scots *oo* corresponding to English 'ou' and 'ow'

out	-	*oot* (rhymes with English 'moot')
our	-	*oor*
round	-	*roon*
house	-	*hoose*
mouse	-	*moose*
about	-	*aboot*
mouth	-	*mooth*
doubt	-	*doot*
cow	-	*coo*
council	-	*cooncil*
now	-	*noo*
town	-	*toon*
allow	-	*alloo*
crown	-	*croon*
brown	-	*broon*
flower	-	*flooer*
plough	-	*ploo*

N.B. Some 'oa' English spellings are also formed with *oo* in Ulster-Scots ('board' – *boord*).

<u>Ulster-Scots *u*, *au*, or *o* corresponding to English 'a'</u>

man	-	*mon* (rhymes with English 'lawn')*
hand	-	*haun*
stand	-	*staun*
salt	-	*saut*
was	-	*wus*
land	-	*laun*
band	-	*baun*

Note: The forms *hann, stann, satt, wuz, lann* and *bann* are also found for the above examples.

<u>Ulster-Scots *ai* or *e* corresponding to English 'a'</u>

This contrast of vowel sound can be represented by a spelling change to *e* or to *ai*:
sharp   - *sherp, shairp*

Before 'r' the *ai* form is preferred (except before final 'r'):

cart	-	*cairt*
sharp	-	*shairp*
arm	-	*airm*
harm	-	*hairm*
part	-	*pairt*
hard	-	*haird*

and in others the *e* form is found: eg after – *eftèr*; was – *wes* (also *wus* and *wuz*); bag – *beg* (also *bahg*).

In words such as 'page', 'game', 'face', etc, where 'a' is followed by a consonant + 'e', the 'a' can be 'glided' into a double vowel sound in Ulster-Scots [ee-ya], and can be written -*ai* + consonant + *e*:

paige [pee-adge]
gaime [gee-am]
faice [fee-ass]
raige [ree-adge]

<u>Ulster-Scots *i* corresponding to English 'e'</u>

There are some words where the English 'e' is pronounced indistinctly in Ulster-Scots, and this sound is usually written as an *i*:

ever	-	*iver* (rhymes with English 'river')
never	-	*niver*
every	-	*ivery*

N.B. These words can also be pronounced [avver] [navver] and [avvery].

Ulster-Scots *u* corresponding to English 'e'

were	-	*wur* (rhymes with English 'our')
when	-	*whun* (also *whan, quhan*, etc)
where	-	*whur*

N.B. Ulster-Scots *u* can also be used for English 'i', particularly when 'i' follows 'w-' or 'wh-', eg *wutch* ('witch'), *twust* ('twist'), *whun* ('whin', ie gorse), *furst* ('first') etc. However, see also the use of *ä* for this distinctive feature as described below in section 1.4.

Ulster-Scots *a*, or *au* corresponding to English 'e'

when	-	*whan*
west	-	*wast*
where	-	*whaur* (rhymes with English 'or')

Ulster-Scots *a* corresponding to English 'o'

prop	-	*prap* (rhymes with English 'trap')*
sob	-	*sab*
long	-	*lang*
off	-	*aff*
open	-	*apen*
drop	-	*drap** (in north and mid-Antrim pronounced [dhrawp])
shop	-	*schap** (also [shawp])

Note: 'Hot' is *het* in the older Ulster-Scots poetry, while 'let' is *loot*.

Ulster-Scots *-ae* or *-a*, corresponding to English '-o' or '-oe'

no	-	*nae* (also *na*)
do	-	*dae*
so	-	*sae*
to	-	*tae*
toe	-	*tae*
foe	-	*fae*
who	-	*wha*

Ulster-Scots *a-e*, corresponding to English 'o-e'

home	-	*hame*
stone	-	*stane*
bone	-	*bane*
one	-	*ane*
rope	-	*rape* (also *raip*)

Ulster-Scots *-aw* or *-aa*, corresponding to English 'ow'

| snow | - | *snaw, snaa* |
| blow | - | *blaw* (also *bla*) |

Ulster-Scots *i* corresponding to English 'u'

just	-	*jist* (rhymes with English 'list') (also *jaist*)
run	-	*rin*
sun	-	*sin* ('son' is often written as *sinn*)
summer	-	*simmer*
such	-	*sic, sich* (pronounced [sitch]).

1.4 Problem vowel sounds in Ulster-Scots

Since the vernacular revival of Scots and Ulster-Scots literature in the early 1700s, 'English' vowel sounds (both as individual letters and in combinations) have been used to convey an approximate Scots pronunciation. However, several distinctive vowel sounds have proved to be difficult to represent, and such problems have given rise to a host of spelling variations for these words in Ulster-Scots. During the present century, some innovative devices have been borrowed from languages other than English in an attempt to resolve these questions.

The short 'i' represented by *ä*

For English words spelt with 'i' such as 'pig', 'hit', 'big' and 'pin', a vowel sound is used in Ulster-Scots speech for which there is no appropriate vowel letter. Such words are sometimes written as *pag, hat, bag*, etc, or even *pug, hut* and *bug*, although Ulster-Scots *u* is used for English 'i' more frequently when following 'w-' or 'wh-', such as for *whun*, 'whin' or *wun* 'win'. (The long-defunct Presbyterian paper *'The Witness'* was often derisively referred to as the *'Wutness'*). However, the potential for confusion with English words is obvious when spellings such as *hit, hat* and *hut* are used for the same pronunciation. One revised spelling system developed in the early 1960s by Professor Robert Gregg and Brendan Adams used an umlaut accent over the letter 'a', (ie *ä*), giving *päg, bäg, hät*. While the only earlier use of the umlaut in Ulster-Scots literature is with *owër* ('over'), this device has proved useful to modern Ulster-Scots writers.

The long 'a' represented by *á*

The use of 'accents' above vowels to indicate change of stress or sound was first successfully employed in Scots literature by William Lorimer for his *New Testament in Scots*. Although accents have not been adopted widely by other Scots writers, Lorimer's acknowledged masterpiece of Greek-to-Scots translation continues to exert an outstanding influence on all Scots and Ulster-Scots writing.

In Ulster-Scots (and in Scots), the letter 'a' is generally pronounced [ah] (rhyming with 'ma' and not with 'may'). However, a standard 'a' sound in words such as *ava* (pronounced [a-va]), can contrast with a longer or more stretched 'a' sound in other words such as *awa* (pronounced [awah] or [awaa]). A limited use of an accent to indicate the lengthened sound of this vowel may be justified:

awá	-	away
twá	-	two

However, in many situations, perfectly suitable conventions already exist:

caa, caw	-	call

aa, aw	- all
aaboadie	- everyone
anaw, anaa	- as well ('and all')

Stressed vowels represented by *í, ý, á*, etc

Another situation where an accented vowel was used by Lorimer was when he wished to indicate which particular vowel is stressed in speech. For example the word 'minister' has been often written **meenister* in Ulster-Scots, following a Scots convention. In Ulster-Scots speech the pronunciation is closer to [manny-stther] or [mineestther] with some stress along with a change in pronunciation on the second vowel. It would be acceptable to render this *minístèr*, and similarly with words such as *advertísement* where the Ulster-Scots stress is on a different vowel from the British English: 'advertisement'. In the same way, *accídent, barrístèr* and *covénentèr* are pronounced [akseedent] etc.

Ulster-Scots vowel pronunciation is complex and varied, to the point where single vowels can be glided so that they sound as double vowels. 'Belfast', for example, has sometimes been written *Baelfawst*, and is pronounced [Bay-aal-fawst] or [Billfaw-ast]. Sometimes, in east Antrim, an exaggerated form of [Bay-aal-faw-ast] is pronounced as a 'put on'. Words such as 'face' and 'page' are pronounced [fee-ass] and [pee-adge], but in this book spellings such as *faice** and *paige** are used, rather than **fyace* or **fiáce*. Similarly, words such as 'post' and 'pot' can be pronounced [po-ast] and [pawit], and are then spelt *poast** and *poat** or *pawt**.

Words with an 'oa' in English spelling such as 'road', 'boat', 'goat', 'coat' etc, are pronounced locally [row-ad], [bow-at], [go-at], [co-at] in Ulster-Scots. In these situations, the use of an accent appears to be the only satisfactory way of indicating a vowel which is pronounced distinctly and separately from an adjacent vowel.

roád*
boát*
goát*
coát*

Loss of initial vowel before 'l'

Several words such as 'elastic' and 'electric' (which begin with a vowel, followed by 'l' or 'll', and then another vowel), can lose the initial vowel sound to become *lastic* and *lectric*. Although this does not happen with all words with a 'vowel-l-vowel' beginning, the following list represents those where this feature occurs most commonly in Ulster-Scots:

lastic	- elastic
lectric	- electric, electricity
lapse	- elapse (eg *a lang time's lapsed fae ye wur hame*)
leven, leiven	- eleven
legiance	- allegiance
lotment	- allotment
luminate	- illuminate

| *Lympics* | - Olympics |
| *ledge* | - allege, declare. |

In the opening line of James Orr's poem 'To the Potatoe' (written in Ballycarry 200 years ago), we find *ledge* used: *I ledge we'd fen gif fairly quat o* ('I declare we'd survive if completely rid of').

1.5 Modified consonants in Ulster-Scots

Several consonants, including the letters 's', 't', 'l', 'w' and 'd', are modified in Ulster-Scots when combined with 'h'. These modifications contrast with English usage.

's' 'sh' and 'sch' in Ulster-Scots

The behaviour of the consonant 's' in combination with 'h' and 'ch' in Ulster-Scots has already been examined in the light of the documentary and historical record (section 1.2). On occasion, the English 'sh' spelling is written as in its historical 'sch' form in Ulster-Scots, while the English 's' spelling is written as 'sh' in Ulster-Scots if it is modified to this sound in Ulster-Scots only. For example, English 'short' can be written *schoart* or *schairt* in Ulster-Scots, while 'soon' is *shuin* (usually pronounced [shane]). The surname 'Shaw' was frequently written *Schaw* or *Schae* in the 17th century.

In the example given above, 'soon' is often written *shuin* in Ulster-Scots, but just as frequently *shune* or *shane*. The plural of shoe ('shoes'), however, is also written *shune* in most of the traditional literature. If the above 'rules' were to be consistently applied, only the spelling of the English word 'shoes' in Ulster-Scots should be *schune* – and in the historical record this form is well attested.

In terms of general pronunciation, the 's' sound in Ulster-Scots is very often modified to 'sh' when compared to the comparable English word. A 'pussy-cat' is a *wee pushie*, *harnish* is 'harness', *shoo* is 'sew', *shooper* can be used for 'super', a 'lease' is a *leash* and a 'vessel' is *veshel*. Even with consonant groupings of 'st' and 'sl', the actual sound of words like *stour* or *slabber* can approach [sshtoor] or [sshlabber]. *Rubbisch* ('rubbish') is pronounced [rubbitch], but other words ending in -*sch*, such as *fäsch* ('fish') are pronounced with a final [-sh] sound. *Pusch* ('push') differs from English in the vowel sound rather than the 'sh' sound, as it rhymes with English 'slush'.

Several English words such as 'school' and 'schedule', are pronounced with a [sk-] rather than a [sh-] sound. In Ulster-Scots an 'sc-' spelling is used: *scuil* ('school'), and *scedule* ('schedule'), although 'sk-' and 'sch-' spellings also occur.

'wh' and 'quh' in Ulster-Scots

In the 'standard' pronunciation of English words such as 'where' and 'were', there is no sound difference between the 'wh' and 'w'. In Scots and Ulster-Scots, however, when a word is spelt 'wh-', there is a marked [hw] sound as the 'w' is aspirated. The historical Scots orthographic form of *quh* for 'wh' has presumably been revived by some modern Ulster-Scots writers partly to emphasise this pronunciation. In this book this usage has been followed only for pronouns and adverbs such as 'who' *quha*, 'when' *quhan*, 'where' *quhar*, and so on – but not for words such as *wheen* ('some'), *whun* ('gorse') etc.

'tw' and *'qw'* in Ulster-Scots

The [kwa] sound appears to have been very extensively used in Older Scots. Indeed, it appears that the *quh-* orthographic convention in Scots (for 'wh-') originally indicated a [kwa] pronunciation. The 'q' sound emerges in unexpected circumstances – for example the name 'Hugh' can be rendered [shooey] [queue] or [queuey].

Historically, the 'tw' consonant combination was not only also represented as 'qw' in Older Scots, but was pronounced as such as well. The best known examples of this are in the *aqween* and *aqweesh* forms for 'between'. In South-West Scotland and parts of Co Antrim, this also survives in the (now rare) forms of *qwa, qwarthie, qwonnie* and *qwal* ('two' 'two or three', 'twenty' and 'twelve'). *The Hamely Tongue* also records in current Antrim speech *quust* for 'twist' and *quuster* for a straw-rope 'twister'.

Modification of the consonants 't' and 'd'

The English consonants 't' and 'd' are often modified by sounding with the tongue between the teeth (ie interdentally) in Ulster-Scots to sound very close to 'tth' and 'dh', – or their sound can even be lost altogether. Most noticeably and commonly these changes happen when the 't' or 'd' is followed by the consonant 'r'. The consonant 't' can also be replaced by a glottal stop (a catch in the throat). When 'th' occurs in English in the middle of words, the Ulster-Scots form may lose the consonant sound altogether. 'Father', 'brother', 'mother', 'bother', and 'rather' are not always pronounced [faither], [brither] etc as in Scots, but sometimes as [faa-er], [brae-er], [maw-er], [baw-er], and [raa-er]. This feature is characteristic of Belfast vernacular, but also occurs in some Ulster-Scots speaking areas, although not in the 'core' areas of mid and north Antrim. As in the above sections, an asterisk will be used after such words to distinguish those not found among the broadest Ulster-Scots speakers (where *faither, brither, mither* and *rether* are used).

In some cases use of a 'th' or 'dh' is sufficient to represent the sound of 't' and 'd', so giving us *butther, sthrae* (straw), *dhrap* (drop), *shoodher* (shoulder), but in some cases it is impractical. 'Tractor', for example, would become **thraycther*, and 'tree' would become **tthree*. The Ulster-Scots pronunciation of 'tree' should not be confused with the numeral 'three', because in 'tree' the 'tr' sounds are modified together to 'ttrh-'. In fact, the difference between interdental 't', 'd' and interdental 'th', 'dh' is that the first are stop consonants (sounded by a firm closure of the tongue between the teeth), while the second are spirants (sounded so that the passage of breath does not wholly cease).

In the 1960s Professor Gregg and Brendan Adams addressed this orthographic problem, and advocated capitalising the letters 'T' and 'D' (even in the middle of words) when they were affected along with a following 'r' sound. Thus we find spellings in their transcriptions such as:

DReekh
DReer
DRawin
guTTers
claaTTer
TRue
beTTer
DRänk
TRäcks

However, other writers do not seem to have adopted this convention, and in recent years some have turned to the use of an accent over the vowel immediately following the modified consonants to achieve the same result: *drèekh, drèer, guttèrs, bettèr*, etc.

In this practice 'tree' becomes *trèe* rather than *tthree or *TRee, and 'water' if written *watèr* is pronounced [watther]. In James Fenton's dictionary, *The Hamely Tongue*, this feature is described (see section 1.7 below), but no orthographic device is necessary in his work, where a particular word such as *butter* can have a pronunciation guide inserted after: eg *butter* (-tth-). The use of an accented vowel to indicate modification of the preceding consonant or group of consonants is adopted in this book. It has the advantage of a certain degree of current usage by modern writers, and also has the capability of indicating loss of the consonant sound altogether. The latter is achieved by adding an 'h' to the 't' or 'd', and accenting the following vowel. Thus *watèr*, pronounced [watther], can be distinguished from *wathèr**, pronounced [waa-er].

eg:	other	-	*ithèr* [ei-er]*
	shoulder	-	*shouldhèr, shoodèr,* or *shouldèr** [shouller/shoodher/ shouldher]
	dander	-	*dandhèr* or *dandèr* [danner/dandher]
	brother	-	*braithèr* [bra-er]*
	mother	-	*maithèr* [ma-er]*
	children	-	*childhèr* or *childèr* [chiller/childher]*
	Ulster	-	*Ulstèr* [Ullsther].

Modification of initial 'th' to 'h', represented by *thì, thà*, etc

Certain words beginning with 'th' in their English equivalents are sometimes, locally, pronounced with an initial 'h' sound in Ulster-Scots. This modification is represented by an accent over the following vowel. So 'think' in Ulster-Scots can become *thìnk** (pronounced [hink]). Other examples include thanks – *thànks** (pronounced [hanks]), and 'thing' – *thìng** [häng].

Loss of initial 'h' represented by *hò* etc

Several words beginning with 'h-' have no initial consonant sound in either English or Ulster-Scots (eg 'honest', 'honour' etc), but this can occur also with several other words in Ulster-Scots:

hospital   - *hòspittal* [ospittle] (historically also *spittal*)

hotel	-	*hòtel* [o-tel]
he	-	*hè* [ee] (see section 4.1).

Although 'hour' is not pronounced in English or Ulster-Scots with an initial 'h-', *hoor* in Ulster-Scots is 'whore' and *oor* is 'our'. In this book 'hour' is represented as *hòor*.

It must be remembered that these modifications of initial 'th' and 'h' are exceptional, and the vast majority of Ulster-Scots words beginning with a 'th' or 'h' are pronounced as spelt.

Modification of 'th-' in 'that', 'the', 'them'

In Scots, generally, 'that' is pronounced and spelt *at* (see section 4.3), and so no other device such as **thàt* is necessary to represent the loss of initial 'th'. Only rarely, however, is *thaim* (meaning 'those' or 'them') written *'em*, although this is frequently the pronunciation. This book follows the practice of spelling 'the' and 'them' as *tha* and *thaim* when the 'th' is sounded, and *thà* and *thàim* when there is loss of the initial 'th' sound (see sections 3.1 and 4.3 for a fuller account of these spelling forms). However, the behaviour of these three words is not consistent in Ulster-Scots. *That, tha* and *thaim* lose 'th' and become *at, thà* and *thàim* only when the preceding word ends with a consonant rather than a vowel sound. The loss of 'th-' does not occur at the beginning of a sentence, or of the preceding word in a sentence ends with a vowel sound. For example, we would not find *Get oot o *at* or **Thà Broons is for cumin themorra* but rather *Get oot o that* and *Tha Broons is for cumin themorra*. In contrast, we would find *Get at oot o here* and *Is thà Broons for cumin?*

The glottal stop for 't' represented by *'tt'*

One of the most characteristic features in rural Ulster-Scots speech is the glottal stop. The glottal 't' is sounded by a 'coughing' or catching action which closes the top of the throat, rather than by the action of the tongue touching the roof of the mouth. There are no orthographic conventions to indicate its presence in earlier Scots or in English, so its history cannot be traced from the documentary record. In Danish an apostrophe is used to indicate the glottal stop, but given the conventions adopted elsewhere this would be liable to confuse in Ulster-Scots.

Unlike the circumstances where 't' is sounded similarly to 'tth' in Ulster-Scots (when followed by 'r'), the glottal stop occurs when preceded by a vowel, and especially when followed by 'l'. For example *bottle* and *nettle* usually contain glottal stops, but *bustin* and *nestit* would not. *Buster* would have its 't' modified [bustther], while *bitter* might be aspirated [bitther] or have a glottal stop [bi'er]. Indeed, for words such as *butter, matter, bitter*, many native speakers sound both a glottal stop and an aspirated 'th': [bu'ther], [ma'ther], [bi'ther] etc.

The glottal stop should be assumed when the spelling in Ulster-Scots in this book involves a double 'tt' preceded by a vowel; words with single 't' in English are respelt as 'tt' (eg 'metal' to *mettal*).

In summary, there are five ways in which the consonant 't' may be sounded in a simple word like 'water'. Only the last four of these are characteristic of Ulster-Scots speech.

 (i)   'water': as in English with the 't' sounded by the action of the tongue on the roof of the mouth;

 (ii) *watèr* [watther]: with the 't' aspirated by the action of the tongue between the teeth ('interdental');

 (iii) watter [wa'er]: (or more frequently in words such as *wattle* [wa'el]): with a glottal stop, where the 't' is sounded at the top of the throat, and not with the tongue;

 (iv) *wathèr** [waa-er]: where the 't' is silent and no attempt is made to voice it by the tongue or by closing the throat;

 (v)   *watthèr* [wa'ther]: where a glottal stop is combined with, and followed by, an aspirated 'th' sound formed by the tongue quickly touching the back of the teeth.

The 'interdental' modification of '-nn-' and '-nd-'

Certain words such as 'wonder' can be represented as *wunner* or *wandher* in Ulster-Scots literature. However, the most common pronunciation is not [wunner] (with the 'n' sounded by touching the tongue on the roof of the mouth) or [wun-dher] (with a distinct 'd' audible). Rather, the '-nn-' is sounded by touching the tongue on the back of the teeth, and is represented here as *wunnèr*. This pronunciation is found with many words which – like *danner/dander* – can be spelt either with '-nn-' or '-nd-'. In the Gregg/Adams spelling system described above (where the letters 't' and 'd' were capitalised to represent their 'interdental' – ie tongue between the teeth – pronunciation), they also advocated capitalizing the letters '-nn-' for the same reason: eg *daNNer* and *wuNNer*.

In James Fenton's dictionary, *The Hamely Tongue* (see section 1.7), words like 'under' are represented as *unther*, rather than the more conventional *unner*, to indicate the same pronunciation. The word 'winner' using this spelling system, becomes *wunther, while 'winter' is *wunter, with a pronunciation reminder (-tth-). The 'interdental' sounding of '-nn-' does produce a barely perceptible, soft 't' or 'th' sound, but without allowing a full 't' or 'tth' sound as in *wuntèr* or *wunter* [wuntther]. The following words with '-nd-' spellings in their English equivalents are provided in *The Hamely Tongue*:

under	- *unther* (here spelt *unnèr*)
underground	- *unthergrun* (here spelt *unnèrgrun*)
thunder	- *thunther* (here spelt *thunnèr*)
wander	- *wanther* (here spelt *wannèr*)
Anderson	- *Antherson* (here spelt *Andèrson*)
Connor	- *Conther* (here spelt *Connòr*)
render	- *renther* (here spelt *rennèr*).

The following words with '-n-' or '-nn-' spellings in their English equivalents are also provided in *The Hamely Tongue*:

banner	- *banther* (here spelt *bannèr*)
dinner	- *dinther* (here spelt *dinnèr*)

general	-	*gentheral* (here spelt *genèral*)
honour	-	*onther* (here spelt *hònòr*)
mineral	-	*mintheral* (here spelt *minèral*)

N.B. In all these examples the '-nn-' and '-nd-' modification only occurs when these consonants are followed by an 'r'.

Like *dannèr*, other Ulster-Scots words with no English equivalents can sometimes be spelt '-nd-' or '-nn-', but usually the '-nn-' forms dominate in the literature. *Rander*, or more commonly *ranner* ('to ramble on without meaning'), is given as *ranther* by Fenton, *raNNer* by Gregg/Adams, and in this work, as *rannèr*.

The consonants 'ng'

The present participle ending ('-ing' in English) is always pronounced [-in], and is written *-in* in modern Ulster-Scots (eg *slaepin** 'sleeping', *waakin* 'walking', *footèrin* 'fidgeting' etc). When 'ng' is not in a final position, but is following by 'th' in English words such as 'length', 'strength' etc, it becomes *nth* in Ulster-Scots: *lenth, strenth* etc.

Elsewhere, when the consonants 'ng' occur together in a word, the 'g' is sounded as in English 'singer', and not as in English 'anger' – ie [ang-er] not [ang-ger]. For example, *langle* and *angle* in Ulster-Scots are sometimes spelt **langhle* and **anghle* to emphasise the softer sound of the 'g'. The hard [g] sound, as in words beginning with 'g-' such as *gye, get, gairden* etc, is sounded as in English. However, words which in English retain the hard [g] sound after 'ng', as in 'finger', 'hunger' and 'anger' [fing-ger, etc], are pronounced in Ulster-Scots without the following [g]: [fing-er], [hung-er] and [ang-er]. Modern writers have occasionally omitted the 'e' to give **fingr*, **langl*, etc. In this book, however, an apostrophe is used to represent this modification:

fing'r
hung'r
ang'r
lang'l
ang'l

The consonants 'gh' and 'ch'

The Germanic 'ch' sound, as in 'loch' or 'lough', is one of the most characteristic sounds in Scots and Ulster-Scots. English spellings of words like 'light', 'bright', and 'night' were used by Ulster-Scots writers during the late 1700s and early 1800s, apparently without any realisation that this could be misinterpreted by readers who were not Scots speakers. During the mid-1800s some of our writers such as Robert Huddleston of Moneyreagh began to introduce apostrophes as an indication of the correct pronunciation. Thus we find in some poems of the 1850s spellings such as *li'ght, bri'ght*, and *ni'ght*. However, it is now widely accepted by modern Scots writers that the spellings *licht, bricht* and *nicht* are more appropriate. This principle applies even where the sound for 'gh' is [f] in English but is [ch] in Ulster-Scots, for example 'enough' and 'tough' are *eneuch* and *teuch* (pronounced [enyeuch] and [tyeuch]) in Ulster-Scots.

The loss of the final consonants '-t' and '-d'

Many words which, in English, end in '-st', '-pt', '-ld' or '-nd', lose their final 't' or 'd' sound in their Ulster-Scots equivalents.

The loss of the final 'd' in 'and', 'hand' and 'land' (to give *an*, *haun** or *hann*, and *laun** or *lann*) is, of course, a characteristic feature of all Ulster vernacular speech, both Ulster-English and Ulster-Scots. 'And' is universally spelt *an* (historically *an'*), while 'hand' can be *haun** for both Ulster-English dialect (especially Belfast and mid-Ulster) and some adjacent Ulster-Scots speaking areas, or, *han* in mid and north Antrim. This distinction of pronunciation within Ulster-Scots is not simply a geographical one, as many speakers will pronounce 'land' and 'hand' as *laun* etc in some contexts, but *lann* in others. For example, you might *skail wrack on thà* <u>*laun*</u> ('spread seaweed on the land'), but an 'island' or 'Scotland' would be an *islann* and *Scawtlann*.

Examples of this feature abound in all Ulster-Scots literature, and while it is frequently represented as *-n*, *-n'*, or *-nn*, the '-nn' usage is adopted hereafter, with the exception of the following examples:

land	- *laun** (but also *lann*)
hand	- *haun**, *han*
and	- *an*
pound	- *pun*, (also *poon* and *poun*)
round	- *roon*
ground	- *grun, groon*
hound	- *houn, hoon*
found	- *foon, fan*

For English words ending in '-ind', some Ulster-Scots equivalents end in *-ynn* to avoid confusion with other words, eg *kynn* and *mynn* for 'kind' and 'mind', rather than **kine, *kinn, *mine*, etc. However, other equivalents such as 'blind', 'bind' and 'find' end in *-in* or *-inn*.

Final '-d' is also lost in words such as 'old', 'cold', and 'hold' to give *oul, coul* or *cowl*, and *houl* or *howl*. These spellings and pronunciations are now shared between vernacular Ulster-English and Ulster-Scots, with the Scottish-Scots (and Ulster-Scots literary) forms of *auld, cauld*, and *haud* being rarely heard in speech in Ulster today, apart from in *haudins* ('holdings') and *hauden* ('held'). Typical of the earlier usage by many of the Ulster-Scots poets are the following lines:
> "*Laigh in a vale there <u>hauds</u> a fair*" (Thomson)
> "*But <u>haud</u> ye, a jiffey*" (Sloan)

Other examples of current forms include:

told	- *toul*
bold	- *boul*
fold	- *foul*
mould	- *moul*
gold	- *goul*, also gool(d) (historic and literary form *gowd*)
sold	- *soul* (rhymes with [howl]).

Note: 'Soul' is *sowl*, and also rhymes with [howl]. The consonant 't', when it occurs as the last letter in some English words, is also lost in Ulster-Scots. This regularly occurs with English words which end in '-st' and '-pt'. The '-pt' ending, for example, becomes *-pp* in Ulster-Scots, although *-p* and *-p'* spellings may also be encountered:

apt	-	*app*
kept	-	*kepp*
slept	-	*slepp*
swept	-	*swepp*
tempt	-	*tempp*

Similarly, English '-st' endings can become *-ss* in their Ulster-Scots equivalents:

lest	-	*less*
feast	-	*feess/faiss*, feesht*
beast	-	*beess/baiss*, beesht*
priest	-	*preess, preesht*
interest	-	*intèress*
nearest etc	-	*nearess, neardess* etc
manifest	-	*mannyfess*
harvest	-	*hairvess, hairss*
best	-	*bess*
nest	-	*ness*

The plural forms of words such as 'nests', 'beasts' etc, can simply involve a longer 's' sound at the end of the word ([ness] for 'nests' rather than [nez] for 'nest'), but the *-ss* spelling adopted here remains the same for both.

<u>The loss of the consonant 'l', and the final consonants '-ll'</u>

Perhaps no feature of Scots pronunciation and spelling is better known than the loss of '-ll' from the ending of words such as the following:

all	-	*aa*
ball	-	*baa*
call	-	*caa*
fall	-	*faa*
wall	-	*waa*
hall	-	*haa* (usually *Haw* in place-names)
knoll	-	*knowe* (rhymes with [cow])
pull	-	*pu*
full	-	*fu*
roll	-	*row* (also *rowl*)

When these words are used to form compound words, such as 'altogether', the 'l' or 'll' element can still be omitted even though it is not in a final position *(aathegither)*. There are numerous compound words formed with '-full', which in Scots and Ulster-Scots became *-fu* (eg *nievefu* 'fistful', *poorfu* 'powerful', etc).

When the 'l' is not in a final position, as in the English words 'salt', 'malt', 'multure', 'pulpit', 'gold', 'hold' and 'shoulder', the 'l' can also be lost in the Ulster-Scots equivalents: *saut, maut, mooter* ('miller's portion'), *poopit, gowd* and *haud* (also *gowl* and *houl*), and *shooder*.

<u>The loss of the consonant 'r'</u>

In Scots speech, *fae* is often preferred to the traditional written Scots *frae* ('from'). Indeed, so widespread is the *fae* usage in some dialects of Scots that *frae* is regarded as a 'literary' form, despite the fact that *fae* also occurs frequently in modern Scots writing. In some Ulster-Scots areas, particularly the marginal ones, the situation is much the same, except that a similar dropping of the 'r' can extend to those words which begin 'thr-'. So 'throw', 'through', 'three', and 'throat' can be *thow** (rhymes with 'so'), *thoo**, *thie** and *thoát** in some local Ulster-Scots dialects. This feature is also common in Belfast speech, and in urban Ulster-Scots. Similarly, *throughither* ('untidy') is sometimes pronounced [thoo-irr]* and the spelling *thouithèr** may be occasionally used in this book. The 'r' can even be lost, albeit rarely, after initial 'b', for example, 'brigade' is sometimes *bigade**, and 'British' *Bitisch**.

<u>The reversal of 'r' and adjacent vowel</u>

In words such as 'children', 'brethren', 'apron', 'modern', 'pretty', 'grass' and 'western', the Ulster-Scots forms often involve a reversal of the position of the letter 'r' and the adjacent vowel; *childern, brethern, apern, modren, purtie**, *girse* and *wastren*.

1.6 <u>Representation of the 'Yogh' or 'y' sound</u>

The 'y-' sound in Ulster-Scots was once represented by the letter 'yogh', firstly as *ʒ* and then *z* in historical documents (see section 1.2). It is represented only rarely in this way in modern writing, apart from its use in placenames and surnames. The sound, however, remains in the spoken language, sometimes being represented as 'y' in a similar way to the way 'y' is used in the beginning of some English words such as 'year' and 'yellow'.

<u>'Yoghing' after the consonants 'm', 'n', 'd', 't', 'l', 'c' and 'g'</u>

The English pronunciation of certain words like 'new', 'tune' and 'Duke' include the 'y-' sound after the consonants 't', 'n' and 'd'. This, of course, also applies in Ulster-Scots, but it extends here to words like *neuk* ('nook'), *teuch* ('tough') and *deuck* ('duck'). While some writers have revived the Older Scots letter 'yogh' in modern Ulster-Scots (and this includes *ze* and *zeir* for 'you' and 'year' etc), the existing spelling conventions of *'neu-'* or *'new '*, *'deu-'* or *'dew-'*, and *'teu-'* are adequate in most cases. Similarly, when the consonant 'f' is 'yoghed' in Ulster-Scots, a 'feu-' spelling is often sufficient, eg *feuggie* ('left-handed').

The word *tulzie* ('dispute', 'quarrel'), pronounced [tul-yeh], is found in an early Donegal Ulster-Scots poem of 1720: *"To redd the Royal tulzie sets thy muse"*, while over a century later (in 1846) Robert Huddleston of Moneyreagh in county Down penned the line: *"Or else the tulzie gangs mair t'ugh"*.

The consonant 'l' can be followed by a 'yogh' sound (and by the letter *z*) in certain

Older Scots words such as *tulzie, culzie* ('welcome') and the north Antrim forms of *caylie – caylzie* ('ceildhe', 'visit'). Some writers use 'y' in these circumstances, but it is not always clear that a 'yogh' sound is intended. For example, the surname *Bailzie* is pronounced [bail-ye], while the placename *Bally* is pronounced [bel-ey]. In these cases, where an *-ly-* spelling might be misleading, the *-lz-* spelling is used in this book. Words like 'include', 'influence', 'cruel' or 'local' which can be pronounced [inclyude], [inflyuance], [cruyel] and [lok-yal] are spelt with a 'y' rather than 'z': (*inclyude, cruyel** and *locyal* inflyuance*).

However, some writers also prefer to represent the ('y') yogh sound in words like *feuggie, teuch* or *eneuch* by using a 'j' or a 'y'; *fjuggy, tjugh, enyuch*. Indeed, a considerable number of Ulster-Scots words are best spelt with the consonant followed by a 'y'. Examples include:

flyue	-	flu
flyute	-	flute
glyue	-	glue
myooly	-	chilblainy
myoother	-	millers portion of meal
myowt	-	whisper, small sound
nyaff	-	a perky wee nuisance
nyim	-	a tiny piece
nyir	-	a nuisance
nyirm	-	whinge
nyirps	-	annoyance
nyitter	-	complain
nyuck	-	steal (in some areas this is pronounced to rhyme with English 'tuck', and slightly differently from *neuk* – a 'nook or hiding-place', which rhymes with English 'took'.)

In this book, a *'nue-'* type spelling is used rather than *'ny-',* except where a subsequent vowel cannot be avoided, or where confusion with another English word might result. For example, *neuk*, not **nyook*; *speuch*, not **spyooch*; *nyuck*, not **neuock*; *feuggie*, not **fyoogy*; and *nyirp* not **neuirp*. The English word 'hook' is <u>not</u> **huik* or **huk* in Ulster-Scots, but is pronounced [hyuk] and is spelt here *heuk*. Similarly, 'book', 'shook', 'took', and 'look' were written as *beuk, sheuk, teuk* and *leuk* by many Ulster-Scots poets of 200 years ago (in addition to *heuk* for 'hook').

Words beginning with a hard 'g' or 'c', and followed by a rounded [a] or [o] vowel sound such as 'cart', 'garden' 'cat' often have their initial consonants 'yoghed' in Ulster-Scots to give *cairt* [kyaert], *gairden* [gyaerdin] and *cát* [kyawt]. It should be noted, however, that this particular feature is more characteristic of Ulster-English dialects in mid and south Ulster, where it is more clearly and more frequently pronounced. Some Ulster-Scots writers have written words such as 'cat' and 'car' as *kat* and *kar*, not simply to 'make a difference' with English, but to suggest the 'kya' pronunciation. Some words actually spelt with a 'k', such as *kepp* ('kept') or *kennel* may also display the 'kya' sound in speech, as may similarly voiced words beginning with *sc-* and *sk-*.

'Yoghing' vowels at the start of words

When certain words begin with a vowel letter they are spelt *y-* if they are pronounced with an initial y- sound in Scots and Ulster-Scots. For example, 'ewe' and 'use' are *yowe* and *yuise*. These words have a 'y' sound at the beginning in English too, of course, as do words such as 'you', 'your', 'year' (*ye, yer, yeir*).

Some other words which do not begin with a 'y-' in English, and which do not have a 'yogh' sound at the start in English, are nevertheless modified in traditional Ulster-Scots. So 'ale' occurs as *yill* in some Ulster-Scots poems, and in earlier documents 'earl' becomes *yirl* or *yerl*. More familiarly, 'earth' becomes *yirth* or *yird*. Some Scots and Ulster-Scots words which are not shared with English are also modified in the same way. 'Eagle', which is *earn* in Scots, can also be *yirn* or *yearn*; *ae*, which is the adjectival form of 'one' or 'a single' is often *yae*; 'one', otherwise, has become *yin* in Ulster-Scots although the 'standard' Scots form is *ane*, and 'once' is *yinst* (see section 2.7).

The words *thon* ('that') and *thonder* or *thonner* ('over there') are used interchangeably with *yon* and *yonner*.

The use of a 'y' sound in front of an initial vowel is even more widespread in the spoken language than the written conventions used in this book suggest. However, the pronunciation of such words depends on the context of the word in speech, and is not consistent. When words like *Ulstèr, hòspittal, ootbye* etc are preceded in speech by another vowel sound they are 'yoghed' and the initial vowels are not sounded 'glottally' as would be the case in English. For example *tha hale o Ulstèr* ('the whole of Ulster') is pronounced [tha hail a-yullsther], and *hè aye cums oot o tha hòspittal* is pronounced [ee yaye cums oot a tha yoshpi'le]. However, when these words are voiced singly, when they begin a sentence, or when they are preceded by a consonant at the end of the previous word in a sentence, then the 'yoghing' of the initial vowel does not occur. It must be remembered that these 'rules' govern the spoken language only, and are not represented orthographically. However, this point will help the reader understand why *o* ('of') is pronounced variably as [o], [a], and [e] in Ulster-Scots speech, and that there would be no difference in speech between *"Tha yin abain tha yirth"* and *"Tha ane abain tha earth."*

Loss of 'l' after 'b', 'p', and 'f'

Some words which begin with the consonants 'bl', 'pl' or 'fl', and are then followed by an [ou] vowel sound, are pronounced without the 'l' sound, and in its place a 'yogh' sound is added. Thus 'blue' becomes *blyeu* or *beu*; *ploo* ('plough') becomes *plyeu* or *peu*; and 'flu' becomes *flyue* or *feu*.

1.7 The spelling system and pronunciation guide of *'The Hamely Tongue'*

The recent publication of James Fenton's *The Hamely Tongue: a personal record of Ulster-Scots in County Antrim* requires special mention in this chapter. Not only is it an authoritative record of contemporary Ulster-Scots as a living tongue in the stereotypical core area of County Antrim, but the book itself, like this present one, carries the *imprimatur* of the Ulster-Scots Academy and the Ulster-Scots Language Society.

James Fenton's objective was to present the vocabulary and illustrative examples of speech he collected over a lifetime (and authenticated by a representative group of native speakers distributed throughout the county). This he accomplished by using his own spelling system which was "... designed to give, as far as practically possible, a direct guide to pronunciation, avoiding the use of the phonetic alphabet and the technical language of the phonologist."

The Fenton spelling system is 'user friendly', and not markedly different from the spellings adopted by some early 20th century Ulster-Scots writers. It avoids awkward orthographic structures, making pronunciation self-evident to the reader who may not be familiar with spoken Ulster-Scots. Because the work is a 'dictionary', with an alphabetical list of head-words, aids to pronunciation can be inserted after the main word entry in a way that is not possible in creative writing. For example, the interdental 'd' and 't' forms (giving *dh* and *tth* pronunciations) are explained in the introduction, but in the text of the dictionary itself, only occasional 'reminders' are given, such as *efter* (-tth-).

Inevitably, some 'eye dialect' or pronunciation spellings tend to differ from traditional Scots spelling conventions, or, more properly, they can contrast with etymologically 'correct' alternatives that survive as historical spelling forms. This problem, of course, has always been present with Scots writers who have frequently had to invent spellings to represent what (to them) was known only as an oral language. *The Hamely Tongue*, to give one example, employs the letter 'z' in words such as *wuz* ('was') and *iz* ('us'). This particular spelling form has also been adopted by some modern Scots writers in South-West Scotland, but has been criticised by modern Lallans 'purists' as a move away from standardisation for Scots spellings because it has no historical precedent in Scots literature. This is not the case for Ulster-Scots, however, since our late 19th century writers such as W G Lyttle, and others following him, regularly employed this particular device. This book employs some such spellings. Indeed, as far as the word *sez* ('says') is concerned, this form is almost universal in modern Ulster-Scots (and Ulster-English dialect) prose. Jim Fenton does, however, extend the use of 'z' in his spelling system to words such as *hoozes* ('houses') and *jalooze* ('suspect, imagine': Std Scots *jalouse*).

Given the immediate popularity of *The Hamely Tongue*, and the fact that the creation of spelling precedents in Ulster-Scots is a process subject to continuing evolution, even those spellings which are unique to this dictionary will probably be adopted by future writers.

It is important, therefore, that a description of the spelling system and pronunciation guide used in *The Hamely Tongue* be included in this chapter. Undoubtedly *The Hamely Tongue* will prove to have had enormous influence on future creative writing in Ulster-Scots, and indeed, readers of this description of the Ulster-Scots language should refer to Fenton's work for accurate contemporary pronunciation of particular words. A unique characteristic of this dictionary is a supplementary list of words which differ from Standard English in form and pronunciation only, but not in meaning. Any future 'standard' for Ulster-Scots will inevitably be based on the dominant Antrim dialect he describes.

Contained in the introductory chapter of *The Hamely Tongue* is an important spelling and pronunciation section (pp ix-xi) which explains not only the word forms and pronunciation common to the whole study area, but also some of the variations and exceptions found within Co Antrim. This is reproduced below:

The representation of consonants in *The Hamely Tongue*

(i)   *d* and *t* have the widespread 'interdental' pronunciation when followed by *r* (*dhrive* for *drive*, *destthroy* for *destroy*). Since this is always so, no special indication is given in the text when they occur. However, they are often, but not always, similarly pronounced when followed by a vowel and an *r*, in these cases this is indicated as in **batter** *(-tth-)*. Pronunciation is often conventional for comparatives, such as *whiter* and *broader*, and almost always so for words denoting agency, such as *reader* and *writer*.)

(ii)   *ch*, when preceded by a vowel (or vowel-sound, as in *yowch*), is, unless otherwise indicated, pronounced as in *loch*; following *u* only, and only where indicated, *gh* is used instead to represent this guttural sound.

(iii)   *th* in *ther* is always pronounced as in *the*.

The representation of vowels and vowel sounds in *The Hamely Tongue*

(i)   Short, stressed *i* (as in *bit*) is equivalent, or very close, to Standard English short, stressed *a* (as in *bat*); thus **niver** *(never)* is pronounced as (or close to) *navver*. Again, since this is always so, no special modification is made to spelling in dialect words or in Standard English words where this *i* is retained. (This short *i* sometimes replaces and is replaced by other vowel-sounds – eg **shilter** for *shelter*, **twust** for *twist* – but these substitutions are made directly in the spellings used.)

(ii)   *i* and *y* in certain words are pronounced as broad *aai* (the most commonly cited example being *maaine* for the pronoun *mine*, as distinct from *mine* for the noun or verb). This variation is not confined to Ulster-Scots, but the *aai* form is so strong there as to be treated in the text as a distinct vowel-sound. (The vowel-sound in the second *mine* also differs from Standard English in being somewhat 'narrower', but the variation is much less marked and is ignored in the text.)

(iii)   *a* when stressed (whether conventionally short as in *cat* or long as in *harm*) is always long; where necessary, it is shown as *ah*, whether in the headword itself, as in **cahse** for *cause*, or as in **wrang** *(-ah)* for *wrong*. (*Note:* always *uh* in *wa-*, *whu-*, etc.)

(iv)   *ow* in dialect words is, unless otherwise indicated, pronounced as in *how*, in words which retain their standard form but which have additional dialectal meanings, pronunciation is, again unless otherwise indicated, conventional. Where there is any possibility of confusion, further guidance is given.

(v)   Other vowel-sounds – notably *eh* as in *net*, *au* as in *pot* and *ae* as in *case* – are usually long (and often markedly so in mid-Antrim and locally elsewhere), but this has no special indication in the text.

(vi)   The pronoun *I* presents particular difficulties. Unstressed, its pronunciation ranges from a short *a* to a muted or quite neutral sound; stressed, it is a broad *ah* in some districts (especially in the central and southern parts of the area) and an equally broad *aai* elsewhere (especially in the east and north). Here, **A** is used for the unstressed form and **I** for the stressed.

(vii)   **o'** is used for *of* throughout, again to avoid confusion, even though the unstressed form is usually completely neutral.

(viii)   r (= 'rhymes with') is sometimes used as the simplest guide to the pronunciation of vowel-sounds, as in: **pull** (r. *hull*).

Variations of pronunciation within Co Antrim

(i)   The substitution of vowel-sound *eh* for *a* (whether short or long) in certain groups of words – in particular, those having *ack, ag, ang, ank, ap, ar* – is common throughout the county (**tex** for *tax*, **fairm** for *farm*). With many such words, however, there is a divergence of practice from district to district, and especially from urban/suburban to rural districts. In the eastern, central and northern rural areas especially, the change often takes the form of a marked lengthening and 'broadening' of the *ah* sound – as in **blak** (-*ah*) for *black* but **seck** for *sack*; **bag** (-*ah*) for *bag* but **fleg** for *flag*; **wart** (-*ah*) for *wart* but **smairt** for *smart*. (The urban/rural divergence is noted by Gregg in the paper cited. However, while it is most marked with words having *ang* or *ank* – urban **benk**/rural **bank** -*ah*), urban **tengle**/ rural **tangle** (*tahng'l*) – his long list of 'urban' forms contains many common in Ballinaloob and other rural districts: eg **kep** for *cap*, **dreg** for *drag*, **ect** for *act*.)

Where two forms of such words occur in the area, both are given, one usually being a minority form and labelled 'local' *(loc.)*.

(ii)   The substitution of vowel-sound *eh* for *ae* in certain words (eg **becon** for *bacon*, **plen** for *plain*) is found in many districts in the northern part of the county, from (roughly) Ballyweaney through Ballyknock to Armoy, and over a widening area that includes Topp, The Ganaby, Drumdo, etc. These are given as local variants in the text.

(iii)   Four minor variations are noted here but ignored in the text. (a) The substitution of short *i* for short *u* in some words (eg **pliver** for *plover*, **rin** for *run*) is widespread, but is more common in the extreme north of the county (**ip** for *up*, **kim** for *come*, **stiff** for *stuff*, etc.). (b) Here, and in some eastern districts, short *i* is also sometimes substituted for vowel-sounds *u* and *oo* (**bill** for *bull*, **schill** for *school*, **giss** for *goose*). (c) The glottal stop (as in *wa'er* for *water*) is particularly noticeable in mid-Antrim but detectable to some degree over a much wider area. (d) The occasional addition of an extra ('glide') vowel (as in *pawit* for *pot*) is found very locally, sometimes confined to individual families.

. . . .

The spelling rules adopted in this present book (like those of *The Hamely Tongue*) are not prescriptive, but choices have been necessary to achieve some sort of internal consistency. For example, limited use has been made of the '*quh-*' for '*wh-*' spellings, and only in very rare circumstances has the '*z-*' for '*y-*' change been adopted. Limited use is also made of three accent marks over vowels:

á, í, ý, etc   to indicate a stressed or lengthened vowel;

à, ì, etc   to indicate that the previous consonant must be 'modified' by 'h', or its sound lost altogether, and

ä   to indicate the distinctive vowel sound for short 'i' in Ulster-Scots.

This book is intended to help people learn to speak, as well as write, Ulster-Scots. For those not familiar with the sound of Ulster-Scots, the spellings should provide a fairly consistent guide to pronunciation. But this book cannot be a complete guide. The closeness of the relationship between English and Ulster-Scots cannot be denied, and so the author has attempted to minimalise spelling variations between equivalent words in the two languages. A word spelt with '*-ui-*' such as *guid* can be readily related to its English counterpart 'good'. However, as an attempt has been made to minimise innovation, the author reminds the reader not to assume that spellings give an accurate or consistent indication of pronunciation. In limiting to a minimum the use of *ä* to represent the short 'i' in Ulster-Scots (for example to such words as *pän* – 'pin'), it must be remembered that words such as *in, it, is* are pronounced [än], [ät or hät] and [äs], despite their 'standard' spelling.

The written language is a very restricted representation of the spoken tongue, and spelling conventions are only a tool to help this process.

Pronunciation can vary from dialect district to dialect district within Ulster-Scots, and even between speakers in the same area. It is a characteristic of Ulster-Scots to use as few words as possible in formal situations – to the point of bluntness. Indeed, native speakers may not articulate sounds distinctly except when asked to repeat themselves (and then they usually "correct" to Ulster-English anyway). The same word may be pronounced completely differently by the same speaker depending on the degree of emphasis, the context of the word in relation to those preceding and following words, and even the sense. In a language so long dependent on its oral form alone, intonation changes – some subtle, some less so – play an enormously important role.

An elderly friend of the author, now long dead, rarely used more than half a dozen words in "conversation". His usual response to a question or statement was one word: "*ay*". This word could mean anything (depending on pronunciation, intonation, facial expression and emphasis), from; "I couldn't agree more"; "I suppose you're right"; "I don't really think so"; to "Not at all", or "Catch yourself on". The same word is used in other ways too – "Ay!" is a common greeting to anyone met in the street, – and what else would an Ulster-Scot call out on catching a miscreant red-handed but "Ay!"?

CHAPTER 2:
NOUNS AND NUMBERS

Nouns are words that stand for animals, places, people or things (and even for abstract concepts such as 'fear'). More words act as 'nouns' than 'adjectives', 'verbs' or any other part of speech. The range of Ulster-Scots nouns is enormous, and it would require a work of dictionary proportions to provide a comprehensive listing. For example, the words used for parts of the human body provide us only with a glimpse of a few familiar terms:

heid	-	head
bap	-	crown of head
fizog	-	face
clock	-	face (slang)
bake	-	face, mouth (slang)
broo	-	forehead
mooth, mou	-	mouth
gub	-	mouth (slang)
weeks	-	creases from corner of mouth down to chin
neb	-	nose
snoot	-	nose (slang)
cootèr	-	nose (jocular: 'coulter' of a plough)
lug	-	ear
ee/een	-	eye/eyes
chollers	-	jowls, cheeks
gowl	-	throat, jaws, jowl
craa	-	gullet, throat
thrapple	-	throat
*shoodèr, shouller**	-	shoulder
airm	-	arm
oxtèr	-	armpit
*hann, haun**	-	hand
fing'r	-	finger (rhymes with 'singer')
thoom	-	thumb
nieve	-	fist
loof	-	palm
*fit, fut**	-	foot
*faet**	-	feet
shanks	-	legs
hinches	-	haunches, thighs
hunkers	-	backs of thighs
hurdies	-	hips
wame	-	stomach, belly
breesht, breist	-	breast, chest

airse   - bottom, backside (N.B. airse is not a 'naughty' word in
                                       Ulster-Scots and is used metaphorically for the 'back'
                                       or 'bottom' of anything)

Note: Words used in this and the following chapters may be archaic (that is only
recorded in the written record and not in modern speech). These 'literary' forms are
identified as such in the glossary at the end of the book only. Words and/or pronunciations indicated by spellings which are 'dialectal' within Ulster-Scots (ie not used
in the traditional speech of the 'core' Ulster-Scots area in mid and north Antrim), are
identified throughout by an asterisk <u>following</u> the word, eg *fivver** ('four'), *fut**
('foot') (where the 'standard' Ulster-Scots words for these examples would be *fower*
and *fit*).

Consider which words in a sentence might be nouns:
      Oor ain <u>kye</u> aye aits <u>hay</u>.
      'Our own <u>cattle</u> always eat <u>hay</u>.'

Here there are two nouns, with *kye* operating as the 'subject' of the sentence, and *hay*
as the 'object'. The construction of this sentence in Ulster-Scots is similar to its construction in English, where in simple terms we would expect a Subject-Verb-Object
(S-V-O) word order, and where the subject and the object are often 'nouns'. For
example, in the simple English sentence; 'The <u>cat</u> (Subject) has eaten (Verb) that little <u>mouse</u> (Object)', the noun 'cat' is the subject and 'mouse' the object.

In Ulster-Scots grammar a construction is often preferred which puts the object to
the front of the sentence (and at the same time keeps a pronoun object), and part of
the verb is moved to the end; *See thon wee <u>moose</u>* (Object), *tha <u>cat</u>* (Subject) *haes it
et* (Verb).

However, before considering in some detail how Ulster-Scots sentences are actually
constructed (chapter 10), we must establish how the parts of sentences operate. As
far as nouns are concerned, this means establishing whether they act as subjects or
objects.

Subjects and objects of a sentence can be either a noun or a 'noun phrase'. A noun
phrase must contain at least one noun (or a 'pronoun') within the group of words
which functions as the subject or the object. For example, the noun phrase *thon wee
moose* contains the noun *moose*, while the whole phrase may act as subject or object.

Some words can be used not only as nouns ('naming' words), but also as verbs
('doing' words). The words 'walk' and 'work', for example, can stand for the things
or 'nouns' that we know of as 'a walk' or 'his work'. On the other hand, 'to walk' and
'to work' are verbs. In an Ulster-Scots phrase such as *a wee dannèr*, the *dannèr*
('walk' or 'stroll') is a noun, although we might <u>dannèr</u> *intae toon* where we are
using <u>dannèr</u> as a verb. As in Standard English, both options are available, but most
Ulster-Scots speakers prefer the noun usage, so we would *hae tuk a wee <u>dannèr</u> intae
toon* rather than *hae <u>dannèrt</u> intae toon*. The Ulster-Scots forms of 'work' include
wark and *darg*. In general *darg* is used only when the noun is intended: *hè's hìs day's
<u>darg</u> daen* ('he has finished his day's <u>work</u>'), while *wark* is preferred when the verb
is the given sense: *an quhit daes hè <u>wark</u> at?* ('and what does he <u>work</u> at?', that is,

'what is his job?'). *Wrocht* is the past tense verb form of 'work': *hè <u>wrocht</u> aa nicht.*
Rather than say 'worry' in Ulster-Scots, *fash* or *trouble yer heid* is common (for
example, Savage-Armstrong: *"tae trouble me heed aboot deein"*). Here a noun
('head') is introduced where it would be unlikely in English.

The Ulster-Scots grammatical preference for nouns rather than verbs (although of
course both are necessary in the grammar of all languages), is really a preference for
certain core verbs that are 'simple' ('have', 'put', 'take', 'give', etc), along with an
extensive use of nouns to form phrases. So we will *pit in an apologie* for someone,
rather than 'apologise' for them. We will *tak a scunner* (or a 'sickener') *at* or *agin*
something rather than *be scunnert wi* it. A clergyman will *mak a prayer* rather than
'pray', and we will *gan for a swäm in thà wattèr* rather than 'go swimming in the
water'.

2.1 Verbal nouns

Another way in which nouns are regularly formed from verbs in English and Ulster-
Scots is by use of the '-ing' form of the verb. These are known as 'verbal nouns'. In
Ulster-Scots, this is really the *-in* form, as the final 'g' is dropped in this verb form
when used as a present participle eg *A'm <u>dauncin</u>* ('I'm <u>dancing</u>'). The same word
form is used as a verbal noun, eg *A'm larnin thà <u>dauncin</u>* ('I'm learning <u>dancing</u>'),
but studies of Scots grammar have revealed that with verbal nouns the 'g' can sometimes be retained: *tha dauncing*. A possible historical precedent for this distinction
may be found in Older Scots and Ulster-Scots writings, where 'verbal nouns' ended
in *-ing* while present participles ended in *-and*.

> eg: *Hè's awa til thà <u>dauncing</u> at thà scuil-hoose thenicht*, but,
>   *Hè's aye <u>dauncin</u>.*

Nevertheless, in contemporary Ulster-Scots speech, it must be observed that the final
'g' is rarely sounded in either circumstance. Indeed, when it is sounded as a form of
corrected speech, it seems to apply equally to the present participle. This is because,
despite the historical precedents, both '-ing' forms are used today by importation
from Standard English.

Note that the definite article *the* or *tha* is often used along with a verbal noun in
Ulster-Scots where it would be unusual in English. This serves to emphasise the use
of the word as a noun.

2.2 Quantifiers

'Quantifiers' are used in the noun phrase to indicate the amount or quantity of whatever is referred to by the noun itself. They can indicate the approximate amount, for
example 'some' houses, or the exact quantity, for example, 'four' houses. Because
quantifiers have some 'adjectival' properties, they are also known as 'determiners'
(see section 5.1). When they do not indicate the actual number or exact amount of
the noun, they are known as 'indefinite determiners' (such as 'all', 'few', 'several',
etc).

A wheen o something is one of the most widely used general quantifiers or 'indefinite
determiners' in Ulster-Scots. Depending on the context, a *wheen* can mean 'a

couple', 'some', 'a few', 'a number' or even 'a good quantity'. *Some* is used in Ulster-Scots with the meaning 'a surprisingly large amount of'; eg *thon wuz some rain last nicht.* Another widely used word for 'an amount' or 'number' is *feck*; eg *wuz thar onie feck o fowk at it?* The *maist feck* means the 'majority' or the 'greater part'.

If the intended meaning of the indefinite determiner is 'some', 'occasional' or 'a few', then *antrin* can be used, for example, *A tuk thà antrin slug o wattèr* ('I took an occasional swig of water'). However, *antrin* is an historic and archaic Scots form, today in literary use only (such archaisms are distinguished from current usages for the reader in the glossary). In everyday speech *tha odd* is more often used: *Hè wud cum roon thà hoose thà odd Settèrday* ('He comes to our house some Saturdays', or 'the occasional Saturday'). *Thar wuz thà odd wee dràp o rain yestreen* ('There was an occasional shower yesterday'). In Ulster-Scots we might *hae tha odd pun*, meaning 'several' pounds (although, given that this might be a characteristic under-statement, it could actually mean 'have a good few pounds'). To express 'few' in the sense 'not many', some sort of negative phrase would be used such as *A hinnae owre monie puns left.* Note that 'odd' meaning 'peculiar' is sometimes *orra* in Ulster-Scots literature: *a gye orra mon* ('a very odd man').

The most common quantifying adjectives (or, more properly, 'indefinite determiners') used in Ulster-Scots are as follows:

little, small – *wee*
[a little bit – *awee* (eg Orr: *"turn'd his head awee"*). However, this is an adverb here, not an adjective (see Section 5.2)]
all – *aa, aw, a'*
any – *onie*
many – *monie* (eg Thomson: *"Right monie a hurchin I hae seen"*)
much, many – *muckle* (eg *muckle guid thon'll dae ye*)
more – *mair*
most – *maist*
about, approximately – *or sae* (eg *twa dizzen or sae*)
enough – *eneuch* (pronounced [en-yugh])
some, a good few – *wheen, lock*
some, an amount – *thing* (eg *thar's nae coals in thà hoose, bot thar's thing oot in thà shade*)
a lot of – *some*
some, occasional – *antrin* (archaic/literary), *tha odd*
such – *sic* (archaic/literary), *sich, seetch*
other – *ither, tha tither*
every, each – *ilk, ilka* (archaic/literary)
every day – *ilkaday*
few, a small amount – *pickle*
roughly, round about – *in or aboot*
whole/whole amount – *hale, halewar* (eg Thomson: *"The halewar o' them clean awa"*)

Some of these quantifiers can sometimes (but not always) function in Ulster-Scots without '...of' added (when it would always be expected in English):
          a <u>wheen</u> prittaes   'a <u>number of</u> potatoes'

    a pickle saut   'a pinch of salt'
    a wee dràp tay   'a small drop of tea' (eg Herbison: *"A wee drap tea they be to gie them"*, also *"an' taks a drap whiskey"*)
    A hae plentie cattèr   'I have plenty of money'

Note: A 'little' can be a *wee bit*, also without '... of', eg *"Your bonnie wee bit bigged nest"* (Herbison).

Conversely, *eneuch* ('enough') does take an '... of' in Ulster-Scots:
    A hae eneuch o cattèr   'I have enough money.

A *nievefu* is a handful or fistful, while a *gopin* or *gowpin* is an amount that would fill two cupped hands held together.

Muckle ('much') appears in the Ulster-Scots literature with various spellings, including *mickle*:
    How hae I leugh a meikle deal
    Wi meikle dole she hosten spat
    He was nae man o' meikle lear
    She ca's the muckle brute her dear
    Sae, when a carle, wi' mickle pains
    I b'live owre muckle o' sic stuff
    White as a mickle skaith
    Jist noo A em muckle tae busy
    So by sic means, I maybe may make mickle mair
    Ye could as muckle bear his bangs
    Ye're got sae mickle gowden gear
    He cared na meikle what he saw
    Ow'r mickle, like ow'r little dreed
    Then hame I goes wi meikle speed

Pickle ('little') occurs less frequently in Ulster-Scots poetry, although in 17th century documents, both *muckle* and *pickle* occur regularly. Some examples of later usages in poetry include:
    To sell a pickle yarn
    That half his pickle peets they tak'

Many of these quantifiers can function as nouns or adverbs as well as adjectives. 'Each', for example, may be *ilk* or *ilka* in an adjectival usage meaning 'each' or 'every'. Ulster-Scots poets alternated between *ilk* and *ilka* without any immediately apparent pattern. When almost 100 examples of these two forms are examined from the different poets writing between 1720 and 1880, it seems that *ilk*, rather than *ilka*, is more often used at the start of a sentence:
    Ilk thing that's about them
    Ilk ane's as feat's a new made prin
    Ilk lassie wi' her dear
    Ilk ferlie ye saw there
    Ilk fairy scene on simmer's morn

> *Ilk ane sinsyne must have his tree*
>   *to speel and spring aff*
> *Ilk wee bird frae its dreary dream*
> *Ilk lass man ha'e a snaw-white gown*
> *Ilk lass, no tald lees on, wha deems*
> *Ilk maid and matron hauds her dear*
> *Ilk short relapse*
> *Ilk day when he did dry the kiln*
> *Ilk coley dog*
> *Ilk farmer man the kintra roun'*
> *Ilk ane I trow*
> *Ilk fearless frien' shall by ye stan'*

On the other hand, when 'each' occurs within a sentence, the form *ilka* is preferred (especially when the following word begins with a hard consonant such as b, c, g, or d):

> *For ilka verse, my social swankie*
> *And ilka bosom kindness shew'd*
> *Remembrance ilka morn*
> *Wad fok at ilka time agree*
> *And ilka wee bird blithely sings*
> *Thou feeds our beasts o' ilka kin'*
> *Twad be fine gif ilka youth ay*
> *The youth on forms sit rang'd roun' ilka wa'*
> *Then men o strength wha bullets play,*
>   *or put in ilka alley,*
> *My head was reft wi ilka cough*
> *Frae ilka neuk the spunkies staucher*
> *The beasts rub doon the cheeks o' ilka door*
> *For ilka draught*
> *Were slung on ilka shou'der*
> *He early rase on ilka morn*
> *Frae ilka bush he taks a few*
> *There's money taxes ilka year*
> *When ilka piper play'd a tune*
> *Ae British shillin ilka day*
> *Then ilka day in sax hours gaun*
> *In ilka gruntle*
> *Then ilka bonnie face I saw*
> *While ilka breath o' wind that blaws*
>   *in ilka way*
> *Wae ilka word my love let fa'.*

Historically, *ilka* is a reduced form of *ilk ane* ('each one'), and appears later in Older Scots than *ilk*. There is some suggestion that *ilk* was used where 'each' might be the expected meaning in English, and *ilka* whenever 'every' would be more usual.

On those occasions where *ilk* rather than *ilka* is used within a sentence, the word following it often starts with a vowel. Of course, this most frequently occurs with *ilk ane*, although the 'incorrect' form *ilka ane* also occurs:

> *But now ilk ane withouten fear*
> *Tears flow freely frae ilk e'e*
> *Clash to ilk ane*
> *Tho' ilk fareweel*
> *Auld mem'rys types ilk image tine*
> *Some stript ilk morn*
> *Their pride ilk day*
> *To check ilk heart an' banish wae*
> *On her laigh floor ilk winter night*
> *Divided roun' ilk hook an' crook*

The choice between *ilk* and *ilka*, in poetry, could also be dictated by metrical considerations, and may be determined only on the basis of fitting the iambic metre.

However, if the English meaning of 'each' is 'to each' such as in a sentence as 'The boys are careless with money, I gave them two pounds each', then *tha piece* or *apiece* is used: *Tha weefellas haes nae had wi cattèr, A gien thaim twa pun apiece.* A *haet* is a 'jot', or a 'scrap' – the 'smallest amount': *A hinnae a haet in thà hoose. Feen (a) haet* or *Deil (a) haet* are common phrases for 'not a jot', ie 'nothing at all' (eg Thomson: *"Diel haet he dow bot girn an spit"*). A *racherie* is a 'large number', usually a large, unsorted collection of something, and a *hattèral* has a similar meaning.

Several compound indeterminate pronouns are formed from quantifiers such as 'any', 'some' and 'every':

> anything – *ocht, oniethin* (also *oniethìn** pronounced [onnyhin]), *oanythin*
> something – *somethin* (also *somethìn** pronounced [som'in], with a glottal stop in place of 'th')
> [Note: *boadie* is used in Ulster-Scots for English 'one', meaning 'person': *A boadie cannae dae ocht these days* ('One can't do anything nowadays')]
> anyone – *onieboadie*
> everyone – *aaboadie, iveryboadie*
> someone – *someboadie*

'Any' as a quantifier in Ulster-Scots is *onie* (pronounced [oany]). However, if 'any(thing)' is meant, eg 'I haven't any(thing) left at all', the appropriate Ulster-Scots word is *ocht*: *A hinnae ocht left ava.*

Similarly, 'too much' can be *iver ocht* or *owre ocht* as well as *owre much* in Ulster-Scots, although this idiom has also been used in Ulster-Scots literature to mean 'so much':

> *hè laucht owre ocht* ('he laughed so much')
> *hè's owre thran gat* ('he has become very difficult')
> *hè's owre ocht thran gat* ('he has become far too difficult')

'How little' is *aa tha much*: *luk at aa tha much ye hae et*, and 'how much' is *tha much*: *luk at tha much laun hè haes. Or sae* means 'or about': *twa dizzen or sae.*

2.3 Diminutives

Nouns are sometimes modified in Scots by the addition of the suffix *-ie* to provide what are known as the 'diminutive' forms: *lammie* ('little lamb'), *birdie*, *laddie*, *lassie* etc. Some of these are well known, and Burns's poem 'To a Mouse' about the wee 'mousey' and its *'wee bit housie'* has provided these forms with almost universal understanding:

> *"Wee, sleekit, cowrin', tim'rous <u>beastie</u>,*
> *Oh, what a panic's in thy <u>breastie</u>!"*

These forms were also common in Ulster-Scots poetry, eg *"but whan the birdie gied a scream"* (MᶜWilliams); *"was bred at Bangor, near the Strannie"* (Boyle); *"I taen a switch 'wee thicker than a roddie, ... right fast alang the roadie"* (Huddleston); *"Then Eppie a drappie o' something was strang"* (Beggs); *"Weds some canker't clownie"* (Orr); *"The snug wee hoosie whaur she lees"* (Savage-Armstrong).

In everyday Ulster-Scots speech, many other nouns can also be modified in this way. As far as people are concerned, besides *lads/laddies* and *lasses/lassies* we can have *girlie* (<u>not</u> with the same connotation as in the modern English adjective), *wifie, sinn/sonnie, ma/mammie, da/daddie, ba/babbie, mon/mannie*, and of course, *grannie* and *auntie* (the short forms 'gran' and 'aunt' are rarely used at all).

In fact, these *-ie* forms are not really 'diminutives' meaning 'small' in Ulster-Scots. More properly they are 'familiar' or affectionate terms, often used (as in English) with children, although the concepts of 'small' and 'nice' are interwoven. For example, we can talk of a lovely *wee hoose* someone has just bought where *wee* does not mean 'small', but instead reinforces the meaning of 'beautiful'. A bag of *sweeties*, a *dollie*, a *marlie*, or a *drinkie* – even if it is a 'wee drinkie' – are not necessarily smaller items than would be otherwise expected if the words *sweets, doll, marble* or *drink* had been used.

Other 'diminutive' nouns with obvious 'base' forms include:
> *duggie* – dog
> *pooshie, pushie** (rhymes with 'hushy') – cat
> *dràppie* – a wee 'drop' of tea, etc
> *loanie* – lane (base form *loanen*)
> *burnie* – stream
> *paddie* – path
> *deuckie* – duck
> *luggies* – ears
> *nebbie* – nose (however, also means 'nosey' as in *nebbie neebours*).

These diminutives are nearly always used along with *wee*, eg *tha <u>wee</u> <u>burnie</u> a-bak o oor hoose* 'the (dear little) stream at the back of our house', or *'tha babbie's gat a wee nebbie jist like his da.'*
Note: Although a *scaldie* is a young, freshly-hatched nestling, this is not a 'diminutive' form as the word *skalled* originally meant 'bald', and so a scaldie is simply 'something bald'. We would not think of a *grumpie* (someone who 'grumps' about) as a diminutive. Similarly, the *poastie* ('postman'), or the *buikie* (the 'book-maker') are really equivalent to the 'nick-name' forms of personal names also found in English, but particularly common in Scots: *Wullie, Rabbie, Fergie, Boydsie*, etc.

Many Ulster-Scots nouns with an *-ie* suffix, like English 'goody' or 'baddy', clearly

have a meaning modified along the lines of 'in the nature of...', or, 'having the characteristics of...'. Obviously, however, the -*ie* suffixes common in 'familiar' names
are perceived to be affectionate forms, rather than 'diminutives'. Regardless of the
physical size of the person the sense of familiarity is increased by referring to
somone as '<u>*wee*</u> *Thompie*' etc. A 'small orchard' is an *orkie**, and a small flat rock
covered at high tide is a *pladdie*. However, *pladdies* and *skerries* are words of
Scandinavian origin, and although like *scaldies* are popularly believed to be 'diminutive' forms (of *plat* 'flat' and *sker* 'rock'), more probably were formed by the addition of the Old Norse word -*ey* 'isle' (eg *sker* + *ey* giving 'rock isle', rather than the
'diminutive' of *sker* giving 'little rock'). Suffice it to say that not all nouns in Ulster-
Scots ending in -*ie* can be described as 'diminutive' forms.

2.4 Plural Nouns

Nouns in Ulster-Scots almost always change their endings in the same way as in
English to indicate if there is only 'one' (singular) or 'more than one' (plural). As in
English, the usual ending for the plural is an -*s*. However, if the singular noun form
ended in a consonant such as the final p, l, g, n, in *schip, farl, lug, toun*, etc, the early
Ulster-Scots literature usually formed the plural by adding -*is*: eg *schippis, farlis,
luggis, tounis* etc. (Note that in some cases the final consonant in the singular noun
is doubled in the plural.)

There are a number of irregular plural noun forms in Ulster-Scots. Several nouns
ending with a vowel, such as *ee* ('eye'), *trèe, shae*, and the noun *hoose* ('house'),
have their plurals formed by adding an -*n*. This is similar to the English 'ox' (singular) and 'oxen' (plural), and so we have in Ulster-Scots *een* ('eyes'), *treen* ('trees'),
schune ('shoes') and *hoosen* ('houses'). The *treen* and *hoosen* forms are both rare
and archaic. The irregular plural of *coo* ('cow') is *kye*, which had a double plural
form *kyen* ('cattle, kine') in early documents that was used when a larger quantity
was referred to – roughly paralleling the English usages of 'cows' and 'cattle'. The
irregular English plural form for 'child' – 'children' – is not used in Ulster-Scots,
where the plural of *chile** is *childèr** (but usually *wean/weans*).

Starn is the Ulster-Scots word for 'star' (singular), and is not an irregular plural.
'Stars' would be *starns*, although these forms also are literary and archaic.

For plural quantities involving nouns of measure, that is, when the plural noun is preceded by a number or quantity, the <u>singular</u> form of the noun is often used:
> *twa pun* (two pounds)
> *a hunner breek* (a hundred bricks)
> *echt mile* (eight miles)
> *fowertie fit lang* (forty feet long)

The behaviour of plural nouns of measurement or quantity as if they were singular
extends beyond the inflection of the noun (*twa mile*, etc). When using the perfect
tense (section 7.13), constructions such as *A'm waitin on hìm <u>this</u> twa hòor* ('I've
been waiting for him [for] these two hours) are common, where the singular demonstrative adjective is used with a plural noun.

Note: In English, 'porridge' (*brochan*), and 'soup' (*broth*) are treated as singular
nouns, but are regarded along with *sowans* as plural in Ulster-Scots:

Them's quaer brochan
'_That's_ good porridge'

A _wheen o_ broth
'some soup'

Hae ye _them_ sowans daen?
'Have you _that_ "sowans" finished?'

'Stew' can be _steuch_ in Ulster-Scots (or _steuchie_ if unappetising), but, occasionally, _stews_ (plural) is used. _Champ_ (mashed potatoes with milk and scallions added) is sometimes referred to in the plural: _like peppers on champs._

Similarly, 'coal' and 'peat' (as fuel) can sometimes be made plural – _coals_ or _couls*_, and _peats_ or _paits*_:
> Thaims guid burnin _paits_
> Pit mair _coals_ on, wud ye

2.5 Noun gender

Unlike most other European languages, but like English, Ulster-Scots makes little use of grammatical gender. Men, boys, and all male animals are of course masculine gender, females are feminine gender and nearly everything else is neuter (see below). Historically speaking, _King's_, with an _'s_ is not a contraction of _his_ but is an ending on the noun inherited from Anglo-Saxon. Nevertheless, in early documents the possessive case of nouns, such as in 'the King's command', was sometimes written as _the King his commaund,_ and sometimes as _the King's commaund._ Indeed, the possessive case was identical often to the older plural form of _-is_ (see section 2.3), so that 'the King's command' might also have been written: _the Kingis commaund._ An inscription of 1625 above the door of Ballygally Castle in east Antrim reads: "_Goddis_ providens is mine inheritans". ('_God's_ providence is my inheritance'). All the following usages: _the Queen her, the Queenis_ and _the Queen's_, are found in Old Ulster-Scots documents. In modern Ulster-Scots, however, the same rules as operate in English are applied for all genders (eg _tha Quaen's commaun_), although the apostrophe is often omitted in writing (_tha Quaens commaun_).

In English, vehicles – especially sailing vessels – are sometimes regarded as feminine in the sense that they can be described as 'she'. This feature also occurs in Ulster-Scots, although the range of 'neutral' nouns which can be used as if they were feminine is much more extensive, and includes mountains, trees, the moon, clouds, rain and other aspects of the landscape and weather:
> eg: _Scho's no that bad theday_ (the weather)
> _Scho cum doon richt owre thà loanen_ (a fallen tree)
> _A biggit thà hoose twa yeir syne an scho's emppie yit_ (a house)

A letter written to the Edmonstons of Ballycarry from Galgorm in county Antrim in 1629 illustrates the use of 'she' and 'her' in reference to a corn mill:
> "... to stay _the mille_ from going gave they could. That day that he cam to stayet _her sho_ vas going tow ours before he cam, for the mellors vas gresting stons. He sad that _sho_ sould not go. I tould him, it is out of tyem for _sho_ had ben going tow ours befor he cam.
> ... to hender _her_ from going ... _Sho_ is going and grend exceding vell."

When nouns have a common gender such as *dominie, weans, fowks* etc, the pronoun 'he' that was used in 'school-book' English for such sentences as: 'Each teacher must leave <u>his</u> room before 8 o'clock' is not good Ulster-Scots, and the traditional 'non-sexist' plural form in English ('they' and 'their') is also the historical Ulster-Scots usage: *Ilk dominie maun laive <u>thair</u> chaummer afore 8 o'clock*.

However, the understanding of *monkynn** or *mankine* and *men* to mean all 'human-ity' and 'people' (male and female) still stands in Ulster-Scots, although these usages are becoming regarded as sexist in modern English.

2.6 <u>Possessive and compound nouns</u>

In fact, the possessive case in the *-'s* or *-s* form as in *tha Queen's commaun* is often avoided altogether by using the construction: *tha commaun o tha Queen*. In English, <u>partitive nouns</u> (particularly collective nouns such as 'herd', 'crowd', etc) are fol-lowed by 'of'. This device is much more extensively used in Ulster-Scots, especially where the noun phrase contains two nouns rather than a noun and an adjective. For example, *a ruif o thatch* or *thà ruif o tha Meetin Hoose* are typical constructions, and the alternatives of *a theekit ruif* and *tha Meetin Hoose ruif* are less satisfactory. So too, we find the *key o tha duir o tha hoose* rather than the **hoose-duir key*; the *scraich-o-day* rather than 'daybreak'; and with the explicit possessive case: *tha coo's eldèr*, the preferred form can be *tha eldèr o tha coo* ('the cow's udder').

Note: This 'rule' breaks down when the two nouns used together in a noun phrase become familiarly associated together to give a compound noun such as *Kirk Session* (rather than **Session o tha Kirk*). When we mean a 'teapot' rather than a 'pot of tea', we use the compound noun *taypot* as a single word to describe the object needed when we decide to *wat* (ie 'brew') *a wee pot o tay*. In earlier times this was the *tay-draa'r* (used to 'draw' the tea). A church organ, referred to derogatively as a *kist* or 'chest' of whistles in Ulster-Scots, is written as a compound noun in the hyphenated form *kist-o-whussles*, rather than as a single word, and so it is also with *paep-o-day* ('dawn').

It should also be noted that the possessive case for 'general' classes of objects involv-ing two nouns in a noun phrase, such as 'dogs' leads', 'car tyres' etc, are constructed using *for* rather than 'of': *laids for dugs*; *tyres for motòrs* etc, eg: *Hae ye onie paiper for lappin in thà schap?* ('Have you any wrapping paper in the shop?').

When a proper, singular noun ends in *-s*, the possessive form is *-s's*, eg *Burns's poems* ('Burns' poems').

2.7 <u>Numbers</u> *(Nummers)*

0	*nocht/ought*	7	*sen/seiven**
1	*yin/ane/ae*	8	*echt*
2	*twa/qwa*	9	*nine*
3	*thrie/thie**	10	*ten*
4	*fower/fivver**	11	*leivin*/livin/elivin*
5	*five*	12	*twal/qwal*
6	*sax*	13	*thirtaen*/thurteen*

14	*fowertaen*/-teen*, etc	70	*seiventie*
15	*fiftaen*	80	*echtie*
16	*saxtaen*	90	*ninetie*
17	*sentaen/seiventaen*	100	*yin hunnèr*
18	*echtaen*	132	*yin hunnèr an thurtie-twa*
19	*ninetaen*	200	*twa hunnèr*
20	*twonnie/qwonnie*	232	*twa hunnèr an thurtie-twa*
21	*yin an twonnie/twontie-yin/twuntie-wan*	1000	*yin thoosan*
22	*twa an twontie/twontie-twa*	1032	*yin thoosan an thurtie-twa*
30	*thretie/thurtie*	1200	*twal hunnèr*
31	*yin an thurtie/thurtie-yin*	1232	*twal hunnèr an thurtie-twa*
40	*fawrtie*	2000	*twa thoosan*
50	*fiftie*	2032	*twa thoosan an thurtie-twa*
60	*saxtie*		

A numeral used to identify the year (eg 1862) is also spoken as *echtaen an saxtie-twa*. Sometimes this is written as *18&62* or even *18 an 62*, for example, at the start of 'fiction' letters written in Ulster-Scots to local newspapers at the end of last century. Some of the numeral forms identified above are archaic, but found in the works of the weaver poets, eg *"This threty year, I'm sure, and three"*; *"For sic a breach this threty year"*; *"These threty year gang whar I may"*; *"This se'nteen owks I have not play'd"*; *"For threty shillin"*.

Note: Numerals ending in *-taen** are pronounced as the spelling here indicates, eg [sax-tain] but only locally, and not in the core Ulster-Scots speaking areas. However, the word *teens*, by itself, is pronounced as spelt; eg *Hè fell intae teens o thoosans* ('He inherited "teens" of thousands'). Note also that *teens* is used in Ulster-Scots in a way in which 'tens' or 'dozens' might be used in English.

ZERO *(nocht)*. The numeral 'zero' or 'nought'. Unlike the other numerals, *nocht* is rarely used except when referring specifically to the number *0*. For example, although *A hae twa schillin yit* (I still have two shillings) can be a valid use of the numeral *twa* in speech, it is not so with the number *0* or *nocht*: (**A hae nocht schillin yit)*. Here we would say *A hinnae ocht left* or *A hae naethin* (or *nane*) *left*. When counting, the numeral 'nought' is *ought*, or *naethin*. *Nocht* is, however, used to mean 'nothing', eg Savage-Armstrong: *"An' think o' nocht but her, sae sweet"*.

ONE *(yin)*. In Mid-Ulster, 'one' is pronounced *wan* and is so written by dialect writers. The pronunciation (and spelling) of 'one' as *yin* is shared between east Ulster and South-West Scotland, although in Older Scots it was always written as *ane*. In Ulster-Scots it is common to add the definite article 'the' before the numeral in speech – eg *Ye cudnae be feart o jist thà yin o thaim* (see section 3.1). The abbreviated form of *ane* – *a'e* or *ae* – is also used for 'one', but is an obsolete adjectival form, and means 'a single -' or 'one (in particular) -'. [Note: The indefinite article 'a' or 'an' in English was also also written in Older Scots as *ane* (see Section 3.2)].

'One' is the only numeral which has two different forms – depending on whether the usage is as a noun (*ane* or *yin*), or as an adjective (*ae* or *yae*):
  Dae ye no ken mair nor yae wee lass?
  Na, A jist ken thà yin.

Cud ye no gie iz tha <u>ae</u> tùrn?
A gien ye <u>yin</u> last nicht.

As with Burns's songs *"Ae fond kiss"*, and *"Let me in this ae nicht"*, *ae* or *yae* often has a sense of 'one in particular, and indeed can mean 'one and only' – *ma yae wee wean*, or *A'm Tam M'Kee's ae ae sinn*. Other (mostly archaic) uses of *yae* include:

(a) the same
   The're aa tha yae breed (also, and currently, *tha yin breed*).

(b) the very
   She's thà yae warst wumman.

(c) about, nearly
   A'm eftèr ae ten ton.

The Ulster-Scots poets rarely wrote 'one' as *yin*, but used the conventional Scots form *ane*. Similarly, they rarely wrote *yae* for *ae*:

   "To town ae morn as Lizie hie'd" (Thomson)
   "Ae day a wan'ring fiddler, lame" (Thomson)
   "Sae a' weel pleas'd, wi ae consent" (Thomson)
   "Thats ae thing in which I am blest" (Thomson)
   "What I hae cost for ae bawbee" (Thomson)
   "Just ae word ere I gang awa" (Thomson)
   "Ae Monday morn" (Huddleston)
   "Gif thou'd withdraw for ae camping" (Orr)
   "The hedge-hauntin' blackbird, on ae fit whyles restin" (Orr)
   "We'se gie them something; ae babee" (Orr)
   "Tho' whyles scarce worth ae bare babee" (Orr)
   "Ae windy Day last owk" (Starrat)
   "To see no yae stane on anither" (Bleakley)

Other 'literary' uses of *ae* in compounds include the following: An *ae-yockit egg* is a 'one-yolked egg', and *ae-haunit* can mean 'single-handed' in the sense of clumsy or 'by oneself'. An *ae-horse peu* is a 'one-horse plough', and *aefauld* ('one-fold') is used to mean 'sincere' – an *aefauld lad* is *aye tha yin wye* ('always the one way' is an idiom used to describe someone who is 'pleasant, trustworthy and sincere').

TWO, THREE *(twa/qwa/thie*)*. The *qwa* (and *qwal, qwonnie, qwarthie*) forms for *twa* etc are rare forms still used in parts of County Antrim. Particularly around Belfast, the letter 'r' is dropped after 'th' in words like 'throw', 'through', 'throttle' and 'three' – which become *thow*, thoo*, thottle** and *thie**. This feature is similar to the way in which *frae* becomes *fae* (and even 'from' becomes *fom**) – see above (section 1.5).

'Several', 'two or three' or 'a couple' is *tworthy, twa-thrie, qwarthie*, etc.

FOUR *(fower, fivver*)*. Although the letters 'v', 'u' and 'w' are often interchangeable in Scots and Ulster-Scots, more often it is 'w' that is substituted for 'v' (eg *owre* for 'over'). The unusual *fivver* form of the Ulster-Scots *fower* ('four') is known to the author only in the Ards area of Co Down. Otherwise it is apparently unknown in Scots or elsewhere in Ulster.

SEVEN *(sen, seiven)*. The shorter form of the Ulster-Scots 'seven' *(sen,* or *sein)* is an archaism which was generally used only in compound words – *sennicht* ('seven nights', ie a 'week'), *sennaker* ('seven acres', as in place-names), *sentaen** ('seventeen'), etc.

EIGHT *(echt)*. The distinctive *-cht* pronunciation of this number is one of the acknowledged 'markers' of Ulster-Scots speech.

ELEVEN *(leivin)*. The initial vowel sound is sometimes lost in a number of words such as 'eleven' in Ulster-Scots (see section 1.4).

TWELVE *(twal, qwal)*. A 'dozen' is used frequently for the number 12, in the form *dizzen*.

Ordinal numbers. The 'ordinal numbers' which define the position of an object in a series; 'first', 'second', 'third' etc are *furst/färss, seconn* and *thurd* in Ulster-Scots. All higher ordinal numbers end in '-th' in English, and in *-tht* in Ulster-Scots:
> fourth – *fowertht*
> eighth – *echt*
> twelfth – *twaltht/twalt*
> eleventh – *leiventht/livintht*
> sixteenth – *saxtaentht*
> twentieth – *twonnietht*
> hundredth – *hunnèrtht*

The abbreviation for these ordinals, for example in giving dates such as the '4th November 1995', is *-t*: *4t Novemmer 19&95*.

Note: The 'length', 'breadth' and 'depth' of anything is the *lenth(t), brenth(t) and the depth(t)*.

'How long is the sixtieth path?' – *Quhit lentht wud thà saxtietht pad be?*
'No more than two miles long' – *Nae mair nor twa mile lang*.

Adverb numbers. 'Once' is *yince* or *yinst*, and 'twice' is *twice* or *twyst* (pronounced [twiced] and not *[twist]). 'Thrice' or 'three times', 'four times', etc are: *thrie tims, fower tims*, etc.

A heerd tell on thà leiventht nicht hè wuz hame thà yinst or twyst jist, bot hè sez hè wuz sax times hame theyeir.

'I heard on the night of the eleventh that he has only been home once or twice, but he said that he has been home six times this year.'

CHAPTER 3:
THE 'ARTICLES' AND MEASURES OF TIME

3.1 <u>The definite article, 'The'</u>: *tha, thà* and *the*

The definite article functions in Ulster-Scots in much the same way as in English. Sometimes, however, its form and the circumstances of its use are distinctive. The Shetland dialect of Scots maintains a *da* pronunciation and spelling for 'the', while in some other areas the 'th' sound is lost. When Ulster-Scots is spoken, 'the' is often not stressed, and is then pronounced as a short [ah] sound, like the 'a' in 'bat'. In certain dialects of Scots this loss of the initial 'th' sound has become established to the extent that the definite article is written as *'e* or *e*. However, it is almost unknown for Ulster-Scots writers to abbreviate the word in this way. In Chapter 1 the pronunciation of 'the' as [tha] or [a] was described as dependent on the context of the word in a sentence, that is, what precedes it in speech. In this book, when the initial 'th' is sounded, the definite article 'the' is written *tha*, and when it is not sounded, the form *thà* is used (section 1.4 above). It should be re-emphasised that there is no historical precedent for the use of any spelling of the definite article other than *the* in traditional, and *ye* in older Ulster-Scots literature, although some modern writers have adopted these *thà* and *tha* spellings.

Thà and *tha* are used throughout this book, except for constructions such as *theday* ('today') where indeed the origin may be 'this day' rather than a direct change from 'to-' to 'the-'. The principal reason for the introduction of *thà* and *tha* into modern Ulster-Scots or Ullans (apart from the fact that these forms may reflect more accurately the spoken language), is to avoid confusion with the Ulster-Scots form of the personal pronoun 'they', which has been represented as *the* since the 19th century by a number of Ulster-Scots poets. The confusion that can arise, for example, in the work of Robert Huddleston makes understanding of some lines difficult:

> "An sae <u>the</u> daunce <u>the</u> nicht awa,
> <u>The</u> morra haes nae cares ava."
> (`And so <u>they</u> dance <u>the</u> night away
> <u>To</u>morrow has no cares at all.')

The can also represent a variant form of English 'there', especially in sentences such as <u>*the*</u> *wuz this stane A haed* ('<u>there</u> was a stone I had'). In Ulster-Scots speech, confusion between the indefinite article *a* ('a') (see section 3.2), and the definite article *thà* (unstressed 'the' pronounced [a]) is also possible, as the two sounds can be virtually identical:

> *A cum roon* <u>*thà*</u> *benn owre quäck* ('I came round <u>the</u> corner too fast')

Roon thà benn can be pronounced [roon-a-ben] by some speakers, so that it is difficult to distinguish whether the definite article 'the' or the indefinite article 'a' is
meant in the spoken language. This difficulty also arises with a number of idioms
such as *monie(s) tha time*, which can also be *monie(s) a time*.

Another confusion in the spoken word occurs between *til thà* and *tae le*, as both have
the same sound. Around Belfast and south Antrim, and in parts of north Down, many
people characteristically pronounce 'the' as [le]. Often this can also be heard in
phrases like *thoo le duir* ('through the door'), and *see ye lemorra* (tomorrow/the-
morra) despite the fact that an 'le' spelling does not show up in Ulster-Scots literature.

[Note: It would be difficult to prove that the French definite article *le* had been a feature of 16th and 17th century English in east Ulster, but although French wasn't spoken, many local documents of the 17th century still used *le* in formal writing as a
legacy of the Medieval period. These documents use only the masculine French form
le (never *la*), and in some cases the *le* form was carried over into English translations
– for example *le Water Street*, *le Session-House* and *le tholsel* in Carrickfergus, and
many townlands such as *Le Cardie* (later 'The Cardy', or 'Cardy') in county Down,
and of course, *Le Forde*, the early medieval name for 'Belfast'. These forms were
still being cited in the 17th century].

Elsewhere in Ulster-Scots there are many circumstances when the word 'the' is used
where it would be omitted, or the indefinite article 'a' used, in Standard English:

(a)   When referring to a meal or drink
      Is thà dinnèr no made yit?
      'Is dinner not ready yet?'
      Hìs wife's gye fonn o tha drìnk
      'His wife's very fond of drink'

(b)   to an illness
      Hè haes thà maisles this fower days
      'He has had measles for four days'

(c)   to an occupation
      Wuz hè larnin thà bricklayin?
      'Has he been learning bricklaying?'

(d)   to an institution
      Hè's no gan tae tha church twyst on thà yin day?
      'He's not going to church twice on one day?'
      Is hè doon at thà scuil theday?
      'Is he down at school today?'

(e)   to a sport
      Hè fair loves thà fitbaa
      'He really loves football'
      Scho'd far rathèr hae tha bowls
      'She'd much rather have bowls'

(f)   to a subject of study
      Tha minístèr's quare an guid at thà Latin
      'The minister's very good at Latin'

(g)   to a cardinal number
      An in cum thà nine o thaim
      'And nine of them came in'
      Thar wuz jist thà yin left
      'There was only one left'

(h)   to time or seasons
      It's gan fower o tha clock
      'It's past four o'clock'
      A cum hame on thà Settèrday morn
      'I came home on Saturday morning'
      A'm aye awa aa tha simmertim
      'I'm always away all summer'

(i)   to places
      Hè cums fae tha Dee in thà Coontie Doon
      'He comes from Donaghadee in County Down'

In the idiom 'saw a time when', this is *saen thà time* or *sa tha time* in Ulster-Scots:

      A sa tha time quhan he hadnae tha yin nor tha tither
      ('I remember a time when he hadn't one or other')

A number of English words that begin with the prefix 'to-', have the definite article substituted in Ulster-Scots.

today	-	*theday*
tonight	-	*thenicht*
tomorrow	-	*themorra, themarra**
together	-	*thegithèr*

'This year', however, is also *theyeir* in Ulster-Scots:

      Theyeir's bin a lang deedle
      'This year has passed slowly'

      Hae ye onie prittas plantit theyeir?
      'Have you any potatoes planted this year?'

The well-known Scots idiom of *the noo* for 'just now' occurs in Ulster as well.
      A cannae gang the noo – A'll see yis aa themarra

*Yer mon** has become a popular catch-phrase to describe somebody from 'Norn Iron'* in Belfast and Ulster-English dialect. *Here cums yer mon wi tha baldie heid.* Here 'your' is not being used in the sense of 'belonging to you', but in place of the definite article 'the' (although a more accurate meaning of this *yer* has a sense of 'that' as well). Of course, it is not only with *yer mon* that we find this usage, but with other nouns:

> *Yer clacks ats made in Swutcherlann is ill on thà wee diamonns*
> 'The clocks made in Switzerland are hard on small diamonds'
>
> *A tuk yer wee lad at cums fae Bang'r*
> 'I took the young boy who comes from Bangor'
>
> *Ye ken yer big hoose near thà tap o tha raa?*
> 'You know the big house near the top of the street?'

In contrast, when referring to parts of the body, and personal possessions, the definite article is sometimes used instead of the possessive pronoun:

> *He's fell aff o tha bike*
> 'He has fallen off his bike'
>
> *Tha secatrie hurt thà airm on thà duir*
> 'My secretary hurt her arm on the door'
>
> *Keep thà heid, wee lad*
> 'Keep your head (keep cool), boy'
>
> *Ay, an keep thà hair on tae*
> 'Yes, and keep your hair on too'.

In some circumstances, the meaning can be ambiguous: *Is thà wife thar?* Depending on the context, this can mean 'Is my wife there?', or 'Is your wife there?'

The definite article can be substitued for 'how', 'what', 'which' etc in the following way:

> *D'ye see tha quäck thae cloods is shiftit?*
> 'Do you see how fast those clouds have moved?'
>
> *Ye saen thà skinnie A'm gat*
> 'You saw how thin I've become'
>
> *D'ye ken thà time hè's cumin at?*
> 'Do you know what time (or when) he's coming?'
>
> *A niver kent thà age he wuz*
> 'I didn't know what age (or how old) he was'
>
> *Luk tha lentht hìs airm is*
> 'Look what length his arm is'
>
> *Hè's aye crawin croose tha big hè's grew*
> 'He's always boasting how big he has grown'.

3.2 <u>The indefinite article: 'a'</u>

The indefinite article *a* is used in Ulster-Scots in some circumstances where it would not be expected in English. For example, there is a tendency for Ulster-Scots to use a noun (combined with the article *a*) where a verb might be more usual in English.

> *hè likes <u>a</u> swim* rather than 'he likes to swim'
> *hè's awa for <u>a</u> swim* rather than 'he's gone swimming'
> *ye no tak <u>a</u> sait?* rather than 'will you not sit down?'
> *gie iz <u>a</u> räng* ('phone me')
> *awa for <u>a</u> dannèr* ('gone walking')
> *haein <u>a</u> sleep* ('sleeping')

Obviously this characteristic means that the indefinite article *a* ('a') may be employed more frequently in Ulster-Scots.

As with *tha*, the indefinite articles *a* and *an* are used in Ulster-Scots in much the same way as in English. The letter 'a' is pronounced in the same way for both words *a* and *an* (ie rhyming with 'ma' and <u>not</u> with 'may'). It has been noted already that in speech it is sometimes difficult to distinguish between the sound of *a* and *thà*. Indeed, these two words are occasionally used interchangeably anyway. For example, in the phrase used to mean 'not one', we find *deil <u>a</u> yin, niver <u>tha</u> yin, niver <u>a</u> yin*, or *deil <u>tha</u> yin*. Similarly, we can have *monie <u>a</u> yin, monies <u>tha</u> yin* etc (eg Huddleston: *"As mony a ane ye've done"*).

The indefinite article can also be added after the 'literary Scots' words for 'each' *(ilk)* and 'such' *(sic)* (see section 2.2).

> *For ilka heidin wud gar ye grue*
> 'As each headline would make you shudder'
>
> *A coontit ilka stìrk amang thae kye*
> 'I counted every yearling heifer among those cows'
>
> *Sicca* (or *siccana*) *thing A niver saen afore, an nae fittin it on*
> 'Such a thing I have never seen before, and no exaggeration'.

In Older Scots, the indefinite articles 'a' and 'an' were nearly always written as *ane* (as was the numeral 'one'), regardless of whether the word was followed by a vowel or consonant. This feature was common in Ulster-Scots writings until the early 18th century. The Scots *ane* is often compared to the French *un*, which can also represent either the number 'one' or the indefinite article. Early Ulster-Scots letters contain numerous examples of the use of *ane*:

> *Sir Hew Montgomere is in building <u>ane</u> fyn housse at the Newton quhairof <u>ane</u> quarter is almost <u>ane</u> verie stronge castell.*
> (From a letter of 1614 from Strabane to James Hamilton of Bangor.)
> [Note: Newtownards is referred to as <u>the</u> Newton.]
>
> *. . . with <u>ane</u> sufficient way for carrying thame*
> (Robert McClelland, north Londonderry, 1614).

> ... *ane* cleashoch or harpe qche (which) *I have*
> (James Boyd, north Antrim, 1624).

> ... *bot thaire come ane bot frome Loche Rying quhairin thaire was ane mane*
> ('but there came a boat from Loch Ryan wherein there was a man')
> (John Hamilton, north Down, 1627).

> *I am far fra sa gud ane gatherer as many are ... giff God hes nocht giffen me ane warldly wyse hairt*
> ('I am far from so good a saver as many are ... if God has not given me a worldly-wise heart')
> (Isobel Haldane, Ballycarry, 1630.)

Although the indefinite article was always written *ane* in older Scots, it is doubtful that it was pronounced in full before a consonant. In fact, in modern Scots *a* is sometimes used in front of a vowel: *hae ye a aipple?*, or *hè's a eejit*, and indeed this is believed to be a long-established feature.

The indefinite article is sometimes inserted in front of numbers: *thar's no a yin o thaim cud bate us*. As in Gaelic, when numbers are counted out, an '*a*' can also be added:

> *a-yin, a-twa ... a-yin, twa, thie*
> *A'll tak a sax or a seven o thaim wi me*

The 'Carrowdore 100' motor-cycle race, for example, is called locally the *Carradòre a-Hunnèr*.

The letter 'Z', when spoken, is pronounced [a-Zed], hence *azoo* ('zoo') and *azinc* ('zinc').

The modern Scots cardinal number 'one' is *ane*, pronounced [yin] in Ulster and south-west Scotland, and is now generally written as it sounds – *yin*. Not only did the indefinite articles *a* and *an* all develop from the Older Scots *ane*, but also so did *yin* and the adjectival form of 'one' – *ae* or *yae* (see section 2.7).

3.3 Units and measures of time

Telling the time in Ulster-Scots is much the same as in English, except that we have *ten eftèr* (rather than 'past') *echt*, and *ten til*, or *aff* (rather than 'to') *echt*. Instead of 'what time is it?', the question *quhit's tha time-o-day?*, or (rarely now) *quhit o clack** (or *o clawk*) *is it?* might be asked. However, the more polite way of asking this is *ye wudnae hae tha time on ye, wud ye?*. If a cardinal number occurs in front of the phrase *o clawk*, this can become *o tha clawk*: *A winnae git hame tae sax o tha clawk*. *Luckie twal o'clawk*, is 'rather more than (just after) twelve o'clock'.

second	-	*saiconn*
minute	-	*männit*
hour	-	*hòor*
half-an-hour	-	*a hauf hòor*
day	-	*day* (as English, but sometimes pronounced [deh])

> *Saxtie saiconn'd mak tha yin männit*
> *Saxtie männit'd mak tha yin hòor*

[Note: *Männit* is used for both senses in English of 'a minute' and 'a moment' eg *houl on a männit* ('wait a moment') – although *houl on a wee* is just as common.] A 'full hour', used figuratively, is a *roon hòor* or a *strucken hòor*: *It tuk me twa roon hòors for tae soart it oot*. The *wee sma hòors* are the 'early hours of the morning'.

Frae yestreen tae themorra morn: parts of the day.

dawn, early morning	-	*scraich-o-day, peep-o-day*
early part of the day	-	*fore-en o tha day, fore-pairt o tha day*
morning	-	*morn*
late morning	-	*forenoon*
mid-day, noon	-	*twal-hòors, heich twal, middle o tha day*
afternoon	-	*evenin, eftèrnoon*
evening, dusk	-	*dailigon, dailichtgan*
late evening	-	*foresupper*
night	-	*nicht*
midnight	-	*mid-nicht, laich twal*

[Note: *Themoarn* can also mean 'tomorrow', eg *wull hè cum eftèr schuil themoarn?*]

yesterday	-	*yestreen, yistèrday, yestrae**
today	-	*theday*
tonight	-	*thenicht*
tomorrow	-	*themorra, themoarn*
this year	-	*theyeir.*

[Note: 'Tomorrow morning' can be *themoarn's moarn* or *themorra moarnin*]

Yestreen is largely a literary form, and can mean either 'yesterday evening', or 'yesterday':

> *"I'm sure ye min' on yester e'en"* (Huddleston)
> *"Yestreen I daftly still'd the clangour"* (Orr)
> *"The Bardie whom thou fill'd yestreen"* (Orr)
> *"This hunted me away yestreen"* (Porter)
> *"Yestreen, sedate I sat beside"* (Porter)
> *"To tell the piper died yestreen"* (Boyle)
> *"Whar cam' it frae yestreen"* (Beggs)
> *"It was but yestreen I had oot my bit claith"* (Sloan).

week – *sennicht, owk* (*owk* is an archaic early literary form, while *sennicht* has had a more recent, and more common, literary usage)

The poet William Starrat of Strabane and Lifford was using *owk* for 'week' circa 1720:

> *"Ae windy day last owk"*
> *"This se'nteen owks I have not play'd sae lang"*.

fortnight   -   *foartnicht*

month   - *month, mond, montht** (a 'month' as a figurative passage of time
           is a *muin-change*)
year   - *yeir, twalmond, towmonn, twal month* (eg *"Three twal month sine
           foretall his deed"*, Starrat; *"For tho' six twomonds they were
           wed"*, Huddleston).

There is very little evidence in Ulster for the use of the Scots words for Monday,
Tuesday and Thursday (*Monanday, Tysday* and *Fuirsday*), although these forms
would have been known from reading Burns and other Scots literature. Instead,
Monday and *Tuesday* (pronounced [chooseday]) and *Friday* are used in Ulster-Scots
as in English. Wednesday is *Waddinsday** or *Wensday* in Ulster-Scots, Thursday is
Thorsday, Saturday is *Settèrday*, and Sunday (occasionally) *Sabbathday*.

The months of the year are as follows (in each case the 'braidest' Scots form is
given): *Jennerwarry**, *Feburie, Mairch, Aprile* or *Aiprae**, *Mie, Juin, Julaai, Ageest,
Sictemmer**, *Uptober, Novemmer* and *Decemmer*.

next Saturday   - *this Settèrday*, or *Settèrday cumin*
a week from Saturday   - *neist* or *nix Settèrday, Settèrday'll be a sennicht,*
                            or, *Settèrday week*
on Saturday   - *a-Settèrday*

Note that a statement such as *themorra wuz a twalmonth* or *towmond* usually means
'a year ago from tomorrow', but it can (rarely) mean 'in a year's time from tomorrow'. When the meaning is 'a year from tomorrow', the more common construction
is *themorra'll be a towmond*. The context will normally reveal the intended meaning:

He cum hame Monday wuz a sennicht
'He came home a week ago last Monday'

The'r flittin Monday'll be a foartnicht (or, more currently, *on Monday foart
nicht*)
'They move house in a fortnight from Monday'

Hè's for cumin hame yestrae wuz a yeir
'He is coming home a year from yesterday'

Yisterday wuz a week
'It was a week ago yesterday'

The seasons are: *Spräng, Simmer(tim), Autumn* (or more often *Hairst* or *Tha bak-en
o tha yeir*), and *Wuntèr(tim)*.

CHAPTER 4:
PRONOUNS AND PEOPLE

'Pronouns' are used in place of a noun, or sometimes in place of a whole noun phrase.

4.1 Personal pronouns: ('I', 'you', 'he', 'she', 'it', 'we', etc).

In conventional grammars, the personal pronouns of a language are introduced by setting out the 1st, 2nd and 3rd 'persons' (singular and plural) in a simple table which relates the personal pronouns to a basic verb. This is done below for the verb *hae* – 'to have' (see Chapters 7, 8 and 9 for the behaviour of Ulster-Scots verbs). However, it must be remembered that in Ulster-Scots literature and speech, the Standard English forms of most personal pronouns are shared and used interchangeably with the distinctive Ulster-Scots forms. The following table summarises, therefore, only the *braid* forms most distant from English:

(1st person, singular)	*A hae*	I have
(2nd person, singular)	*ye hae*	you have
(3rd person, singular)	*he/scho/hit* haes*	he, she, it has
(1st person, plural)	*we hae*	we have
(2nd person, plural)	*yous/yiz/yous'uns hae*	you (plural) have
(3rd person, plural)	*the/thaim'uns hae*	they have

Sae A̲ jist tell't him sez I̲, "A̲ hae heerd it a' afore". In this short piece taken from a 100 year-old County Down novel you can see that the writer (W G Lyttle) uses both *A* and *I* for the first person pronoun 'I'. Although many Ulster-Scots words are different from their English equivalents, in certain circumstances an apparently 'English' word (such as 'I') can also be the correct Scots form.

I (or sometimes *me*) is used in Ulster-Scots as the emphatic form of *A* (ie when there is a heavy stress or emphasis placed on the word). When 'I' is not emphasised, the usual form of the word in Ulster-Scots is *A*, although other writers have used such spellings as *Ah, a'* or even *a*. In the phrase: *'Quha's lukin me̲? sez I̲'*, both *me* and *I* are used emphatically – but in exactly the same way as they would be found in English. However, in the phrase *'him an me̲'s lukin oot, sez me̲ til hìm'*, *me* is being used where 'I' would be the Standard English form ('he and I̲ want out, I̲ said to him').

The modern Scots word *A* (meaning 'I') can be pronounced either with the 'a' sound found in 'pat' or 'mat', or even with a longer sound as at the end of 'paw' or 'raw'. This distinctive pronunciation probably has a lengthy history, but it is only over the past 150 years that it has been written as *A*. The Rhyming Weavers of 200 years ago always wrote thus: *"I̲ didna care ava"* (Thomson, 1793).

[Note: The sound of the letter 'a', when spoken by itself – such as in spelling out 'A.B.C.', or even in saying 'Amen', – is a long and drawled 'Ahh' as in *'pan'* or *'bar'*. This contrasts with the English pronunciation which rhymes with 'say' or 'pay'.]

The difference between emphasised and unstressed words such as *I* and *A* can also be seen in the way in which *ye* and *you* are used.

> *Quhit-for daed ye apen yer bake an tell on me? A niver let on at ye wurnae oot theday – an quha sez you shud a?*
> 'Why did you open your mouth and inform on me? I didn't tell that you weren't out today – and who said you should have?'

Exactly the same situation exists with the plural forms of 'you' in Ulster-Scots – *yiz* and *yous*.

> *Yiz see yous boys – qu' she – yiz ir aa daft.*
> 'You see you men – she said – you are all daft'.

Again, 'she' in Ulster-Scots is only written in the archaic, literary form *scho* by some modern writers when it is unstressed, and as *she* when it is intended to be emphasised. *Scho* is pronounced [shuh] and *she* (emphatic) as [shee].

> *Scho's for thà schaps themarra.* ('She's going shopping tomorrow')
> *Quhit! Is she goin an aa?* ('What! Is she going too?')

[Note: In the Scots written in Ulster 300-400 years ago 'she' was always written *scho*. This spelling has been common in Older Scots since 1375, but is rejected by some modern writers as archaic, while others use it as the 'standard' Ulster-Scots form in all circumstances regardless of emphasis. Burns used it in his poem 'There was a lad': *"Quo' scho – wha lives will see the proof"*.]

It is the common form of the neuter pronoun today, but the medieval Ulster and Older Scots form of 'it' – *hit*, is still used in the east Donegal dialect of Ulster-Scots. *Hit* is occasionally used in this book as it is the author's objective to be inclusive of the different varieties found throughout Ulster.

Although the pronouns *he, him, her* and *his* are spelt similarly in Ulster-Scots to English, they are often pronounced, especially when not stressed, without the initial 'h', and may be written *hè* [ee] etc (see section 1.5).

'First person' pronoun forms vary as follows:

'I' (personal pronoun – subject)	-	*A* (emphatic – *I*)
'me' (personal pronoun – object)	-	*me* (sometimes *iz*)
'mine' (possessive pronoun)	-	*mine* (sometimes *mines*)
'myself' (reflexive pronoun)	-	*masel*

[Note: 'My' in Ulster-Scots is *ma* (emphatic form *mae*) although in the written record *mine* occurs frequently. 'My own' can be *mine ain* as well as *ma ain* in Ulster-Scots literature, and *iz* ('us') can be used to mean 'me' (singular) in phrases like *let iz in, gie iz that*.]

In English, the personal pronouns 'I', 'he', 'she', 'we' and 'they' are used when the pronouns are the <u>subject</u> of the sentence, while the forms 'me', 'him', 'her', 'us' and 'them' are used when they act as the <u>object</u>. The equivalent forms of the personal pronouns in Ulster-Scots (when they act as the <u>object</u>) are *me* and *iz* (for 'me'), *you* (for 'you', singular), *him, her* and *hit* (for 'him', 'her' and 'it'), *iz* (for 'us'), *yous* or *yous'uns* (for 'you', plural) and *thaim* or *thaim'uns* (for 'them').

The following sentence includes all the rest of these Ulster-Scots usages:
> *Sez <u>me</u> til <u>ma</u> da – <u>A</u> ken thon's no <u>mine</u>, for <u>A</u> hinnae gat yin <u>masel</u>.*
> (<u>I</u> said to <u>my</u> father, <u>I</u> know that's not <u>mine</u>, as <u>I</u> don't have one <u>myself</u>.)

And so with 'you', 'he', 'she', etc:
> *Sez <u>you</u> til <u>yer</u> da – <u>Ye</u> ken thon's no <u>yours</u>, for <u>ye</u> hinnae gat yin <u>yersel</u>.*
> *Sez <u>him</u> til <u>his</u> da – <u>he</u> kens thon's no <u>his</u>, for <u>he</u> haesnae gat yin <u>hissel</u>.*
> *Sez <u>iz</u> til <u>wor</u> da – <u>we</u> ken thon's no <u>oors</u>, for <u>we</u> hinnae gat yin <u>worsels</u>.*
> *Sez <u>yous</u> til <u>yer</u> da – <u>yiz</u> ken thon's no <u>yours</u>, for <u>yiz</u> hinnae gat yin <u>yersels</u>.*
> *Sez <u>thaim</u> til <u>thair</u> da – <u>the</u> ken thon's no <u>thairs</u>, for <u>the</u> hinnae gat yin <u>thairsels</u>.*

4.2 <u>Reflexive pronouns ('myself', 'yourself', etc)</u>

The '-self' pronouns ('-selves' for plural forms) are called 'reflexive' pronouns, and take *-sel* (singular) and *-sels* (plural) endings in Ulster-Scots:
> eg: *He gien <u>hissel</u> a dunt.* ('He gave <u>himself</u> a nudge'.)
> *The saen <u>thairsels</u> oot.* ('They saw <u>themselves</u> out'.)

[Note that both of these forms differ from Standard English in their base (*his/thair*) as well as in their second element (*sel/sels*), although the *himsel* and *thaimsels* forms are, of course, also used].

When the word 'myself' is intended to mean 'by myself (alone)', the usual form in Ulster-Scots is *ma lane* (eg *A'm for comin hame ma lane*). For 'yourself', 'himself', etc, with the same meaning, the equivalents are as follows:

myself *(masel)*	-	*ma lane*
yourself *(yersel)*	-	*yer lane*
himself *(hissel)*	-	*hìs lane*
herself *(hersel)*	-	*her lane*
itself *(itsel)*	-	*its lane*
ourselves *(worsels)*	-	*wor lane*
yourselves *(yersels)*	-	*yer lane*
themselves *(thairsels)*	-	*thair lane(s)*

4.3 <u>Demonstrative</u> <u>pronouns</u> ('this', 'that', 'those', 'these')

'Demonstrative' pronouns are used to indicate distance (near or far) from the speaker. In English, the 'near' demonstrative pronouns are 'this' and 'these' (singular and plural), and 'that' and 'those' (singular and plural) are the 'far' pronouns. The Ulster-Scots equivalents are as follows:

that	-	*thon*
those	-	*thae, thaim (thar), thon*
this	-	*thir* (rare, even in traditional literature, usually: *this*)
these	-	*thir*

When these words occur directly in front of a noun, they are 'determiners' and function more as adjectives than pronouns (see 5.1).

Thon

thon buik thonner ('that book (over) there')
'That' in the sense of 'that man', 'that building' etc is *thon* in Ulster-Scots (*thon boy, thon biggin*, etc). *Thon* can also be used in a more abstract sense, meaning 'it':
thon scunners me ('it sickens me')
thon's a guid day theday ('it's a nice day today')

Less commonly, *thon* can also be used with a plural meaning, in place of 'those' (eg Savage-Armstrong: *"Owër me heed in thon firs"*, *"An' if ony yin pokes in thon ruins for pelf"*).

Thae

thae wee biggins ('those little buildings'); also *thon wee biggins, thaim wee biggins*.

'Those' in the sense of 'those men', 'those books' etc is *thae* in traditional Scots (*thae boys, thae buiks* etc). Today, however, colloquial Ulster-Scots speech usually has *thaim*, or *thaim thar* for 'those'. The following examples show how *thae* was used by the Ulster-Scots poets:
> *"Whar thae twa suckers, lucky pair, erect their snouts"* (Thomson)
> *"But thae daft days are chang'd"* (Orr)
> *"And brought hame wonders, but thae wonders lies"* (Anon-Laggan)
> *"Then let me tell thae worthless men"* (Anon-Laggan)

Thir and This

thir muckle buits ('these large boots')
The use of *thir* for 'these' (and sometimes for 'this') is historic, literary and archaic, and is probably now extinct in spoken Ulster-Scots. Examples from Ulster-Scots poetry include:
> *"Thir twa or three lines I pen"* (Huddleston)
> *"Mair lown, quo' she – thir's woefu' times"* (Orr)
> *"Thir births beside us are the Lockes"* (Orr)
> *"O Village fam't for scenes like thir"* (Orr)
> *"If thir three tons ware aff my han"* (Boyle)
> *"And lilted owre thir twa three lines to you"* (Starrat)

The forms *this (here)* and *these (here)* are now widely used. eg: *this (here) mait's aff* ('this food has spoiled').

The intrusive *here* and *thar* found in *this here* and *thaim thar* are probably used to reinforce the meaning of the English forms 'this' and 'them' when used in mixed English/Scots speech ('broken Scotch') by Ulster-Scots speakers.

There are several characteristic ways in which the word *this* is used in Ulster-Scots:

(a) *Eftèr thà war, the brung in this new law.*
     ('After the war, they brought out a [particular] new law')
This is often used in storytelling and recounting the past in place of 'a', 'the' or 'that'

and carries the meaning of 'a particular', that is, it functions as an adjective to draw attention to a particular noun.

> *This* wee lad jist cum oot afore me.
> A wuz aitin ma piece an *this* flee lit on it.
> See *this* oul bothèr we're haein wi tha polis?

(b) *A'm stuid here this twonnie männit waitin on ye.*
     ('I've been standing here waiting for you for twenty minutes'.)

Here *this* is used in place of 'for' or 'these' in sentences which have a 'present perfect' tense meaning in English (see section 7.13). It is important to note that *this* (which is only singular in English, 'these' being the plural form), is used in Ulster-Scots for both singular and plural forms.

> Tha oul doll *is* sut here girnin *this* twa hòor, fae quättin-tim.
> Ma motòr's rinnin wi a flat tyre *this* sax mile.

(c) *Quhits this the caa hìm?* ('What *is* it [remind me] that he is called'?)

This is also often used in place of 'it' in a question where the speaker is trying to remember something.

> Quhar's this ye cum fae?
> Quhan's this the'r cumin?

(d) *A'm cumin this Settèrday.* ('I'll be coming next Saturday'.)

When *this* is used as an adjective in front of a day, or month, or even year, it means 'this day (etc) coming' or 'next' Tuesday and so on. *Nix* or *neist Settèrday*, which of course literally translated means 'next Saturday', actually means 'a week from Saturday', as, of course, does *Settèrday week*.

> Ye daein muckle theyeir?
> ('Are you doing much *this* year?')
> Quhit daeins is on *this* Friday then?
> ('What'll be happening next Friday then?')
> An quhit aboot *nix* Settèrday anaa?
> ('And what about Saturday week as well?')

Because of the obvious potential for confusion with *this* meaning 'next', such statements as *A'm scoorin oot a wheen o sheuchs this yeir* would usually be rendered: *A'm scoorin oot a wheen o sheuchs this yeir cumin*. ('I'm going to clean out a number of drains next year').

Note: If the speaker had intended to mean this ('present') year, it would have been – *A'm scoorin oot a wheen o sheuchs theyeir*.

[N.B. Although *naix* or *nix* is the current speech form of 'next', the traditional form in Ulster-Scots poetry is *neist*:

> "Neist morn the o'erseen fellow fan" (Thomson)
> "Neist name this day" (Huddleston)
> "An' neist in text, comes wabster Jock" (Huddleston)
> "She sidelin steppit up neist me" (Huddleston)
> "When neist ye gang to mount Parnassus" (Carson)
> "Nor saw the sairs neist day they'll reap" (Orr)
> "Then, sick neist day, poor Mary boost disburse" (Orr)
> "When tald o' a' neist morn he'd tremble" (Orr)
> "An wha I may belang to neist" (Porter)

"The reaming bicker neist gaed roun" (Boyle)
"There's ither pleughs are cried up neist" (Boyle)
"But the neist morn" (Anon-Laggan)
"But, Lad, neist mirk we'll to the haining drive" (Starrat)
"Neist tales o' ghaists" (McKinley)]

4.4 Interrogative pronouns ('who', 'whom', 'whose', 'which', 'what')

The 'interrogative' pronouns are used to ask questions. When they occur in front of nouns they are considered to be 'determiners' rather than pronouns (see section 5.1). If the questions are about people, then *wha* is used in Ulster-Scots for English 'who', 'whom' and 'whose'. As explained in section 1.4, *quh-* spelling forms, rather than *wh-*, are used in this book for pronouns and determiners.
Quha cum til thà meeting? ('Who came to the meeting?')
Quha daen at? ('Who did that?')
Quha belangs thà motòr oot-bye? Quhas is thà motòr oot-bye? Quha daes thà motòr oot-bye belang til? ('Whose is the car outside?')
Quha haes thà wee dug? Quhas is thà wee dug? ('Whose is the small dog?')
Quha like is cumin? ('Just who is coming?')

The formal English 'whom', as in 'whom do you have in mind?' is again constructed using *wha* or *quha* in Ulster-Scots: *'quha wud ye hae in mynn'?*
         'which' – *whilk, quhilk.* The spelling form *quhilk* was often abbreviated in Ulster-Scots manuscripts as *qlk*, and was used in this form by Ulster scribes of Kirk Session minutes long after it had become obsolete in Scotland.
Quhilk o thae kye wud be yours? ('Which of those cows are yours?'). *Quhilk*, like 'which' in English, can ask questions as a singular or plural pronoun.
         eg: *quhilk is thà biggist yin?* (singular)
                  quhilk o tha kye haes ['have'] *bin milkt?* (plural)
Note: *Whilk* is also used in the 'for which' type of sentence, eg Thomson: *"For whilk she freely fed unfetter'd"*.

In speech, the interrogative pronoun *quhilk* is often replaced with *quhit yin* ('what one') or *quhit aa* – depending on whether the question is posed of a singular or plural subject.
         quhit yin is thà biggist?
         quhit aa o tha kye haes ['have'] *bin milkt?*

Note: 'all' is not normally used in British English immediately following a pronoun, although this is not necessarily the case in American English. In Ulster Scots this is common:
         Quha aa is comin? ('Who are coming?')
         Quha aa cum in late? ('Who came in late?')
         Wud yis aa houl yer whist! ('Would all of you be quiet!')
         Quhit aa hooses is biggit? ('What houses have been built')

[*yis aa* compares exactly with the southern American-English *y'all* ('you all') which, in turn, probably derives from this characteristic of Ulster-Scots grammar.]
         quhit – what?

an quhit wud ye dae wi it?
('and what would you do with it?')

quhit kynn o a bein is scho?
('what sort of a person is she?')

quhit's thà time noo?
('what time is it now?').

The construction *quhit* + noun is usual when questioning measurements:

Quhit lentht is hit?
('How long is it'.)

Quhit wecht is hit?
('How heavy is it'.)

However, the definite article *(tha)* is often used in these circumstances: *Quhits <u>tha</u> lentht o hit? Quhits <u>tha</u> wecht o hit?*, etc (see Section 5.3).

A (rare) shortened phrase used as a determiner (see section 5.1) in Ulster-Scots is *quhitna* or (with plural nouns) *quhitn*:
   Quhitna breid's at? ('What kind of bread is that?')
   Quhitn fowks is leevin yit? ('What people are still living?')

4.5 <u>Relative</u> <u>Pronouns</u>

When the pronouns 'that', 'who', 'whom' and 'which' are used to stand for a noun in an English sentence, the relative pronoun *at* ('that') is used in Ulster-Scots. The interrogative pronoun forms *quha* and *quhilk* are <u>not</u> used.
   Yer boy <u>at</u> haesnae onie cattèr.
   ('The man <u>who</u> hasn't any money.')

   Thonner's yer boy <u>at</u> A saen in thà toon.
   ('There's the man <u>whom</u> I saw in town').

   Aa tha kye <u>at's</u> oot in thà fiel.
   ('All the cattle <u>which</u> are out in the field'.)
[Note: It has often been observed, in regard to this usage in Scots, that Burns's *"Scots wha hae"* would be 'more accurate Scots' if it had been rendered *"Scots at haes."*]

The Ulster-Scots relative pronoun *at* can be regarded as a shortened form of *that*. It should be noted, however, that some speakers understand it to represent 'what', as in Belfast and Ulster-English dialect, giving rise sometimes to 'corrected' forms in Ulster-Scots speech today such as:
   Aa the kye <u>quhat's</u>* oot in thà fiel.

Another Ulster-Scots form of the relative pronoun *at* is *as*.
   Aa'<u>s</u> A hae is ma ain.
   ('All <u>that</u> I have is my own'.)

Weemin as haes nae daicent claes maunnae gang.
('Women who have no good clothes mustn't go'.)

See thàim'uns as daesnae ait thair tay ....
('As far as those who don't eat their tea are concerned ...')

Both *as* and *at* can be used interchangeably as Ulster-Scots forms of 'who', 'which' or 'whom'.

'Whose': The interrogative pronoun *quhas* ('whose') is not used as a relative pronoun or adjective in Ulster-Scots. Instead the form *ats* is used.

Tha wee fella ats da is deid.
('The boy whose father is dead'.)

Tha fowk ats heid-yins is daen oot.
('The people whose leaders are finished'.)

'That', or *at* can be followed by a possessive pronoun to substitute for 'whose':
Tha weans at thair bus bruk doon on wuz late.
('The children whose bus broke down were late.').

On the other hand, when the relative pronoun is the subject of a secondary clause, it can sometimes be omitted altogether:
Tha weans cum in this bus wuz a double-decker.
('The children came in a bus which was a double-decker').

This feature also occurs in the traditional poetry: *"Lord help them weds sic Misses"* (Huddleston); *"Then Eppie a drappie o' something was strang"* (Beggs).

When the relative pronoun is the object, it may be omitted (as in English): *Thonner's yer man (at) A sa in tha toon.*

In English, relative clauses of the '... who are asleep above' type can be reduced by omitting the pronoun and verb: 'Quiet! there are children (who are) asleep above'. This contraction is also common in Ulster-Scots: *Whisht! thar's weans sleepin abain.* However, this reduction of the relative clause can also extend in Ulster-Scots to a single word:
Thar's a wheen o prittas (ats) spoilt.
Tam sez thar's baith rid an bue flooers (ats) wantit.

4.6 People

'A person' – *a boadie*:

This is used in compound words, wherever 'one' is used in English:

someboadie	(someone)
iveryboadie, aaboadie	(everyone)
naeboadie	(no-one)
onieboadie	(anyone)

Obviously, these are also equivalent to English 'somebody', 'everybody', etc. 'One', used in the formal English sense as in: '<u>One</u> always is embarrassed there' can be rendered in Ulster-Scots using *a boadie*: *<u>A</u> <u>boadie</u> wud aye be affrontit thonner*, although in speech it would more often occur as *ye* ('you'): *<u>Ye</u>'d aye be affrontit thonner*.

When 'each' is used in English to mean 'each one' or 'every individual', the literary Ulster-Scots form is *ilk yin* or *ilkin (ilk ane)*. In colloquial speech *thaim aa* would be used.

> *A gien <u>ilkin</u> a wee dicht*, or *A gien <u>thaim</u> <u>aa</u> a wee dicht*
> ('I gave <u>each</u> a small wipe'.)

'People'

A 'crowd' of people is a *thrang* in Ulster-Scots, but *crowd* or *crood* is sometimes used where 'group' or 'attendance' might be expected in English (eg: *Wuz thar a big <u>crood</u> in tha hoose last nicht?*). *Crowd* is also used sometimes to refer to a sizeable collection of objects as well as people: *Yer mon haes a hale crowd o tràictèrs forbye*. ('He has a whole lot of tractors as well'.)

When 'people in general' is meant, the English word 'people' is not used, but rather *folks* or *fowks*. Sometimes, *fowk* or *fowks* is used (rather than *ain yins*) to imply that the people are related:

> '*Wud thon be yin o his <u>fowks</u> at's alang wi hìm?*'
> ('Is that one of his <u>relations</u> with him?')

While a person's *ain yins* would be related, their *ain fowks* or *ain folks* are simply 'friends and neighbours'.

Note: *Freen* or 'friend' can also mean a relation: *Him an thà wee fella fae Carrick wud be freens*. ('The boy from Carrick and he are related'). A *cousin* can mean any sort of blood relation: *Him an thà wee fella fae Carrick wud be soart o cousins*.

'People' in the sense of 'a people' (or 'nation') is *leid* in Scots, although *leid* can also mean 'language'.

humanity	-	*mankynn*
people	-	*fowks, folks*
person	-	*boadie* (also *crittèr, thing*, etc)
relations	-	*freens, cousins*
man	-	*man, mon*, boy, fella, oul lad, oul fella*
		(eg Thomson: "*Gies her auld mon the youthfu twine*", Savage-Armstrong: "*A deed mon's banes A'll gather*").
men	-	*menfowk, boys, fellas*
woman	-	*wumman, doll** (also *wee doll, oul doll**, etc)
women	-	*weeminfowk, dolls*, wifies*
baby	-	*ba, babbie, bairn*
child	-	*wean, chile* (often *wee chile*)
children	-	*weans, childèr**
boy	-	*lad* (also *wee lad*, wee fella*), *loon*
girl	-	*lass* (also *wee doll, wee thing, hizzie*), *quaen*

Mrs	-	*Miss* – Note: The respectful address for a 'lady of the house' (especially the landlord's, or minister's, wife) is *Mistrèss*. *Miss* is an abbreviated form and does not imply a lack of marital status. It is also used to address female school teachers (whether married or single). It can be used by itself *(Plaise <u>Miss</u>, can A laive tha room?)* or with surname *(<u>Miss</u> Boyd)*.
mother	-	*ma, mither*
grandmother	-	*grannie, graunie* (eg Thomson: *"An' social graunie taks her smoak"*)
father	-	*da, daddie, faither*
brother	-	*braither*
brothers, brethren	-	*braithern*
sister	-	*sistèr*
wife	-	*guidwife* (eg Boyle: *"Whan a guidwife cries out and squeels"*)
husband	-	*guidmon, man,* etc (eg Thomson: *"Our auld gude-man haf tynes his wit"*, *"Her guidman lean't against the wa"*; Boyle: *"Come tell me then, the guidman said"*; Huddleston: *"How this guidman and that guidwife"*; Savage-Armstrong: *"The guid-mon: Dinnae darken my Eden, guid-wife"*).
son	-	*son, sinn*
daughter	-	*dauchter*. Note: In the same way that the term 'son' is used in colloquial speech as a familiar form of address to any young male, so *dauchter* is used in Ulster-Scots for any young girl or lady.

'Else' – *ither*

'Who <u>else</u> is coming?' In general, this use of the word 'else' is avoided in Ulster-Scots speech, in favour of 'other': *Qua aa ithèrs is cumin?*, or *Quhit ithèr yins is cumin?*

> 'I couldn't remember anything <u>else</u> to bring'
> *A cudnae mynn ocht <u>ithèr</u> tae bring*

> 'What <u>else</u> needs done?'
> *Quhit <u>ithèr's</u> t'dae?/Quhit <u>mair's</u> needit daen?*

Similarly, the 'or else' usage of 'else' is often avoided in Ulster-Scots, and can be replaced with *(or) less*, (probably derived from 'unless' or 'lest'):

> 'Come back immediately, or <u>else</u> I'll thrash you'
> *Cum bak richt noo, or <u>less</u> A'll gie ye a guid whalin*

> Do it, or <u>else</u>!
> *Dae it, or <u>less</u>!*

> I saw him, <u>else</u> I was mistaken
> *A saen hìm, <u>less</u> A'm wrang*

CHAPTER 5:
ADJECTIVES, ADVERBS AND ASKING QUESTIONS

'Adjectives' are words which, along with 'determiners', are used to qualify the meaning of nouns and pronouns. The noun *coo*, by itself refers to any type of cow. When adjectives such as *wee* and *broon* are added, the meaning becomes much more specific: *wee broon coo*.

'Adverbs', on the other hand, modify the meaning of the other parts of speech such as verbs, adjectives, other adverbs, clauses or whole sentences. The verb *gang* ('go') has its meaning made more specific when an adverb such as *quäck* ('quickly') is added: *gang quäck*.

5.1 <u>Adjectives</u>

Adjectives are used to modify the meaning of nouns and pronouns and to make their meaning more precise. They often give specific information about nouns such as the size, colour, type and nature of an object.

(i)	size:	*bäg mon**	('big man')
		wee hoose	('small house')
		laich brig	('low bridge')
(ii)	colour:	*beu sey**	('blue sea')
		broon lemonade	('brown lemonade')
		rid boag	('red bog')
			(The Older Scots form *reid* is now rarely heard except, of course, in the surname 'Reid')
		graen gussgabs	('green gooseberries')
		yella bellie	('yellow belly, or coward')
		greh lift	('grey sky')
(iii)	type:	*Scotch car*	('Scotch, or spoked-wheel cart')
		wud pue	('wooden plough')
(iv)	nature:	*sair heid*	('sore head, or head-ache')
		daft notions	('silly ideas')
		fait hoose	('neat or tidy house')
		lacken day	('rainy day')

Of course, many adjectives are used to describe the 'nature' of people. Within the range of 'pure' Scots and Ulster-Scots words (that is, words which occur in Scots only, and <u>not</u> in English as well) we find many times more words dealing with negative ideas (ie poverty, dirtiness, bad behaviour etc) than those dealing with 'good' or pleasant characteristics. This is a feature shared by many heavily stigmatised languages which are regarded in themselves as vulgar and ignorant 'dialects'. So, as far as adjectives describing people are concerned, 'pure' Ulster-Scots words certainly follow this pattern. The ratio of about six negative words to one positive given in the examples below is true of Scots generally. Some common adjectives used in Ulster-Scots to describe people include:

fait	-	neat, tidy
croose	-	cocky, impudent
thaveless	-	incompetent
sleekit	-	sly
unkit	-	shy
throughither, thooithèr*	-	untidy
mingin	-	dirty, smelly

'Determiners' are words which determine the number or definitions of nouns and pronouns. They can appear to function as adjectives; eg _thon_ *sheuch* ('that drain'), _oor_ *hoose* ('our house'), _twa_ *pun* ('two pounds'), etc, although some of the same words can also function as pronouns, eg *thon's oors* ('those are ours').

Some grammarians do not regard 'determiners' as true adjectives because they do not describe nouns and pronouns and they do not have finite content or meaning when they stand alone. In this book some determiners are considered separately as follows:

(i)   numbers, amounts and indefinite determiners ('one', 'twelve', 'many', 'both', etc) are dealt with in chapter 2;

(ii)   definite and indefinite articles ('a', 'an', 'the') are dealt with in chapter 3; and

(iii)   demonstratives ('this', 'that', 'those', etc) and possessives ('my', 'your', 'our', etc) are dealt with in chapter 4.

The interrogative 'adjectives' *quhilk* ('which') and *quhit* ('what') are used in questions to ask for information about nouns; eg _quhilk_ *buik hae ye bocht?* ('_which_ book did you buy?'), _quhit_ *plons* haes yer weans gat?* ('what plans have your children?').

Once again, some grammarians do not regard these as true adjectives, and interrogatives are dealt with in this book in section 4.4 (Interrogative Pronouns).

Certain word endings commonly indicate an adjective (many of the following examples are firmly authenticated only in the written record. See glossary to determine which forms are still in current speech):

-in The '-ing' or verb participle form of some words can also be used as an adjective (as in Standard English).

coupin *cairt*	'_tipping_ cart'
speelin *bairs*	'_climbing_ bears'
beelin *hurt*	'_festering_ wound'

-rife The *-rife* suffix indicates 'liable to' or 'full of the quality of'.

caulrife	'susceptible to cold'
	lee tha windaes apen, we'r no _caulrife_ fowks
	'leave the windows open, we're not _cold_ types'

oulrife (Scots form *auldrife*)	'ancient, very old'
	sic <u>oulrife</u> gates bisnae roon theday
	'such <u>old</u> ways aren't to be found today'
salerife	'easy to sell'
	thae <u>salerife</u> prittas is aisie cattèr
	'those "<u>sellable</u>" potatoes are easy money'
wakrife	'wakeful', 'having difficulty sleeping'
	A'm <u>wakrife</u> this twa yeir
	'I've not been sleeping properly for two years'

Examples in Ulster-Scots poetry include: *"And cauld-rife mountains, wild an' hiegh"* (Thomson); *"At sic a sober cauld-rife rate"*, *"He hears the wakerife rail"* (Porter).

-some The *-some* suffix implies the production of a condition or state.

lonesome	'lonely'
	mair lang <u>lonesome</u> nichts
	'more long <u>lonely</u> nights'
dairksome	'dark'
	thon hoose haes powerfu <u>dairksome</u> chaummers
	'that house has very <u>dark</u> rooms'
lichtsome	'cheerful, pleasant'
meddlesome	'meddling'
hairtsome	'heartening, pleasurable'
teedisome	'tedious'
willsome	'wilful'
langsome	'tedious, wearisome'

Examples in Ulster-Scots poetry include: *"A leesome wee hizzie is Betty MacBlaine"*, *"Ye cannae dec'ave her, ye're fearsome tae lee"*, *"A'd scoor the roads wi' lightsome fit"* (Savage-Armstrong); *"Changes are lightsome"* (Bleakley); *"Twas heartsome to see on a Saturday morn"*, *"An ne'er before's been cheersome"* (Herbison).

-like The *-like* suffix gives the adjective a more general meaning of 'tending to be ....'

dirtielike	'dirty'
	Thair weans is aa <u>dirtielike</u> childèr
	'Their kids are all dirty children'
daftlike	'silly'
	Yer heids fu o <u>daftlike</u> notions
	'Your head's full of <u>silly</u> ideas'
thranlike	'awkward, obstructive'
	He's ae <u>thranlike</u> bein
	'He's one <u>awkward</u> person'

-art	*thrawart*	'difficult'
		Monies thà <u>thrawart</u> task A daen
		'I have done many <u>difficult</u> tasks'
	hameart	'homely, traditional'

A lowe tha oulrife <u>hameart</u> daeins
'I love the old homespun things'

-fu   The *-fu* suffix implies a subjective condition in an adjective:

powerfu   'powerful, very exceptional'
                             Thon's a <u>powerfu</u> boy
                             'He's an <u>amazing</u> man'

waefu   'sad'
                             Oul billies haes <u>waefu</u> pairtins
                             'Old friends have <u>sad</u> partings'

carefu   'caring, compassionate'
                             Tha <u>carefu</u> neebors cum til thà wake
                             'The <u>caring</u> neighbours came to the wake'

Examples from literature reveal that *fu* can be used as a suffix or can precede an adverb to modify it: *"The thoughtfu' class consider poor folks need", "They ken fu' braw'ly whare we stay", "Fu' aft I've pass'd the wa'-stead whare he leev'd", "an unco dolefu' ditty"* (Orr); *"A ken fu' weel the wee thing sits"* (Savage-Armstrong); *"I marched in fu' stately and throwed the dud down"* (Herbison).

-lins   The *-lins* suffix indicates a direction, way or condition.

haaflins   'half-grown'
                             In cum this wee <u>haaflins</u> skitter
                             'In came a small, <u>half-grown</u> runt'

norlin   'from the north'
                             Aa thae <u>norlin</u> billies stick thegithèr
                             'All those <u>northern</u> friends stick together'

middlin   'poorish, mediocre'
                             Thon's a <u>middlin</u> day
                             'It's a <u>poor</u> day'

ochtlins   'in any way'
                             He's no <u>ochtlins</u> thran
                             'He's not <u>at all</u> difficult'

hidlins   'secret, on the sly'
                             Scho'll no dae ocht apen, bot be warkin awa in <u>hidlins</u>
                             'She'll not do anything openly, but works away in <u>secret</u>'.

Airslins ('backwards') occurs in Ulster-Scots poetry (eg Thomson *"But wad auld Hornie arslins draw thee"*), as do other similar forms:

    "Tis aiblins (from 'able' + *-lins* = 'possibly') *less remark"* (Huddleston)
    "She sidelins steppit up neist me" (Huddleston)
    "Or you may aiblins get a thrashin" (Leech)
    "That darklins came their haste to spy" (Leech)
    "An' when the spae-wife to the Mill-town in hiddlins slips" (Orr)
    "But aiblins she'll return again" (Boyle)
    "The being oughtlins obligated" (Anon-Laggan)
    "Tho' haflins cauld an' blin" (Beggs)

-en The *-en* suffix indicates an adjective derived from a material or substance, and was frequently used in older documents:

beechen	'beech'
aischen	'ash'
leiden	'lead'
whaiten	'wheaten'

However, 'wooden' can be *wud* or *wudden* in Ulster-Scots. The archaic English adjective 'olden' is still frequently used in Ulster-Scots speech, particularly in the phrase *tha oulen days* ('the olden days').

-less	*fuitless*	'clumsy footed'
	haunless	'clumsy handed'
	uiseless	'useless'
	gormless	'stupid'
-ie	*graedie*	'greedy'
	aisie	'easy'
	birsie	'hairy, bristly'
	rucklie	'wrinkled'

'Comparative' and 'superlative' forms:

One characteristic of 'true' adjectives which is not usually shared with determiners or interrogatives is that they can have 'comparative' and 'superlative' forms. For an adjective such as *wee* ('small'), the comparative form is *wee'r* ('smaller') and the superlative form is *wee'est*.

	comparative	superlative
some ('some')	*mair* ('more')	*maist* ('most')
ill ('bad')	*waur* ('worse')	*warst* ('worst')
wee ('small')	*wee'r* ('smaller')	*wee'st* ('smallest')

[Note that *wee'r* and *wee'st* are pronounced with a 'y' sound at the apostrophe [wee-yer] and [wee-yest], and not with a glottal stop (see section 1.6). The same pronunciation 'rule' applies to any adjective which ends with a vowel, eg *yella* ('yellow'), *yella'er* [yellayer] (comparative form), and *yella'est* [yellayest] (superlative form)].

There is a much wider and freer use of *-er* and *-est* suffixes to form comparatives and superlatives in Ulster-Scots than in English, giving words such as *wunnerfuller* ('more wonderful'), *wunnerfullest* ('most wonderful'), *Scotchier* ('more Scottish') and *Scotchiest* ('most Scottish'). Of course, the words *mair* ('more') and *maist* ('most') can be added in front of adjectives to form comparatives and superlatives, eg *mair wee nor her dauchter* ('smaller than her daughter'), and frequently double comparatives are formed such as *mair wee'r nor her dauchter*. For superlative forms with *maist*, double superlative forms can also be formed, rarely, such as *tha maist laichiest an thà maist wee'st duir in thà hoose* ('the lowest and the smallest door in the house').

Superlatives can be formed with the suffix *-maist* as well as *-est*:

hinnèrmaist	'last, final'

benmaist, inmaist	'innermost'
bunemaist	'uppermost'
nethermaist	'lowest'
heichmaist	'highest'

However, *heichess*, or *heechest*, is the common form of 'highest'. The '-est' suffix is sometimes *-ess* in Ulster-Scots (see section 1.5).

Laich ('low') has two comparative forms for 'lower' – *laicher* and *nether*. In general, *nether* is the preferred form, especially in place-names and for all literal senses of 'lower'. *Nethermaist* or *maist laich* can be used for 'lowest', besides *laichest/laichess*. Other examples of comparative and superlative adjectives include:

oul, ouler, ouless: 'old', 'older', 'oldest'
>   *'Andrae haes gat <u>oul</u> schune'*
>   'Andrew has <u>old</u> shoes'
>   *The'r <u>ouler</u> nor Peties*
>   They're <u>older</u> than Pat's
>   *The'd be tha <u>ouless</u> schune in thà hoose*
>   They're the <u>oldest</u> shoes in the house

guid, bettèr, best: 'good', 'better' 'best'
>   *Thon's a <u>guid</u> day*
>   'That's a <u>nice</u> day'
>   *Hits a <u>bettèr</u> day nor tha Sabbath*
>   'It's a <u>better</u> day than Sunday'
>   *Hit wuz tha <u>bess</u> (sometimes best) day o tha hale sennicht*
>   'It was the <u>best</u> day of the whole week'.

ill, waur, warst: 'bad', 'worse', 'worst'
>   *Thon's an <u>ill</u> yin*
>   'He's a <u>bad</u> one'
>   *Hè's <u>waur</u> nor his da*
>   'He's <u>worse</u> than his father'
>   *He's tha <u>warss</u> (sometimes <u>warser</u>, or <u>waur</u>) o tha hale hirsel*
>   'He's the <u>worst</u> of the whole gang'

affen, affener, affenest: 'often', 'more often', 'most often'

Comparative forms indicating a lower degree often avoid the use of **less...*, preferring *no sae... (as)* instead:
>   *oor grcss wud<u>nae</u> be <u>sae</u> grüen <u>as</u> yer ain*
>   'our grass is <u>less</u> green than yours'

>   *<u>no sae</u> muckle rain theday!*
>   '<u>less</u> rain today!'

'Attributive' and 'predicative' adjectives:

Adjectives can occur in different positions in relation to the nouns they describe. Often they are placed before a noun and in this position they are known as 'attributive' adjectives: *a brave day, a yella ba*, etc.

Attributives may be 'piled' up in front of the noun, as in English:
>*Hè's a <u>powerfu, bäg, strang</u> mon*
>'He's a <u>powerful, big, strong</u> man'

However, as we shall see in the next section, certain words such as *powerfu* can also function as adverbs, in which case their meaning can alter.

Adjectives can also be joined to their nouns by a verb. In that case they occur after the noun (and verb), and are known as 'predicative' adjectives:
>*tha dug is <u>broon</u>*   ('the dog is <u>brown</u>')
>*tha owresettin wuz <u>wrang</u>* ('the translation was <u>wrong</u>')
>*A wuz <u>stairvin caul</u>*   ('I was <u>cold</u>')

These adjectives should not be confused with present participles in similar constructions:
>*tha wean wuz <u>scraichin</u>*   ('the child was <u>screeching</u>')
>*ma heid is <u>birlin</u>*   ('my head is <u>spinning</u>')

Adjective phrases usually occur after the noun they describe:
>*tha rodden <u>owre tha moss</u> is lang*
>'the lane <u>over the bog</u> is long'

>*thae schune <u>rucklet wi age</u> bisnae tha richt size*
>'those shoes <u>wrinkled by age</u> aren't the right size'

Compound adjectives are formed quite freely in Ulster-Scots, as they are also in Standard English:
>*guid-leevin*   ('religious, born again')
>*gospel-greedie*   ('churchy')
>*ill-got, ill-gatten* ('improperly gained')
>*aff-hann, aff-loof*   ('offhand')
>*near-begaun*   ('miserly')
>*close-fistit*   ('miserly')
>*up-kintra*   ('from inland')
>*bäg-heidit*   ('big-headed, proud')

5.2 Adjectives and adverbs

The function of adjectives and adverbs is to qualify, or modify, the meaning of other words in the sentence. In the case of adjectives it is only nouns or pronouns whose meaning is qualified, while adverbs can modify other parts of speech such as verbs, adjectives, other adverbs, clauses or whole sentences. The main function of an adverb, however, is to modify the main verb in a sentence – hence its name.

Intensifiers

Adverbial forms such as *terrible, powerfu, dead, rail* and *desperate* are used in Ulster-Scots to modify adjectives in such a way as to increase the 'power' of the adjective. They are known as 'intensifiers' and often equate to the adverb 'very...' (see section 5.6).

Some words which would be used as adjectives in English, are used as 'intensifying' adverbs in Ulster-Scots: _terrible_ nice, _powerfu_ nice, _dead_ nice, _rail_ nice, _desperate_ nice (all meaning 'very nice...'). These forms can change their meaning when functioning as adjectives, and their 'English' equivalents are also expressed differently:

'(to have a) great hunger'	_hae a desperate hung'r_
'terrible news'	_desperate news_
'very handsome'	_dead guid-lukin_
'dead fox'	_deid tod_
'really sick'	_rail bad_
'real money'	_ectual cattèr_
'very hot'	_powerfu wairm_
'powerful arms'	_strang airms_

'A terrible day' might be expressed as _a desperate day_ or _a desperate oul day_.

'A very old man' might be expressed as _a terrible oul mon_ but this could be confused with the meaning 'a wicked man', so a construction such as _a mon at's terrible oul_ ('a man who is very old') is preferred. Such confusion is unlikely when _terrible_ is used as an adverb with a positive effect; eg _a terrible guid day_ ('a very nice day'), or _a terrible guid mon_.

Thon's a brave day. _Brave_ here is an adjective meaning 'nice, good, reasonable'. Similarly, the words _guid, quaer_ and _powerfu_ can be used as adjectives with much the same meaning – 'That's (or, It's) a nice day':

> _Thon's a brave day_
> _Thon's a guid day_
> _Thon's a powerfu day_
> _Thon's a quaer day_

Indeed, the word _some_ can also be used, without the indefinite article, to convey the same meaning:

> _Thon's some day._

Each of these 'adjectives' can also be used as adverbs. They can modify adjectives in such a way as to increase or 'intensify' their power.

Certain adverbs of degree (see section 5.6) such as _brave, guid,_ etc equate in meaning to the adverbs 'very', 'really', although with a change in intonation, or less emphasis, these same intensifiers can mean 'pretty, fairly, moderately'.

> _Thon's a brave guid day_
> _Thon's a powerfu guid day_
> _Thon's a quaer guid day_
> _Thon boy's some guid age noo_

Some of these adjectives and adverbial uses of the same word forms can be reversed, eg:

> _Thar's a guid brave lenth o road tae go yit_

However, we do not find reversals such as *guid quaer...*, or *guid some*.

The following combinations can also be found:
> Thon wuz <u>some</u> quaer bargain he gat
> Thon wuz a <u>quaer</u> guid nicht
> Thon's a <u>quaer</u> brave nummer o folk

Only with *quaer, brave* and *guid* can the word *an* be added as a suffix to distinguish the adverbial function from the adjectival:
> That day's <u>brave an</u> wat
> That day's <u>guid an</u> wat
> That day's <u>quaer an</u> wat

This feature also serves sometimes to distinguish the 'very...' meaning from the less intensifying 'fairly...' meaning:

Thon's a brave guid day   ('That's a very good day')
A jalouse it'll be brave an guid aa simmer   ('I suppose it'll be pretty good all summer')

In response to a question such as 'what is the day like?', the adverbial form of these words is not used (**brave guid*), but the adverb + *an* form is:

> brave an guid   ('fairly good')
> quaer an guid   ('fairly good')

If the response to the same question was to be 'very good', a different adverb would probably be used – for example *powerfu guid*.

There are two other intensifiers, *gye* and *rail*, which can be used with *an*.
> Thon's a gye guid day
> Thon day's gye an guid
> Thon's a rail wet day
> It's rail an wet the day

Gye and *rail* (meaning 'very' and 'really') are used mostly as adverbs, but also have a limited use as adjectives. Although we cannot have:

> * *Thon's a rail day*   *That's a <u>really</u> day
> * *Thon's a gye day*   *That's a <u>very</u> day,

it is possible to have:

> A <u>gye</u> lump o a load   'A <u>considerable</u> load'
> Yer man's a <u>rail</u> eedyit   'He's an <u>utter</u> fool'

Oul ('old') is widely used in Ulster-Scots as a 'prop' or an adjectival aid to intensifiers. As an adjective it can mean 'old', of course, but it can also mean 'same...', for example, in a disapproving comment such as *ye'r no raidin thon <u>oul</u> buik again?* ('you're not reading that <u>same</u> book again'). *Stuepit* ('stupid') is used in much the same way, with a similar negative meaning: *ye're no raidin thon <u>stuepit</u> buik again?* However, again as an adjective, *oul* can also be used to mean 'nice, familiar, favourite...' in a more positive sense: *A love til hear tha <u>oul</u> banjo*. The Americanism of 'good ole boy' may reflect a common usage in Ulster-Scots of *guid oul* and *brave oul* to mean 'nice, pleasing, it's good to see it...': *Thon's a <u>brave oul</u> day theday*.

Wile ('wild') is used as an adjective in Ulster-Scots with the meaning of 'out of the ordinary', similarly perhaps to the now archaic usage of *unco*.

     Thon's a <u>wile</u> price.   'That's an <u>exceptional</u> price.'

Such an observation, depending on context, can mean 'exceptionally good' or 'exceptionally bad'. Of course, it may also mean 'wild', as in English: *Thon's a <u>wile</u> day.*

As an adverb, *wile* acts as an intensifier, to mean 'very'.

     Thon's a <u>wile</u> guid day.

It is possible to say *Thon's a gye <u>wile</u> day theday*, where *wile* is used as an adjective meaning 'wild' ('It's a very <u>wild</u> day today'), but not **Thon's a guid (an) <u>wile</u> day theday.* (*'It's a very <u>exceptional</u> day today').

Rail or *real* is used as an intensifier in Ulster-Scots equivalent to the adverb 'really', but not as an adjective (except of course, when used with the same meaning as English 'real'):

     Thon's a <u>real</u> guid day, but not **Thon's a brave an <u>real</u> day.*

In summary, the intensifiers outlined above are all adverbs of degree which modify adjectives. The degree of meaning implied by the intensifier can vary from 'very', to 'quite' or even 'fairly'. The following list suggests how the usages rank from the 'strongest' intensifiers to the 'weakest':

thon's a terrible wet day	('very, most')
thon's a desperate wet day	('very')
thon's a wile wet day	('very')
thon's a powerfu wet day	('pretty, very')
thon's some wet day	('pretty')
thon's a gye an wet day	('pretty')
thon's a real wet day	('quite, pretty')
thon's a guid an wet day	('quite')
thon's a quaer an wet day	('quite, fairly')
thon's a brave an wet day	('fairly')

These adverbs, many of which can also function as adjectives, are illustrated here in usages where they modify adjectives. Adverbs may, of course, modify most parts of speech (other than conjunctions, prepositions, nouns or pronouns), and it is verbs which they modify most commonly.

Adverbs can modify in terms of <u>manner</u>, place, <u>time</u>, <u>degree</u> or <u>frequency</u>.

5.3 'How' and adverbs of manner

Adverbs of manner indicate <u>how</u> something is done:

     The dannèrt richt ben thà hoose <u>slow as ye like.</u>
     ('They strolled right inside the house <u>slowly</u>'.)

     The rid tha bikes <u>twa abreesht</u>.
     ('They rode their bikes <u>two abreast</u>').

In English, many adverbs are formed by adding '-ly' to adjectives. In Ulster-Scots, to construct an adverb, the adjectival form is used by itself (ie: usually without *-lie*):

> *Tha motòr cum doon tha raa gye <u>quäck</u>.*
> ('The car came very <u>quickly</u> down the street'.)

> *Tha wean wuz spoartin itsel <u>happie</u> eneuch.*
> ('The youngster was playing <u>happily</u> enough.)

So <u>adjectives</u> and <u>adverbs</u>, such as 'powerful' and 'powerfully' or 'wild' and 'wildly' in English, become merged as single words in Ulster-Scots *powerfu* and *wile*. As these words can carry a different meaning in Ulster-Scots (when used as adverbs), this feature has proven to be fertile ground for Ulster humour, giving us adjectives and intensifying adverbs which apparently 'contradict' each other (with their English meanings):

> *a <u>powerfu</u> waik wee man*
> ('a <u>very</u> weak little man')

> *a <u>wile</u> tame wee dug*
> ('a <u>very</u> tame small dog')

> *a <u>desperit</u> aisy-gan boadie*
> ('a <u>very</u> "laid-back" man')

> *a <u>dead</u> active wee mon*
> ('a <u>very</u> active little man').

The same adverbs, when modifying verbs rather than adjectives or other adverbs, are nevertheless used without the '-ly' suffix, preferring the endings *-like* or *-some* where appropriate. Commonly, however, the '-ly' suffixes can be avoided altogether by other constructions:

> *Hè swem <u>powerfu-like</u> til thà boát/He swem rail strang tae tha boát*
> ('He swam <u>powerfully</u> to the boat'.)

> *Mae Auntie Marie is <u>lonesome</u> leevin in Inglann*
> ('My Aunty Marie is <u>lonely</u> living in England')

> *He lasht oot <u>wile-like</u>/He taen a <u>wile</u> leenge*
> ('He lashed out <u>wildly</u>.)

> *Scho scrabbit <u>desperit</u> at hìm/Scho gien hìm a <u>wile</u> scrabbin*
> ('She scratched <u>desperately</u> at him'.)

> *Scho's <u>serious</u> bad.*
> (She is <u>seriously</u> ill.)

> *Hè cud jist slaep <u>restless-like</u>/He wuz <u>wakrife</u>.*
> ('He could only sleep <u>restlessly</u>'.)

Note: The word *like* is a common 'tag', often occurring at the end of Ulster-Scots sentences. Some speakers use it habitually whether or not it makes some sort of grammatical sense. This feature is common in South-West Scotland – especially Glasgow – and is also used throughout Ulster, especially in Belfast.

>   *A'm desperit hung'rie like.*

Here this could be understood as *desperit-like* ('desperately'), but not so with:

>   *A saen yer mon, like, wi the big neb.**
>   ('I saw the man, really, with the big nose'.)

In traditional poetry we find *like* only added to adjectives, not as a 'tag', eg: *"An a' sic like"* (Gilmore), *"But soon the goss grew feeble like"*, *"In siccan garb, mad-like as Caor"* (Thomson), *"Twad be strangelike to see you gang in unexpected"* (Bleakley).

Similarly, *-some* as a suffix is common: *"An' ne'er before's been cheersome"* (Huddleston); *"Gif prudence, wi' a halsome hint, for ance procured thee"*, *"The face ne'er was lo'esome"*, *"Ay when approch't by lasses lo'esome"* (Orr).

'Really', as we observed in the previous section, is *real* or *rail* in Ulster-Scots:

>   *A'm rail hung'rie like.*
>   ('I'm really hungry'.)
>   *Tha waithèr turnit rail sudden-like.*
>   ('The weather changed very suddenly'.)

Rather than use an adverb like 'exactly', as in 'I don't know exactly how it works', it is common to produce an adverbial phrase, so that the word 'exact' appears as an adjective in the clause:

>   *A dinnae ken thà exect wye scho warks.*
>   ('I don't know the exact way it works').

'Exact' is sometimes pronounced [sezaict] in and around Belfast, but is [egzect] in the core Ulster-Scots areas.

Note: There are circumstances when the *-lie* suffix is used with some adverbs in Ulster-Scots. In response to a question such as 'How are you today?' (*Quhit-wye ir ye theday?*), the answer *bravelie* is heard just as often as *brave an weel*. Similarly, *richtlie* (or *richt an weel*) can be used.

'How?': When 'how' (otherwise *hoo* in Ulster-Scots) is used as an adverb of manner, the appropriate form is *quhit-wye* (or *tha wye*):

>   *Quhit-wye ir yiz for comin?*
>   'How are you going to come?'

>   *A niver saen quhit wye he daen it/A niver sa tha wye he daen it*
>   'I didn't see how he did it'

'How much' is *tha much*: (*Is thon tha much ye hae?*). 'How little' is *aa tha much*: (*Is thon aa tha much ye hae?*) 'How well' is *aa tha weel*: (*Is that aa tha weel ye ken me?*)

A statement such as 'see how bright those stars are', would be rendered *Luk tha bricht thae starns is*. Indeed the definite article is frequently used in place of 'how' or 'what':

> *D'ye ken tha time hè's cumin?*
> 'Do you know what time he's coming?'

> *D'ye see tha far it is tae thon toon?*
> 'Do you see how far away that town is?

> *A niver kent tha age he wuz/A niver knowed tha oul he wuz.*
> 'I didn't know what age he was', or 'I didn't know how old he was'.

> *Luk at tha lentht o hìs airm*
> 'Look what length his arm is, or 'Look how long his arm is'.

> *Wud ye luk tha big hè's gat*
> 'See how big he has become'

Note: If by 'which way' in the question 'which way are you coming?' we mean 'which direction or which route', then *quhit roád* is used:
> *Quhit roád are yiz for comin?*
> ('Which way are you going to come?')

Quhit-roád can also be used idiomatically for 'what way', or 'how' instead of *hoo ir ye...?/Quhit-wye ir ye...?*
> *Quhit-roád are ye thenicht?* ('how are you keeping tonight?')

The words *roád* and *gate* do not always mean the physical object 'road' as in English, but can be used metaphorically for 'manner' or 'way'. *Quhit roád are yiz for comin alang?* would be used to make clear the literal meaning of 'which road are you going to come (by)'. *Redd thà roád* is used for 'clear the way'. Indeed, *roád* also operates as a verb, meaning 'to direct': *Hè roadit me tha wrang roád* ('He directed me the wrong way').

> *Quhit-wye daed the thank ye?*
> ('How did they thank you?')

> *Quhit-wye ir ye?*
> ('How are you?').

Sometimes a 'plural' form is used in Ulster-Scots *quhit roáds, quhit gates*, and *quhit wyes* to distinguish the metaphorical from the literal meaning. *Quhit-roáds is it hè cud speel thon trèe?* 'How can he climb that tree?' *Nae roáds!* 'No way!'

'However' can be expressed as *hooiver, hooaniver* or *howsomiver*, although *bot* is also often used (see section 6.4).

[Note: In responding to 'how are you?' questions, the words *ill* ('bad'), *weel* ('well', 'fine') and *richt* ('right') are frequently used. *Aa richt* means 'well enough', rather than 'all right', and the word *eneuch* is often added to ensure the characteristic Ulster-Scots understatement. *Middlin* is another suitably neutral response].

somehow	-	*some-roád(s)*
		some-wye(s)
		some-gate(s)
		somehoo
very	-	*verie, vera*
		unco
		gye
than – compared with	-	*nor, bis (Ye'r bettèr oot daein a tùrn <u>bis</u> stap-pin at hame)*
so	-	*that (scho's gat <u>that</u> fat A cudnae lift her)*
so (much)	-	*thatwye (A'm <u>thatwye</u> used tae it)*

That can also be used in the following ways:

nevertheless	- *for aa that*
immediately, without warning	- *like that (scho jist drapped deid <u>like that</u>)*
indeed	- *that (A wull <u>that</u>)*
or so, about that	- *or that (Hit coast near sax pun <u>or that</u>)*
and so on	- *an that (He lo'es tha fitbaa <u>an that</u>)*

The ending *-lins* is found with certain words to make adjectives and adverbs in Ulster-Scots. Examples of both adjectival and adverbial usages are given above (section 5.1).

partly	- *haflins*
so-so	- *middlins*
perhaps (also 'maybe')	- *aiblins*
backwards	- *airselins* ('forwards' is *forrids*)
sideways	- *sidelins*

Unco, when used as an adverb rather than an adjective, has the meaning of 'very', 'extremely', 'exceedingly' etc. This is its most common use in the traditional literature:

"Yet unco worthless were their beddins" (Huddleston)
"And unco sma' my slumber" (Huddleston)
"Pert, keen an' crouse, an' unco wordie" (Leech)
"Thats seldom unco kind" (Orr)
"Christy wroght unco close, whyles took a gill" (Orr)
"An unco throuither squath'ry" (Orr)
"Ha, Ha, but I'll be unco cheerie" (Orr)
"An' water-spaniels unco few" (Boyle)
"Puir lad, ye'll fin' it unco cau'd" (Savage-Armstrong)
"Tis an unco hard way" (Gilmore)
"Noo, unco low has got my lyre" (Gilmore)
"Is it no makin' unco free" (Gilmore)
"Yet some were unco civil" (Gilmore)

"In warldly wisdom unco weak" (Beggs)
"Tho' unco bare" (McKinley)

On the other hand, when *unco* is used as an adjective (modifying a noun) the meaning is 'strange', 'peculiar', 'extraordinary', 'great', 'awful', or 'unfamiliar':

"An' cute was he when unco folk were there" (Orr)
"That unco day" (Huddleston)
"Wi' unco grace" (Leech)
"But, sir, I'm in an unco fret" (Leech)
"It is an unco law that" (Porter)
"Remembrance gi's him unco pain" (Anon-Laggan)
"I'll gie them a' an unco slip" (Bleakley)

5.4 '<u>Where</u>' and adverbs of place

where	-	*whar, whur, quhar, quhair*
there	-	*thonner, thonder, thar*
here	-	*here*
away	-	*awa*
somewhere	-	*someplace, somefer** (rare, Co Antrim)
anywhere	-	*oniequhar, onieplace, oniegate*
nowhere	-	*naequhar, naeplace, naegate, naefer** (rare, Co Antrim)
everywhere	-	*aaplace, aagates, iveryroád*
in the neighbourhood	-	*here-aboots*
far off	-	*awa*
distance	-	*far*
what distance	-	*hoo far*
all the distance	-	*aa tha far*
at a distance	-	*abeich*
outside	-	*ootbye, oot, athoot, but* (eg Huddleston: *"Auld plenishen outby was strew'd"*; *"When Rorie had little outbye to dae"*)
downstairs	-	*doon thà stairs*
inside	-	*ben* (eg Orr: *"An' to the fire step ben"*; Savage-Armstrong: *"Welcome ben!"*, *"An' yince a corp wuz bowlted ben it cudnae weel get oot"*).

Awa <u>doon thà stairs</u> an pit yer claes on.
('Go <u>downstairs</u> and get dressed'.)

Note that in Ulster-Scots *awá* ('away') is also used as the verb 'go'. Of course *awa* can be an adverb of place and direction as well.

Hè's awa <u>doon thà stairs</u>, <u>oot</u> an <u>awá</u>.
('He has gone <u>downstairs</u>, <u>outside</u> and <u>away</u>.')

Athoot ('without') can be used to mean 'outside' (eg Savage-Armstrong: *"It wuz better athoot an' whun ye cam' ben"*), or 'lacking' (eg Savage-Armstrong: *"A'll climb athoot a lather", "A'll bear athoot yin man".*) An alternative form of 'without' is *withouten*, which, like the similar but more archaic form *forouten*, is only used in traditional literature with the 'doing without' or 'in the absence of' sense:

> *"You would hae got an ample share, withouten fail"* (Herbison)
> *"withouten either whip or spur"* (Thomson)

Forouten ween also occurs as 'without doubt', or 'undoubtedly'. *But*, as in *"but an' ben"*, means 'outer' or 'outside', eg Thomson: *"Gif out he gangs but to the road".*

Some words such as *abain/aboon* ('above'), *owre/athort* ('across'), *ahint* ('behind'), *ayont* ('beyond') and *aneath* ('beneath') are used more often as prepositions than adverbs, and are dealt with as such in Chapter 6. In the traditional poetry, most examples of the use of these words occur as prepositions, with only a few adverbial and adjectival usages:

> *"May a' the powers aboon keep me frae sic a balsom"* (Carson)
> *"Ye'd think that a' the starns abeen"* (Anon-Laggan)
> *"A heerd a hoof ahint"* (Savage-Armstrong)
> *"But whun he got intil the loanin' anayth"* (Savage-Armstrong)

Adverbs of place modify the meaning of verbs, adjectives, other adverbs or even whole sentences, by explaining 'where'.

When 'where' is used to form questions in English, *quhit-place* is sometimes preferred in Ulster-Scots to *quhar* in much the same way as *quhit-wye* is sometimes preferred to *hoo*.

> *Quhar is thon weefla fae?*
> ('Where is that boy from?')
>
> *an quhit-place dae ye cum fae yersel/an quhar ir ye frae yersel?*
> ('and where do you come from yourself?')

5.5 'When', 'while' and adverbs of time

The words 'when' and 'while' – like their Ulster-Scots equivalents – usually act as conjunctions rather than adverbs (see Chapter 6), but in this book these are dealt with in this section.

'When' – *whan, quhan, quhaniver*

The roles of 'when' and 'whenever' in English can be reversed sometimes in Ulster-Scots as *quhaniver* and *quhan*. For example, 'whenever (every time) I see him, I lose my temper', is *iverytim*, or *quhan A see him, A aye loass thà rag*. However, when a single occasion is referred to such as 'I couldn't take it any more when he came in drunk last night', we find 'whenever' used: *A cudnae thole it nae lang'r quhaniver hè cum in blootèrt last nicht.*

Questions of the 'when?' type can be formed by using *quhan?* or *quhit-time?* but only with the latter usage if a specific 'time' is appropriate.

Quhit-time's thà weemin cumin hame thenicht?
Quhar ir yiz aa gan on yer holídays?

'While', 'whilst' – *quhan, quhaniver*

Can ye spaik* quhan ye're aitin yer mait?
('Can you speak while you're eating your food?')

Hè cum in quhaniver A wuz aitin ma mait.
('He came in while I was eating my food.')

Besides the normal use of *quhan* and *quhaniver* for 'while', the alternative form *as* also occurs frequently: *Hè cum in as A wuz aitin ma dinnèr*. If the intended meaning is 'at some point during' (rather than 'together, at the same time'), we find the construction .. *as A wuz in thà middle o*. This is often alluded to in the humorous 'saying':

Hè cum in as A wuz sittin in thà middle o ma dinnèr.

Quhiles, whyles etc in Ulster-Scots means 'sometimes' or 'occasionally'.
A'm aff quhiles at nicht.
('Sometimes I get off work at night.')

Literary examples from Orr of Ballycarry include:
"*With them galore, an' whyles a plack*",
"*An' drink whyles, an' think whyles*",
"*Tho' whyles scarce worth ae bare babee*",
"*On ae fit whyles restin*".

Other time adverbs in English and their Ulster-Scots equivalents:

English		Ulster-Scots
ever, always	-	*aye*
sometimes	-	*quhiles, betimes* (eg Gilmore: "*Altho betimes I like to try it*")
often	-	*affen*
after	-	*eftèr*
once	-	*yinst, yince, a-tim* ("*The wur thrie hoozen thar a-tim*")
now	-	*noo, tha noo*
soon	-	*shuin, shane, bedeen* (eg Thomson: "*Then sigh an' sob an' mourn bedeen*")
ago, thereupon	-	*syne*
never	-	*nar, niver*
next	-	*neist, nix, syne*
immediately, soon	-	*belyve* (eg Orr: "*Belyve an auld man lifts the Word o' God*", "*Belyve he staid hale days an' nights frae hame*")
early	-	*airlie*
finished, all over	-	*daen, aa by* (It'll be *aa by* afore we get thar)
later	-	*eftèr, latèr*
occasionally	-	*betimes*

| at last | - *at lang lenth* |
| since | - *fae, frae, sin* |

Although *syne* and *sin* are regarded as different forms of the same word in the major Scots dictionaries,[1] their use is distinguished in Ulster-Scots literature. Sin, or sin' often occurs at the beginning of a sentence with the meaning 'since', 'because', or 'seeing that'. It is quite possible this usage is confused sometimes in modern speech with seein ('seeing'):

"*Sin' natures gi'en me wit an' fire*" (Huddleston)
"*Sin' he by devils' han' was ta'en*" (Huddleston)
"*Sin' sunrise drudgin i' the moss*" (Orr)
"*Sin' I was born*" (Porter)
"*Sin' Mary's dead*" (Boyle)
"*Weel quo' the gout, sin' baith are sae*" (Anon-Laggan)
"*Sin' it has tin'd the very wale o' men*" (Anon-Laggan)

Syne, on the other hand, is used with the meaning of 'thereupon', 'next', 'then – right away', 'afterwards', 'so' etc:

"*And syne began to fa*" (Thomson)
"*Syne speel the side, an' down the hatch*" (Orr)
"*Syne wi anither glass they hail day-light*" (Orr)
"*Syne took it hame*" (Orr)
"*Syne wash the dishes, milk the kye*" (Gilmore)
"*I'll syne hae nane o't ava*" (Beggs)
"*For syne thou'lt hae nane to gie*" (Beggs)
"*Yet syne they got up an' they took the road*" (Beggs)
"*Syne oot wi his snoot-cloot and dighted his nose*" (Huddleston)

Langsyne means 'long ago' or 'a long time' (or as an adjective it can mean 'ancient'). For example, Orr: "*An leugh, langsine, to hear his strain*", Thomson: "*Waesucks to think on a lang syne*".

Atween ('between') can be used in a time sense in the phrase *atween an ...* ('between now and ...'), eg Orr: "*Atween an' day*", ('until the morning'), "*Atween an' May, gif bowls row right*".

A'm for seein her eftèr.
('I will see her later.')

A'll see ye anithertim
('I'll see you on some other occasion.')

A hinnae saen her fae yestreen.
('I haven't seen her since yesterday'.)

---

[1]The treatment of *syne* and *sin* or *sen* as one word in the *Concise Scots Dictionary* is regarded by a former editor of the *Dictionary of the Older Scottish Tongue* as an error (letter, Professor A J Aitken to author 18/3/97). Professor Aitken would prefer to treat syne and sen separately, since their derivations, though connected, are divergent, as are their uses.

Some of the most used adverbial phrases of time include the measures of time, eg *last nicht, theday, themorra*, etc (see section 2.3).

5.6 'How much' and adverbs of degree

very	-	*brave, vera, verie, real, quaer, unco, gye (Thon's a gye big hoose).*
so	-	*that, at (Hè wuz at hungrie hè cum hame afore nicht).*
nearly	-	*near (Hè near gat hìs heid brustit apen).*
largely	-	*gyelie, maistlie (Ma tùrns is gyelie daen).*
half	-	*hauf*
almost	-	*near, near haun, amaist (A hae amaist twa thoosan breek, an the'r near aa hann-daen), gyelie (A'm gyelie daen. It's gyelie by noo.)*
quite	-	*fair, clean (A'm fair scunnèrt, for A'm clean oot o cattèr.)*
perfectly well	-	*fine (A ken aa that fine).*
also, as well, too	-	*forbye, (Wud ye dae that forbye?), an aa, tae, eke.*
completely	-	*perfaitlie (Scho wuz perfaitlie drookit.)*

The use of *eke* as an adverb meaning 'also' is well recorded, for example, in Samuel Thomson's verse:

> *"That was the herd o' kye an' horse, an eke the safeguard o my purse"*
> *"A social jug here waits my frien', and eke the heel o' an auld cheese"*
> *"Destroy the lambs and eke the hens"*
> *"At early morn, and eke at e'en"*
> *"And eke o' poor, decayed mortality".*

In current speech, *tae, an aa* and *forbye* would be used for 'also'.

'Too' meaning 'excessively' is usually *owre* in current speech (although *iver* is also used), and in the traditional poetry:

> *"He's far owre wise to jibe; but no owre grave to joke"* (Orr)
> *"I b'live owre muckle o' sic stuff"* (Porter)
> *"Ow'r mickle, like ow'r little dreed"* (Anon-Laggan)
> *"I'm owre young for married gates"* (Huddleston)

How much?

> *Quhit daes thae sweeties coast?*
> ('How much do those sweets cost?')

> *Quhit lenth o ma taak daed ye unnèrstaun?*
> ('How much of my lecture did you understand?')

> *Tha maist o it wuz blethers*
> ('It was largely nonsense.)

Cud ye no tak mair?
('Could you not take more?')

Na, it wuz owre ocht: tha heid cannae tak in mair nor tha airse can thole.
('No, it was too much: my head can't take in more than my backside can stand.')

Sometimes, superlatives are formed in Ulster-Scots using an *-est* suffix (such as *miserablest, powerfulest*, etc) which would be irregular in English (see section 5.1).
In Ulster-Scots, *a hauf-* is used rather than 'half a-'
A'll tak a hauf gless (rather than 'half a glass')
Cum roon in a hauf hòor (rather than 'half an hour') (eg Thomson: *"An' try ae haf hour to be happy"*).
A hauf loaf is bettèr nor nae breid ('Half-a-loaf is better than no bread')

[Note: The idiomatic use of 'half' to mean 'partly', or even 'mostly' as in *hauf-drùnk* also occurs in Ulster-Scots poetry, eg *"Haf deaf, haf blin' my tow I ort"* (Thomson). *Haflins*, also meaning 'half' or 'partly' (see section 5.1 for adjectives with *-lin* endings), was also used in the same way:
"The haflins blin' descry at ance the man o' ment" (Thomson)
"Tho' haflins cauld an' blin" (Beggs).
However, *haflins* can also function as a noun meaning 'a half grown (person)':
"Tho' strife like haflins rises" (Orr)
"Can mair than haflins correct" (Thomson)].

5.7 'Why' and adverbs of purpose

Quhy wudn't A?, Quhit-for wud A no?, or, *Hoo wud A no?*
'Why wouldn't I?'
Hoo me?
'Why me?'

Quhit-for no? means 'why not', and *quhit-for* is the most common Ulster-Scots alternative (ie Non-Standard English) form of 'why'. On occasion the compound can be split within a sentence (and used as in Standard English): *Quhit wud A dae that for?* ('Why would I do that?')

If the sense of a 'why' question is more a matter of 'what is the reason?', then *quhit-wye?* or *hoo-cum?* can be used, the sense being: 'how is it?'

Quhit-wye is it ye'r sae late thenicht?
'Why are you so late tonight?'

an hoo cum (or, *hoo wuz it*) *A wuznae toul?*
'and why wasn't I told?'

For why is used to mean 'the reason why': *A'll shuin tell ye for why.*

5.8 'Please' and 'Thank-you': asking a polite question

In English, many of the 'wh-' adverbs are used to form questions, the other most common method being verb-subject inversion ('Have you ...?', 'Did you ...?' etc). In Ulster-Scots questions are formed in much the same way, although, as we have seen in earlier sections of this chapter, different adverbs to the expected English ones are used to effect the same meanings. Similarly, 'did' and 'have' are used differently. For example, the question 'Did you light the fire?' would be constructed something like: *Hae ye tha fire lit?* (The change in verb position here is dealt with in section 10.11, while this usage of *hae* is dealt with in section 8.4).

The polite adverb 'please' is not used generally in Ulster-Scots when requesting someone to do something. Instead of turning a command such as 'light the fire' into a polite request by adding 'please', a negative question with positive interrogative tag is asked:

> *Ye cudnae gie tha fire a licht, cud-ye?*
> ('Will you light the fire, please?')
>
> *Ye wudnae hae the time on ye, wud-ye?*
> ('What time is it please?')

'Please', as the verb *please*, or *plaise**, is used, however:

> *ye cudnae <u>plaise*</u> hìm*, or, *thar's nae <u>pleasin</u> hìm.*
> ('he is impossible to please.')
>
> *hè wuz weel <u>plaisit*</u>.*
> ('he was very <u>satisfied</u>.')

'Thank-you' is simply *thànks* in Ulster-Scots, sometimes pronounced [hanks], while particular gratitude of the 'a big thank-you' type can be expressed as *monie thànks*, or *guid on ye*.

CHAPTER 6:
PREPOSITIONS AND CONJUNCTIONS

Prepositions are words that are 'pre-positioned', ie they come before nouns, pronouns or noun phrases. They show how two parts of a sentence are related to each other in time, in location, or in some other way.

> eg: *thà saits is <u>unnèr</u> tha table*
> *hìs da cum <u>afore</u> hìs brithèr <u>in</u> thà prizes*
> *hè pit it <u>in</u> thà laft, <u>abain</u> thà byre*

Prepositions may be either 'simple' or 'complex'. 'Simple' prepositions, such as 'in', 'on', 'under', 'before' etc consist of only one word, while 'complex' prepositions, such as 'ahead of', 'close to', 'apart from', 'as far as' etc consist of two or three words.

'Conjunctions' are words such as 'and', 'but', 'before' etc that join together parts of a sentence. Many words can be used as a preposition, adverb or conjunction, depending on their placement.

> eg: *A maun see him <u>afore</u> thenicht.* (preposition)
> *A gien yiz yer tay <u>afore</u> yiz ast for it.* (conjunction)
> *Ye haed yer tay <u>afore</u>. A cannae gie ye ocht mair.* (adverb)
> *Hè's <u>ahint</u> wi hìs darg.* (adverb)
> *Hè's staunin <u>ahint</u> thà duir.* (preposition)
> *A hae <u>aboot</u> echt yeir for tae dae.* (preposition)
> *A'm <u>aboot</u> readie noo.* (adverb)

6.1 Prepositions with spatial meanings (relating to location, direction or position)

across	-	*owre, athort*
above	-	*abain/aboon*
below	-	*alow, ablow*
beyond	-	*ayont*
between	-	*atween, atweesh, aqween, aqweesht*
around	-	*aboot*
from	-	*frae, fae*
beneath	-	*in alow, aneath*

Examples of the use of *aboon* etc (for 'above') in traditional poetry include:
> *"My auld wheel now sits silently, aboon the bed"* (Herbison)
> *"Rolls his huge waves aboon the tide, wi' unco roar"* (Colhoun)
> *"The herd's aboon me on the laft"* (Orr)

> *"Prepar'd for sic aboon the lift"* (Porter)
> *"In gifts you far aboon me soar"* (Kerr).

[Note: see also section 5.4 for adverbial uses of some of these words.]

Ayont, ahint, aneath and *atween* ('beyond', 'behind', 'beneath' and 'between') occur in much the same way in these poems:

> *"Like the silkworms ayont the tide"* (Boyle)
> *"Atween the fu' sacks an' the wa'"* (Boyle)
> *"Ayont the mill"* (Boyle)
> *"The man that stands ahint the screen"* (Boyle)
> *"Some think themsels ayont your reach"* (Anon-Laggan)
> *"The twa ald wives ayont the fire"* (Anon-Laggan)
> *"Nor e'er ayont the parish be"* (Thomson)
> *"Aneath your fauld"* (Thomson)
> *"Ahint her wundee sma', and knits"* (Savage-Armstrong)
> *"Here anayth this shelterin rod"* (Savage-Armstrong)
> *"Atween yer greezly paw an' heaven"* (Savage-Armstrong)
> *"But whun he got intil the loanin' anayth"* (Savage-Armstrong)
> *"Till he come tae a loanen ahint Bellawhite"* (Savage-Armstrong)

If movement 'downwards' is implied, *doon* is used:

> A run <u>doon</u> thà loanen, bot tha motòr cum <u>doon</u> fair on me.
> 'I ran <u>down</u> the lane, but the car came <u>downwards</u> straight at me'.

Note: *clum doon* can be regarded as a verb phrase (meaning 'descended'); see chapter 7. Idiomatic uses of *doon* include *doon thà hoose* (the room beyond the kitchen hearth), and *doon thà toon* (in the town centre).

Several of the following forms (eg *ben, ayont* etc) have already been illustrated as adverbs in the preceding chapter.

'underneath', 'beneath', 'below', 'under' – *unnèr, aneath, ablow, alow*

Ye hae it <u>aneath</u> yer sait ('It's <u>underneath</u> your chair')

A cum in <u>ablow</u> Tam in tha gowf ('I came <u>below</u> Tom at golf')

Hè tuk a sait <u>unnèr</u> thà bortrèe ('He took a seat <u>under</u> the elder').

When 'below' means physically 'under', the Scots *ablow* is rarely used. Rather *unnèr* is used or, on occasion, *aneath* ('beneath').

'below', 'beyond', 'at the far side of' – *ayont, tae tha bák o, a-bak o*

> *Tha tailzer's schap is twa duir doon thà Raa <u>ayont</u> thà Polis Barricks.*
> 'The tailor's shop is two doors down the street beyond/below the Police Station'.

> *Tha toon <u>tae tha bak o</u> tha lough.*
> 'The town <u>at the far side of</u> the lough.'

> *Tha pad <u>a-bak o</u> tha sheuch*
> 'The path <u>at the back of</u> the ditch'.

'up', 'above', 'over' – *up, abain*

Tha hale familie is leevin <u>up abain</u> thà schap.
'The whole family are living above the shop'.

When movement upwards is meant by 'up', this word may be part of a verb phrase: *speel up, climm up*, etc ('ascend', 'climb')

'across', 'over' – *owre, athort* ('from one side to the other')
Tha cat waakit <u>owre</u> tha clain* fluir*.
('The cat walked <u>across</u> the clean floor.')
Thon brig'll tak ye fae Antrìm <u>athort</u> thà Lagan Wattèr til thà Coontie Doon.
('That bridge takes you from Antrim <u>across</u> the River Lagan to County Down.')
Tha Rids is awa <u>owre</u> tha sey.
('The Reids have gone <u>across</u> the sea.')
Hè cloddit tha beef <u>owre</u> tha coontèr.
('He threw the meat <u>across</u> the counter.')

In Ulster-Scots poetry, *athort* is used with the same sense, eg *"An' ride athwart the toun"* (Beggs); *"And neebour loons that come athort"* (Thomson), although *owre* is much more common, eg *"Till yince mair owër Antrim an' Airds an' Lecale"* (Savage-Armstrong).

'next to', 'beside', 'against' – *fornent, fornenst, agin.*
Tha toon <u>fornenst</u> thà Black Wattèr.
A pit thà graip <u>agin</u> thà duir.

'In the direction of' is *in bae: gan <u>in bae</u> tha toon.*
'Out of' is *or: awa <u>or</u> that, get up <u>or</u> that.*
'To the back of' is *behinn, ahint* or *a-bak o*, as in *tha fiel <u>a-bak o</u> tha plantin* ('the field at the back of the wood').

Other prepositions:

'off'	-	*aff*
'out'	-	*oot*
'in'	-	*in* (pronounced [aan])
'through'	-	*throo, thoo**
'along'	-	*alang*
'into'	-	*intae, intil*
'behind'	-	*ahint (A saen hìm <u>ahint</u> thà duir).*
'among'	-	*amang*
'opposite', 'facing'	-	*fornenst, fornent (Tha hoose <u>fornenst</u> thà schap).*
'to'	-	*til, tae*

Note: 'Married <u>to</u>' is *merriet <u>on</u>* in Ulster-Scots.

'inside', 'in'	-	*ben (Hè cum <u>ben</u> thà hoose).*
'from'	-	*frae, fae (He cum up a wee dannèr <u>frae</u> tha toon).*

Note: For 'from' in the sense 'Someone took it <u>from</u> me', *on* can be used: *Someboadie tuk it <u>on</u> me.*

'before', 'in front of'	-	*in front o*

Note: For *afore* see 6.2 below (*afore* is used in Ulster-Scots for 'before' when the preposition has a time rather than a place meaning).

'around', 'about'   -   *aboot, roon (Hè pit thà coát <u>aboot</u> hìs shoodèrs. Pit that <u>roon</u> ye).*

6.2 <u>Prepositions with time meanings</u>

Many of the following are not only shared with Standard English, but there are no distinctive (Non-Standard English) forms:

'at' – *at*
Yer man cum <u>at</u> 6 o'clock.

'in' – *in*
The gat thair new hoose <u>in</u> Aprile.

'on' – *of, a-*
The aye cums <u>of</u> a Tuesday.
Thar's nae schaps apen <u>a</u>-Monday.

'before' – *afore*
A'll be hame <u>afore</u> säx.

'after' – *eftèr*
A cud get oot <u>eftèr</u> wark.

'during' – *throo, th'oo**
A'll call <u>throo</u> tha week.

'since' – *frae, fae*
A hinnae saen hìm <u>frae</u> Settèrday.

'before ever' – *or iver*
It'll be yeirs <u>or iver</u> ye see him agane.

'til', 'until' – *tae, untae*
A wrocht at hame <u>tae</u> A wuz saxteen.
Ye'll no see him <u>untae</u> Settèrday.

'for' – *for* (sometimes spelt *fur*)
A'm stappin at hame <u>for</u> thà simmer.

'by the time that' – *agin, gin*
Hè gat on him <u>agin</u> thà duir apened.
'He got dressed <u>by the time</u> the door opened'.
A shud hae daen <u>gin</u> Settèrday
'I should be finished <u>by</u> Saturday'.

Just as *til* can be used in Ulster-Scots for most English usages of 'to' (eg Orr: *"They'd ca'their mother le'er, an'curse her <u>till</u> her face"*), so *tae* ('to') can be used for 'until' or 'til'.

'until' – *tae* / 'to' – *til*
>   Lee it <u>*tae*</u> A get bák.
>   'Leave it <u>until</u> I return.'
>   Gie it <u>*til*</u> iz themorra.
>   'Give it <u>to</u> me tomorrow.'

If, however, the sense of future passage of time is 'during and throughout the time that', the phrase *aye an while* can be used.

>   Ye winnae paie nae rent <u>*aye an while*</u> A leeve.
>   'You won't ever pay rent <u>while</u> I live.'

The old spelling form of this phrase is *aze and quhile*. It is used in the motto of the Ulster-Scots Academy: *"Thole aye an quhile poustie"* ("Endure til strong"), where the meaning is 'endure as long as health and strength (last)'.

6.3 <u>Prepositions of cause and manner, and other prepositions</u>

'because (of)', 'on account of', 'for' – *for, acause o, oot o.*
>   Scho daen it <u>*for*</u> her man wuz cumin.
>   Hè cum in <u>*acause o*</u> tha coul.
>   Hè daen it <u>*oot o*</u> badness.

'from' (because of) – *wi*
>   Hè died <u>*wi*</u> cancer

'about' (because of) – *wi*
>   Ma da's at thà docters <u>*wi*</u> hìs heid.

'by' – *wi, bae*
>   Ye'll onlie get in <u>*bae*</u> tha bak duir
>   Scho wus stung <u>*wi*</u> a bee
>   He brung it in <u>*wi*</u> horse an cairt

'by' (by way of) – *tae*
>   Tha moiley haed a calf <u>*tae*</u> tha rid bull

'by' (by means of) – *tae*
>   Hè's a cairpentèr <u>*tae*</u> tràde

'with' (support) – *on for*
>   Hè's <u>*on for*</u> ye an aa yer pairtie.
>   'He supports (is <u>with</u>) you and all your party'.

'with' (accompany and possession) – *wi*
>   Ye maun gan <u>*wi*</u> hèr.
>   Gie iz tha wee bahg <u>*wi*</u> tha broon haunnle.

'with' (for) – *tae*
>   Tak a egg <u>*tae*</u> yer tay.

(also *at*, eg Savage-Armstrong: *"Fur the herrin' he'd et <u>at</u> his breakfast wuz red"*)

'too' – *owre*
> Hit's <u>owre</u> lang.

'rather more than' – *luckie*
> <u>luckie</u> twal o'clock

'as far as' – *tha lenth o*
> Ye cudnae see <u>tha lenth o</u> thae hoozes.

'against' – *agin, agane*
> Hè's aye <u>agin</u> thà heid-yins o tha cooncil.

'letting (one) down' – *on (ye)*
> It brustit <u>on</u> me.

'also', 'as well as' – *forbye*
> Thar's twa weans <u>forbye</u> tha mithèr.
> A bocht new claes, an a wee pair o schune <u>forbye</u>.

'for' – *tae*
> Hè wrocht <u>tae</u> a fairmer.

'of' – *o*
> A hae yin <u>o</u> thaim oul dunchers.

'of' (about) – *on*
> Thon mynns me <u>on</u> a guid yarn.

'regarding', 'concerning' – *anent, aboot, adae wi, as regairds*
> A'll taak til ye <u>anent</u> thà price themorra.
> Tha polis wuz tellin lies <u>on</u> me.
> He gien iz a taak <u>as regairds</u> oor historie.

'so that' – *tae, til*
> cum owre <u>tae</u> A see ye.

'than' – *as, nor*
> A'll no gie nae mair <u>nor</u> sax pun.
> A'd rathèr hae a buik <u>as</u> thà wireless.

6.4 <u>Co-ordinating conjunctions</u>

'Conjunctions', or words used to link together different parts of a sentence, can be either 'co-ordinators' or 'subordinators'. 'Co-ordinators' join units of equal status (eg two words or two clauses) and in English include words such as 'and', 'but', 'yet' etc.

'and' – *an*

The conjunction *'an'* is used to join words and clauses of equal importance. If the subject of both clauses is the same, it does not have to be repeated in front of the second verb.

eg: *Tha oul fella tuk hìs duncher aff thà peg <u>an</u> set aff for hame.*
'The old chap took his cap off the peg <u>and</u> set off for home'.
Hi! wud ye cum awa <u>an</u> tak tent o me.
'I say! will you come here <u>and</u> pay attention to me'.

The units of equal 'status' joined by co-ordinators may be single words: eg *lads <u>an</u> lasses*. Sometimes *an* is used in idioms in such a way that it cannot be properly regarded as a conjunction at all (see section 5.2).

brave <u>an</u> guid
sic <u>an</u> a thing
gye <u>an</u> oul

In speech, *an* is often used to begin sentences:
<u>An</u> *in A cums wi ma claes drookit.*
Obviously, *an* is not used here as a 'conjunction', but helps to indicate the 'narrative mood' (that a story is being told), which is signalled by the verb form (see Chapter 7).

'but' – *'bot'* (N.B. This spelling has been used in Scots since medieval times).

As in English, *bot* is a conjunction used to join clauses where there is a contrast:

Scho's lukin tae buy new schune <u>bot</u> scho haesnae onie siller.

Unlike in English, *bot* in Ulster-Scots can be placed at the end of the clause expressing the contrast:
Scho's lukin new shune for thà weans, scho haesnae onie siller bot.
Mynn, hè's no sae weel hissel bot.

It is doubtful if the word *bot*, positioned at the end of the sentence, could be always regarded as a re-positioned conjunction, rather than as an adverb meaning 'however'.

ach ... bot! Sometimes 'but' is used to introduce an expression of dissent, disgust or contradiction:
'<u>But</u> what would I have been able to do?'
'I know he's your dad, <u>but</u> I can't stand him'.
'<u>But</u> sure he's always whinging'.

In Ulster-Scots the interjection *ach* (which expresses impatience, annoyance, etc) is used, often along with *bot* in a final position:

Ach, quhit cud A hae daen bot?
A ken hè's yer da, <u>ach bot</u> A cannae bide hìm.
<u>Ach</u> *sure hè's aye chirmin, he didnae cum <u>bot</u>.*

Indeed the two words *ach* and *bot* are often used jointly as an argumentative interjection:

Ach bot! (eg Orr: *"But och! 'tis owre like Bedlam wi' a' this day"*).
Note: It will be obvious to students of Irish Gaelic that there may be some connection with the Gaelic word *ach* ('but'). It will be equally interesting to students of Old and Middle English that the Anglo-Saxon word for 'but', 'however' and 'but on the contrary' *(àc)* was still being used in medieval Ulster-English writings.

'however', 'yet' – *yit, bot, still, like*
The use of *bot* at the end of a statement gives emphasis when the usage is definitely adverbial and the meaning is 'however': *A niver meant it, <u>bot</u>. Bot* also provides emphasis without necessarily being positioned at the end of a sentence:

> *Boys bot scho's yin sair eejit.*
> *Ye'd wunnèr bot hè wud gie up.*
> *Dear knows bot A cud dae wi a hann.*

Bot can be used to 'soften' or ameliorate the force of a sentence as well as to provide emphasis. *Like* is used in this particular way also:

> *A wuz lukin a wee haun, <u>like</u>*
> *A hut hìm, <u>like</u>, bot it wuznae a-purpose*
> *Scho cud dae wi a visit, <u>bot</u>, gif ye wudnae mynn, <u>like</u>*

In a sentence such as 'It is cold today <u>yet</u> I feel warm', *bot* would be used in Ulster-Scots:
> *Scho's caul theday <u>bot</u> A'm wairm eneuch.*

An alternative is *still*:
> *Scho's caul theday <u>still</u> A'm wairm eneuch.*

In the same way that *bot* can be positioned differently in an Ulster-Scots sentence, *still* and other 'conjunctions' can be placed at the end of the relevant clause, rather than at the beginning:
> *Scho's caul theday, A'm wairm eneuch <u>still</u>.*

N.B. In Ulster-Scots, *yit* can be used as an equivalent to 'still' in the English adverbial sense of 'I've <u>still</u> got a pain':
> *A hae a pain on me <u>yit</u>.*

Yit is, of course, also used in the same sense as English: *A'm no daen yit.*

6.5 <u>Subordinating conjunctions</u>

These are used to join subordinate or dependent clauses (ie not of equal status) to the main clause of a sentence.

'after' – *eftèr*
> *Hè gien it til thà wean <u>eftèr</u> hè haed it near brok.*
> 'He gave it to the child <u>after</u> he had nearly broken it'.

'although' – *the mair*

'because' – *becahse, acause, for, seein, bein, as, sin*

> *Hè speelit tha brae <u>seein</u> as hè cudnae get roon hit.*
> 'He climbed the hill <u>because</u> he couldn't get around it'.
> *Hè cum oot <u>acause</u> tha reek haed him blint.*
> 'He came out <u>because</u> the smoke was blinding him'.
> *The aa cum til thà daunce <u>for</u> it wuz free.*
> 'They all came to the dance <u>as</u> it was free'.
> *<u>Bein as</u> we wur aff wark, we aa cum.*
> '<u>Because</u> we were off work, we all came'.

'before' – *afore, or*
> *Gie iz yin mair <u>afore</u> ye gan.*
> *It'll be lang hòors <u>or</u> we'r daen.*

Ere is often used in Ulster-Scots literature, with the meaning 'before':
> *Ere in some neuk, wi' goose and gander* (Orr)
> *Just ae word ere I gang awa* (Thomson).

This spelling – taken as the obsolete literary English word 'ere' – was apparently used by these writers for the related borrowing from Old Norse *ár* ('early'), which gives us the current Ulster-Scots *or.*

'more ... than' – *mair ... nor*
> *A hae <u>mair</u> prittas <u>nor</u> A cud ait.*

'when', 'while', 'whilst' – *quhan, quhaniver*
> *A wuz ootbye quhaniver tha snaa wuz cumin doon.*
> 'I was outside while it was snowing'.

(see the fuller discussion of 'when', 'whenever' and 'while' in section 5.5).

The verbless subordinate clause is a feature of Scots, used when expressing surprise or indignation. In particular, the verbs 'was', 'had' etc can be omitted in Ulster-Scots if *an* or *wi* is used to introduce a clause which expresses such contrast: 'as, while, when, although ... was, had' etc – *an, wi.*

> *A wuz ootbye <u>an</u> it snaain.*
> 'I was outside <u>as</u>/<u>while</u>/<u>when</u> it was snowing'.

> *Hè cum in <u>an</u> me in thà middle o ma dinnèr.*
> 'He came in <u>as</u> I <u>was</u> eating my dinner'.

> *A wuz oot in thà snaa <u>an</u> nae coát on me.*
> 'I was out in the snow <u>although</u> I <u>had</u> no coat'.

> *Scho wuz dauncin <u>wi</u> tha bann stapt.*
> 'She was dancing <u>when</u> the band <u>had</u> stopped'.

In each of these examples, *an* and *wi* can be used interchangeably: *Hè cum in <u>wi</u> me in thà middle o ma dinnèr, Scho wuz dauncin <u>an</u> tha baun stapt*, etc.

Note: If *quhaniver* is used rather than *an* or *wi*, the implied verb must be reinstated. Otherwise the meaning changes as in English:

Scho wuz dauncing quhaniver the baun wuz stapt.
'She was dancing <u>when</u> the band <u>had</u> stopped'.

Scho wus dauncin quhaniver the baun stapt.
'She was dancing <u>when</u> the band stopped'.

'since' – *frae, fae, sin*
     A'm at scuil <u>fae</u> A wuz five.

'so that' – *sae as*
     Hè wrocht aa Settèrday <u>sae as</u> hè cud hae tha Monday aff.

'that' – *at, as*
     Tha mon <u>as</u> wuz lukin ye.
     Wha wud a thocht <u>at</u> aa wuz loast
     Yer man hissel sez <u>as</u> hoo the wur bait

'til' – *tae*

'than' – *nor*
     Tha soo wuz bägger <u>nor</u> A thocht.

'by the time that ... had' – *agin, gin*
     I hae tha claes brocht in aff thà line <u>agin</u> it haed stairtit tae rain.

(Note that *agin* and *gin* can be used with an implied or missing auxiliary verb in Ulster-Scots, similarly to the examples for *an* and *wi* above: *scho wuz dauncin gin tha bann [haed] stapt*).

It is obvious that a large number of words can be used in Ulster-Scots as adverbs, prepositions and/or conjunctions. The most important task, however, is not to determine the function or 'part of speech' of each word by itself. Instead, the key to understanding Ulster-Scots syntax lies in deciding what is the purpose in the sentence of each clause or phrase. In this process, the first step is to determine whether a particular clause modifies the <u>Subject</u>, the <u>Object</u> or the main <u>Verb</u>. A 'word-for-word' translation of prose from English to Ulster-Scots is likely to be unsuccessful if there is not an understanding how each clause functions. Ulster-Scots syntax will be discussed in more detail in chapter 10, following an exploration in the next three chapters of how Ulster-Scots verbs operate.

CHAPTER 7:
THE VERB IN ULSTER SCOTS

Verbs, the 'doing and being words', are the most important elements of a language. A verb is the basis of every sentence: It gives sense to a group of words, for without a verb all there can be is a phrase (which cannot make sense by itself), or a meaningless collection of words. 'The black cat' is a phrase, and 'the cat black' is only a collection of words. However, when a verb is added we have a true sentence: 'The black cat *ran*' or 'The cat *is* black'. In different languages verbs are usually capable of being altered in form so that they can carry additional information – not just telling what action is implied by the 'doing' word. For example, changes in the verb form can indicate more information about the sense of time of what is happening, whether the event is in the present (The cat *is* black), the past (The cat *was* black) or the future (the cat *will be* black). Changes in verb form can also tell us about the subject – whether the person or thing 'doing' the action is plural or singular, 1st, 2nd or 3rd person, etc (I *am* black; it *is* black; all the cats *are* black.)

In Ulster-Scots grammar, the behaviour of the verb is most important, but for students learning it as a new language, the different verb forms can be difficult to learn. To understand Ulster-Scots properly, however, we must understand its grammar, and the key to understanding Ulster-Scots grammar is to understand how its verbs are used.

In Ulster-Scots the verb sometimes has a different ending in the present tense according to the person of the subject (*A am, ye ir, hè is; A hae, ye hae, hè haes*, etc). There are three persons. The FIRST PERSON is, or includes, the person speaking, eg *A dae* ('I do'), *we dae* ('we do'). The SECOND PERSON is the person spoken to, eg *ye dae* ('you do'), and the THIRD PERSON is the person spoken about, usually requiring *-s* on the verb, eg *hè daes, scho daes, hit daes, yer mon daes, tha wee lad daes* etc. These are easily remembered using the old adage that "anybody who always talks in the 1st person (about himself) is a bore; the person that talks in the 3rd person (about others) is a gossip, and the person that talks in the 2nd person (about you) is *'guid crack'* ".

Number can also affect verb endings in the present tense (*hè haes, the hae*). Number is either SINGULAR or PLURAL, so the subject of the sentence (the person or thing 'doing' the action told about by the verb) will be either only one (singular) or more than one (plural). first Person Plural would therefore be: *we dae*, Second Person Plural: *yous dae*; and Third Person Plural: *the* ('they') *dae*. However, as we shall see, in some circumstances plural verb endings can also take the *-s* form (eg *them yins daes, yer men daes, tha wee lads daes* etc).

In the simplest of sentences with only a subject (eg 'The cat') and a verb (eg 'eats'), it is the verb form which is changed to indicate the tense – 'The cat <u>eats</u>'; 'the cat <u>ate</u>'; 'the cat <u>has eaten</u>'; 'the cat <u>will eat</u>'. In the first example ('the cat eats'), the verb is in the present tense and is 3rd Person Singular. In English, (except for 'was' as the past tense of 'be') only, 3rd Person Singular verb forms, in the present tense, use the 's' ending, although both Ulster-Scots and English share a 'narrative' mood which also involves using present tense verb forms to recount past actions. The different ways in which these -s endings operate for verbs in Ulster-Scots will be described below in section 7.7.

Some languages (such as Latin) express nearly all verbal features by changing the single verb word, or by adding suffixes, a process called inflection. Other languages (such as English and Scots) more often add other words, called helping or auxiliary verbs, to the 'main' verb to construct compound forms and phrases.

As we shall see from the spoken language, Ulster-Scots often does not always follow the usual sentence construction (or word order) pattern of English. In informal conversation, it is possible to hear, for example, a statement like *"naethin bot broon fäsch, thon cat haes"* where the object *fäsch* is followed by the subject *(thon cat)* and ends with the verb *(haes)*. In English the construction is Subject-Verb-Object ('that cat has nothing but brown fish').

English and Ulster-Scots share the pattern of having minimal use of inflection when it comes to verb words, eg with the verb *tae tak* ('to take') there are only 1 base and 4 inflected verb forms in English, and 1 base and 3 inflected forms in Ulster-Scots:

> *tak* (take)
> *taks* (takes)
> *taen* (took and taken)
> *takkin* (taking).

[N.B. The Ulster-English dialectal form *tuk** ('took' and 'taken') is also used by some speakers as an alternative to *taen*.]

However, when we think of inflecting compound verb <u>forms</u> (rather than simple verb words) we find such constructions as: *is takkin* ('is taking'), *is for takkin* ('is going to take/will take'), *cud hae tuk* ('may have taken'), *maun hae taen* ('must have taken'), etc.

It is obvious that the verbal forms used in Ulster-Scots are usually <u>groups</u> of words, as in English, rather than a single, inflected verb word, as in Latin. However, the Ulster-Scots verb forms must still vary to imply a range of information about time, tense and 'mood'.

Obviously 'tense' (ie the time of the action indicated by the verb) is a fundamental feature.

7.1 <u>Expressing future events</u>

There are a number of ways in which future action can be indicated through verb modification, or by the use of adverbs which clearly set the time being referred to in the future.

(a) using *for*:

> *Ir we for rain theday? Wud we be for rain theday?* ('Is it going to rain today?')
>
> *A'm for sayin nae mair* ('I am going to say nothing more.')

Gangin (contracted forms *ganin* and *gan*) in Ulster-Scots literally means 'going' in the English sense of movement (rather than of future tense). So we can be *for gangin intae toon*, meaning 'going to go to town'. However, 'going to ...' is more usually *gan tae* or *gonnae**.

The word *for* is often used to indicate an intention to do something, rather than a future event over which there is no control. However, *for* is used more widely than an 'intend to' or 'plan to' translation might imply. So it is that we can certainly ... *be for cuttin thà gress themorra* (meaning we intend to cut the lawn tomorrow), but we can also say *thae wee fellas is for haein a accídent* ('those wee boys <u>will have</u> an accident'), indicating a sense of likelihood.

Ye'r for it, wee lad*. The idiomatic use of the compound *for it* is widespread in Ulster-Scots. It means 'in trouble', or 'going to get punished'.

(b) using *wull* or a modal verb + *be*:

Wull, like 'will' in English, can operate as a modal verb to indicate future tense:

> *A'll loan ye it on Settèrday* ('I'll lend it to you on Saturday'.)

Modal verbs + *be* can indicate future time, but may require an adverb of time to make this clear:
> *A micht/wull/shud/cud be late themorra* ('I may/shall/ought to/might be late tomorrow.')

It should be noted here that *wull* is used as a modal verb in Ulster-Scots for <u>both</u> 'will' and 'shall' in English. Different usages of modal verbs such as *wull* (or 'shall' in English), *can* and *cud* ('may' or 'might' in English), will be explained more fully in chapters 8 and 9.

(c) Using present tense *be* + main verb (usually present participle) and a qualifying adverbial phrase.
> *A'm loanin* ye it this Settèrday, am A no?*
> ('I'll lend it to you on Saturday, won't I?')

This form of future tense construction, which uses the present tense but qualifies it with a clause or phrase to indicate its future tense meaning, is very common in Ulster-Scots speech, and is similar to ways in which past tense meanings can also be formed (see section 7.13).
> *A'm lukin thon buik bak afore thenicht.*
> ('I'll be wanting that book returned before tonight'.)
> *Quhit lentht o time ir yiz aa stappin themorra?*
> ('How long will all of you be staying tomorrow?')

A wuz thar aa last week, an A'm stuid thar thenicht again.
('I was there all last week and I'll be standing [waiting] there again tonight'.)

Note that in the last example the past rather than the present participle is used (see section 7.11).

Sometimes, this type of future tense construction is preferred to that using *for*, and can be formed by substituting an adverbial phrase for the *for* eg:

A'm for saying nae mair.
A'm saying nae mair thenicht.
('I'll be saying nothing more tonight.')

(d) Other uses of *be* to express future.

The subjunctive mood (section 7.10) is used when a statement expresses doubt, uncertainty or even hope. For example, in the statement *Yiz ir intae wark themorra*, the present tense of the verb *be* is used in the form *ir* ('are'). However, when uncertainty is introduced, the form *be* is preferred.

Gif yiz aa <u>be</u> intae wark themorra. This is the subjunctive or conditional mood, and occasionally can be used to express future time as well:

A hope ye <u>be</u> aa richt quhaniver thà doctòr cums.

Be is used in this way in Ulster-Scots for all persons <u>except</u> the 3rd person (singular and plural), where *bis*, *bees*, or *is* is preferred.

Gif A <u>be</u> at thà schaps thenicht (1st person)
Gif ye <u>be</u> at thà schaps thenicht (2nd person)
Gif hè <u>bis</u> at thà schaps thenicht (3rd person singular)
Gif the <u>be/bees</u> at thà schap thenicht (3rd person plural)
Gif thà oul fella an thà wife <u>bis/is</u> at... (3rd person plural)

7.2 <u>Present tense</u>

In Ulster-Scots there are two principal ways of expressing present time, depending on whether the present state is temporary/momentary, or whether it is a habitual or permanent state.

(a) Passing or 'temporary' sense of the present:

eg: *Thon's a graun day theday* ('It's a nice day today')
or (emphatic) *Thon <u>is</u> a graun day ...* ('It is indeed a nice day...')

(b) Permanent or 'habitual' sense:

Christmas'd be a big day wi tha Amerícans ('Christmas is an important day with Americans')
or (emphatic) *Christmas <u>wud</u> be a big day.*

Although *is* is used in the same way as in English, Ulster-Scots has also a number of different ways of expressing, in verb form, these different nuances of present tense meanings.

Christmas daes be a big day wi tha Américans.
This is a more dogmatic form than *wud be* as used above. Its negative form is *niver (Niver a big day wi iz, Christmas)*, or *disnae be (Christmas disnae be a big day wi iz)*. The negative form of *wud be* is simply *wudnae be (Christmas wudnae be sich a big day wi iz)*. In Chapters 8 and 9 these auxiliary verbs are discussed in detail.

Ulster-Scots has also the 'habitual' and 'proverbial' form of verb words which employs the *-s* ending (eg *taks*, for 'take', *bees*, for 'am', etc). Another circumstance where verb words employ *-s* endings is in the story-telling, or 'narrative' style, where it can be difficult to distinguish the tense. The *-s* endings in the following examples are not always used in everyday speech, and in some cases only rarely so.

> **eg: (narrative)**
> *A <u>cums</u> in thà hoose wi nae claes on an sez ...*
> ('I <u>came</u> into the house with no clothes on and said ...').
>
> **(habitual)**
> *A aye <u>cums</u> in thà hoose tha bak roád.*
> ('I always <u>come</u> into the house the back way').
>
> **(proverbial)**
> *Quhiles A sits an thìnks, ithèr times A jist sits.*
> ('Sometimes I sit and think, other times I just sit').

This *-s* ending can also be used to indicate an 'habitual' sense in Ulster-Scots with the verb *be*, where it would be equivalent to 'am', 'is', etc in English:

> *He aye <u>bees</u> bad wi a sair heid in thà sin.*
> ('He <u>is</u> always ill with a headache in the sun').

The way in which the verb *be* behaves in Ulster-Scots is particularly complex and is dealt with in detail in chapter 8. For the moment, it should be noted that *be* (with or without the *-s* ending) can be used sometimes to indicate an 'habitual' sense or to emphasise the point.

> **eg:** *Thae chickens fae tha market bis aff.*
> Habitual: ('Those chickens that you get from the market are (usually) "off", ie bad'), or
> Emphatic: ('Those chickens you got from the market are (this time, definitely) "off" ').
>
> Non-emphatic and Non-habitual: *Thae chickens fae tha market is aff.*
> ('Those chickens that you got from the market are (this time) "off" ').

In speech the different meanings would also be distinguished by intonation.

7.3 <u>Past tense</u>

Verb forms used in Ulster-Scots to express past tense can indicate two different types of events: one that is 'continuing' past, or one that is completed. Also the habitual moods described above can also be used in the past tense. Compare for example:

A wuz aitin* ma dinnèr quhaniver ...
('I had been eating (but not necessarily finished) my dinner when ...')
A hae ma dinnèr et ('I have eaten (all) my dinner')
A'm at ma dinnèr this twa hòors
('I have been eating my dinner for two hours'),
A bin aitin ma dinnèr at mae ma's ('I have been (regularly) eating my din-
ner at my mother's').

In the last three examples we begin to encroach on the 'perfect' tenses, which will be
dealt with in section 7.13.

The English forms such as 'took' and 'have taken' are, however, usually merged with
a single form such as *taen* in Ulster-Scots eg: *A (hae) taen thà offer up* means 'I
accepted (took up) the offer', or 'I have taken up the offer'. If an Ulster-Scots speaker
wished to distinguish the nuance of meaning here, a 'tag' can be used at the end of
the sentence: *taen thà offer up, sae A daed* (for the first sense), or *taen thà offer up,
sae A hae* (for the second sense). This becomes more clear in the negative forms: *A
didnae tak thà offer up, sae A niver*, and *A hinnae taen thà offer up, sae A hinnae*
(here it is implied that I might still change my mind). An alternative is to change the
word order to *A hinnae tha offer taen up*. This feature can be associated with a different sentence construction, one which places part of the verb at the end: *Hè is gye
hungrie gat* (see chapter 10).

Ulster-Scots speakers will also use what appears to be present tense verb forms to
indicate an ongoing past that continues to the present:

A'm at scuil twa yeir noo.
('I've been at school two years now'.)

Hè's waitin on yous aa sin yestreen.
('He has been waiting for all of you since last night'.)

Of course, as well as the different verbal phrase forms indicating a sense of time or
'tense', the verb words themselves are often 'inflected' (or changed). This is most
often achieved in English by adding a '-d' or an '-ed' to the end of the verb (eg
walk/walked, talk/talked, etc), or by a vowel change (eg swim/swam, run/ran,
eat/ate, etc), or, indeed, by both (tell/told). In traditional Scots, the vowel changes are
sometimes different from English (eg *rin/run*), and *-t* or *-it* endings used (eg
change/changit, stairt/stairtit etc) in place of the 'd' or 'ed' endings.

7.4 Past tense verb endings: *-it, -t* and *'t*

Although verbs which end with a stressed vowel such as *caa* ('call') or *dee* ('die')
take a *-d* ending to form the past tense (*caa'd* and *dee'd*), the use of *-it* endings on
past tense verbs which end in a consonant (equivalent to '-ed' endings in English) has
been a feature of written Scots, both in Scotland and Ulster, for centuries. Verb stems
which end in a liquid or nasal consonant take a *-t* rather than *-it* ending (eg *kilt*
'killed'). The general rules in Ulster-Scots for which verbs take *-ed, -d, -t, -'t, -it* or -
et endings are discussed more fully in section 7.5.

In English the past tense and part participle forms of 'learn' can be either 'learnt' or 'learned'. Remembering that in Ulster-Scots the verb *larn* means 'to teach' as well as 'to learn' (and so is not exactly the same verb), both past tense and part participle forms are represented by *larnt*, eg *A larnt hìm hìs sums*. When the equivalent of 'learned' is required (as with the adjective in 'a very learned man'), the spelling in Scots is *larnit*.

In modern Scots writing the *-it* ending is used only where the vowel is sounded before the 't'. So for 'rented', 'salted', 'nudged' etc we have *rentit, sautit, duntit*. Ulster-Scots poetry often included *-et* spellings which suggest that the last vowel was pronounced where it would not be in English, (eg Orr: *"Wifes baket bonnocks for their men"*, *"A henpecket taupie"*, *"A forket flash cam sklentin' thro"*, *"He weav'd himsel', an' keepet twa three gaun"*.) In some cases this pronunciation is still marked, as in *droondit* ('drowned'), eg Savage-Armstrong: *"Peg's Jamie that wuz droondit in the say"*.

When in English the verb ends in '-nd' or '-ld' (as in 'mend') the past tense should not necessarily be written in Ulster Scots as *mendit*, for the consonant sound before the '-ed' is often lost. For 'mended', 'sounded', 'rounded', 'banded' and 'sanded' we have *ment, soont, roondit, bandit*, and *sannit*. 'Moulded' becomes *mouled* or *mouldit* and 'folded' becomes *foulit*. 'Minded' (in Ulster-Scots meaning 'remembered') presents a particular problem, for **minnit* suggests a pronunciation that would rhyme with 'linnet'. Many Ulster-Scots speakers 're-introduce' the 'd' to say *minded* for the past tense form, while others use *mined*. The spelling form *mynnit* has been used by some modern writers to avoid the use of the apostrophe in an alternative form **min'it*. However, the use of the apostrophe cannot always be avoided. 'Walked', 'talked', and 'banned', for example, have often been written as *waakit, taakit* and *bannit*. Modern Scots writers are presented with a dilemma in these cases. The *-it* endings here suggest an archaic pronunciation of the last vowel, while on the other hand, apostrophes have been studiously avoided in modern Lallans literature. So it is that **waak't* and **taak't* are also disliked forms. On the question of apostrophes, however, the objections seem to be based on whether or not the 'missing' letter is 'English' (as with **fu'* rather than *fu* for 'full'). If this is the principal reason, there should be no objection to using apostrophes to indicate missing 'Scots' letters (as with *walk't* for *walkit* etc). The alternative, of course, is to simply use a *-t* ending (*waakt, taakt, bannt* etc). This is correctly applied anyway to verb forms such as *coupt* ('overturned'), *stapt* ('stopped'), *dandert* ('ambled'), *telt* ('told'), *felt* ('felled') and, of course, *larnt* (eg Savage-Armstrong: *"An' he rides roon' the Airds whaur his feythers helt sway"*).

7.5 Verb inflection to indicate past tense

At this point a distinction must be made between 'full' verbs, or single words that take on the full verb function, and compound verbal forms that consist of groups of words. With full verbs sound and spelling changes occur within the word itself (inflection) to indicate past tense. In Ulster-Scots there are a number of full verbs, such as *taak* ('talk'), which are inflected and used in much the same way as in English: *A taak't til thà wee lad* ('I talked to the little boy'). Other English full verbs are rarely used in Ulster-Scots, eg 'bellow' (*baw* or *rout* in Ulster-Scots), while some are similar to Ulster-Scots verbs, but have a different past tense inflection (for example, the past tense of 'run' in English is 'ran', but in Ulster-Scots the present tense is *rin*, and the past tense *run*. Examples of irregular English past tense forms which are represented differently in Ulster-Scots include:

(1) I <u>break</u> stones in the quarry.   A <u>breks/busts</u>* *stanes in thà quarrie.*
     I <u>broke</u> a stone yesterday.   A <u>bruk</u> *a stane yesterae.*
(2) I <u>teach</u> the children today what I <u>taught</u>   A <u>larn</u> *thà weans theday quhat A* <u>larnt</u>
     them yesterday.   *thaim yesterae.*
(3) I <u>cleared</u> the cupboard and <u>fixed</u> the   A <u>rid/redd oot</u> *thà press an* <u>soartit</u> *thà*
     blender. Would you <u>clean out</u> the   *mäxer* <u>oot</u>. *Ye cudnae* <u>redd oot</u> *thà*
     drawer too please?   *drawer forbye cud ye?*
(4) I <u>ran</u> into the room   A <u>run</u> *in tae thà chaummer.*

Many irregular Ulster-Scots past tense verb forms are the same as the English past participle forms:

      eg: I stink (present)   A *stink*
                 I stank/stunk (past)   A *stunk*
                 I have stunk (past participle) A *hae stunk*.

It is a general rule for verbs that are common to both English and Ulster-Scots, that the past participle form in English will provide the Ulster-Scots past tense <u>and</u> part participle forms. This is a particularly useful rule for verbs whose past tense inflections are marked by vowel changes.

      eg: A <u>cum</u> *in thà chaummer* ('I <u>came</u> in the room')
          A <u>hae cum</u> *in thà chaummer* ('I <u>have come</u> in the room')
          A <u>seen/saen</u>* *hèr cumin* ('I <u>saw</u> her coming')
          A <u>hae saen</u> *hèr cumin* ('I <u>have seen</u> her coming')
          A <u>gien</u> *it til hèr* ('I <u>gave</u> it to her')
          A <u>hae gien</u> *it til hèr* ('I <u>have given</u> it to her')
          A <u>taen/tuk</u>* *it wi me* ('I <u>took</u> it with me')
          A <u>hae taen/tuk</u>* *it wi me* ('I <u>have taken</u> it with me')

In Ulster-Scots poetry the forms *gien* ('gave' and 'given') and *taen* ('took' and 'taken') are found as expected (eg Thomson: *"An' gien us a' cause to bewail"*; Sloan: *"And the verdict they gi'en was"*, *"What was the look that his foremanship gi'en"*; Huddleston: *"In a stiff case too, he could gi'en a pill"*, *"Brave Doddery strowlin' ta'en the gate"*, *"Sin' he by devils han's was ta'en"*; Herbison: *"Lang since this baith are ta'en"*). However, *gied* rather than *gien* is sometimes heard nowadays, and also occurs frequently in the traditional poetry:

      "He gied his hips the farewell cla" (Thomson)
      "To which the muse gied little hearing" (Thomson)
      "Perhaps you gied cause to use sic words" (McWilliams)
      "But whan the bairnie gied a scream" (McWilliams)
      "A gied her the hau'f o' my life" (Savage-Armstrong)
      "If ye gied her yin kiss" (Savage-Armstrong)
      "If yin A gied, ye'd axe fur ten" (Savage-Armstrong)
      "He gied th' affront" (Orr)
      "I coupt it up an' gied a gluister" (Orr)

Another variant of these forms is *took* or *tuk* and *give* or *giv* for 'taken' and 'given' (eg Thomson: *"I kenna whether ye hae took note"*). The 'rule' (whereby the English past participle form gives the basic Ulster-Scots past tense form) does, however, seem to break down with some other irregular verbs such as *gae, gang* or *gan* for 'go'. Although *gaed* and *gaen* are both heard as the past tense and past participle forms, most Ulster-Scots speakers today use *went* in both situations.

> A <u>went</u> tae toon yestreen.
> A <u>hae went</u> tae toon.

> ('I <u>went</u> to town last night').
> ('I <u>have gone</u> to town').

However, when Ulster-Scots poetry is examined, *gaed* is the most usual form:
> *"But aye her tongue gaed at full speed"* (Leech)
> *"He gaed na far for them I 'tweel"* (Boyle)
> *"Whan he gaed up to turn the corn"* (Boyle)
> *"The reamin bicker neist gaed roun"* (Boyle)
> *"Ere he gaed out to theek wet strae"* (Boyle)
> *"And aff she gae'd"* (Anon-Laggan)
> *"Gaed awa to the toun wi' her butter an' eggs"* (Beggs)
> *"An' a's gaed wrang wi' the ferm"* (Savage-Armstrong)

Similarly, *seen* or *saen** is in everyday use in Ulster-Scots and Ulster-English in place of 'saw' (eg Savage-Armstrong: *"A seen yer doom yestreen"*), and is consistent with the other usages of past participle forms for past tenses in Ulster-Scots. However, this use of *seen* (along with that of *done* or *daen* for 'did') is so firmly believed by Ulster-Scots speakers to be nothing more than 'bad' English grammar that it is frequently 'corrected' in speech to *sa* ('saw') and is relatively rare in Ulster-Scots poetry. The much rarer spoken usage of *seed* for 'saw' is, on the other hand, found more often in poetry: *"An' turnin' seed a sicht"*, *"A seed his face"*, *"A year syne A seed him as noo A see you"*, *"Thon nicht that A seed him, A tell't uv jist noo"*, *"Ay, quoth the Goodwife, Jamie seed him tae"* (Savage-Armstrong).

Irregular past tenses:

Past tense forms that in English are formed by changing an '-ide' ending to '-ided' (eg 'divide'/'divided'), are formed in Ulster-Scots by a vowel sound change only. So it is that we have *divid* rather than 'divided' in such idioms as: *tha warl is ill <u>divid</u>* ('the world is unfairly divided').

Some verbs with an '-ide' ending in the present tense have the '-id' past tense ending form in English too, eg:

Verb	Past tense (Eng.)	Past participle (Eng.)	Past Tense & Past Participle (Ulster-Scots)
hide	hid	(have) hidden	*(hae) hid*
slide	slid	(have) slidden	*(hae) slid*

However, with virtually all *-ide* ending verbs in Ulster-Scots, the past tense (and past participle) form is achieved by an *-id* ending.

	Verb	Past tense/past participle
eg:	*glide*	*glid** (not glided)
	ride	*rid* (not rode/have ridden)
	confide	*confid** (not confided)
	reside	*resid* (not resided)
	side	*sid** (not sided)
	chide	*chid* (not chided)

An exception to this rule is 'guide', where the past tense form in Ulster-Scots is *guidit* rather than **guid*. Similarly, verbs with '-ive' endings achieve their past tense and past participle forms in Ulster-Scots through changing the vowel sound rather than adding an ending.

Note: Some speakers pronounce *hid, rid* etc as [hud] [rud] etc, and sometimes spellings will be encountered reflecting this.

	Verb	Past tense/past participle form
eg:	*dive*	*div* (not dived/diven), occasionally *dove*
	drive	*driv* (not drove/driven)
	derive	*deriv** (not derived/deriven)
	revive	*reviv** (not revived/reviven)
	arrive	*arriv** (not arrived)

Note: The past tense and past participle form of the verb *rise* is *riz*, but the verb 'raise' (as with raising children) is *rax* in Ulster-Scots. *Rax* also means 'to reach', but with whichever meaning, the past tense form of *rax* is *raxt*, or *raxed*.

When we consider verbs with '-ite' endings the situation is similar. With 'write', the past tense and past participle form is *writ* (not 'wrote' or 'written'). So it is with *bite* (past tense *bit* and past participle *hae bit*), and similarly:

	Past tense/Past participle
site	*sit** (not sited)
skite	*skit** (not skited)
smite	*smit* (not <u>smote</u> or <u>have smitten</u>)

This last verb is used in Ulster-Scots with the meaning to 'infect' (eg with a cold), rather than 'strike a blow', and the adjectival form meaning 'infectious' is *smittle*. The same past tense verb forms with *-it* endings are also found with some verbs rarely used in Ulster-Scots, such as:

	Past tense/Past participle
ignite	*ignit* (not ignited) (The verb usually used would be *lit*)
incite	*incit* (usually, *egg on*)
unite	*unit* (usually, *pit thegither*)

In English, certain verbs are pronounced as if they end in '-ite', such as 'sight', 'light', 'right', etc. In Ulster-Scots these are pronounced *sicht, licht, richt*, etc and the past tense forms are *sichtit, lichtit*, and *richtit*. So it is that the different usages are in some ways more easily distinguishable in Ulster-Scots, as *site* means to locate (eg a building) and its present and past tense forms *site* and *sit** would never be confused with *sicht* and *sichtit* ('to see someone or something').

In the same way *licht* is used in Ulster-Scots only for the sense of illuminating or setting fire to, not for landing (or as a bird 'alighting' on a branch). We would say that the fire was *lichtit*, but that the bird *lit* or *lut** on the tree. In Ulster-Scots to *light* (on someone) (past tense *lit*) is also used to describe someone accosting another: *Scho lit on hìm afore hè cud get in thà duir*. The past tenses of *hit* is *hut*, and of *spit* is *sput*. While *lut** can be the past tense form of *light* in some areas, it is more often the past tense form of *let*.

Richtit usually means 'corrected' or 'straightened' and *dicht* or *dichtit* means 'wiped'. *flichtit* with the meaning of the flight or movement of people (even moving house) is now more widely used as *flit* in the present, and *flitted* in the past tense.

'fight' is one English verb which behaves inconsistently in Ulster-Scots, for the present-tense form is *fecht* rather than **ficht* and its past tense can be *focht*, or *fit**.

Verbs ending in '-eat' in English usually end in *-ait** in Ulster-English, and this ending and pronunciation is shared by some Ulster-Scots speakers. They normally add -it to form the past tense and past participle, for example *defait** ('defeat'), *defaitit** ('defeated'), or "*A'm jiltit an' chaytit* ('cheated')" (Savage-Armstrong). However, the English verb 'eat' itself is sometimes *ait** in the present tense in Ulster-Scots (but *eat* as in Standard English in the core areas), while the English past tense 'ate' and past participle 'have eaten' are *et* and *hae et* in Ulster-Scots. 'Beat' is *bait* or *bate* in Ulster-Scots for all tenses, past and present.

'Heat' is *hait**, for present tense, *het* for past tense and past participle, while 'bleat', 'repeat' and 'cheat' are *blait**, *repait** and *chait* respectively for the present tense, and *blaitit*, *repaitit* and *chaitit* for the past tense and past participle. Note: 'Bleat' would more typically be *meh* and 'repeat' *cum owre*.

The past tense form of *greet* ('cry') can be *grat* (eg Orr: "*The weans grat*"). In contrast, while the past tense of 'catch' in English is the inflected form 'caught', in Ulster-Scots it is *catched* (eg Thomson: "*Death wha the noblest ay has catch'd*").

The past tense of 'begin' is *begoud* ('began'), eg Huddleston: "*The e'enin sun begoud tae lo'er*", Orr: "*Begoud to be less lazy*", "*The lift begud a storm to brew.*"

Verbs in *-ell*:	past tense	past participle
sell	*soul* ('sold')	*hae soul*
tell	*toul/telt*	*hae toul/hae telt*

Verbs in -oul:	past tense	past participle
foul ('fold')	*fouldit* ('folded')	*hae fouldit*
houl ('hold')	*hel/helt*/hoult** ('held')	*hae hel/helt*/hoult**
moul ('mould')	*mouled/mouldit*	*hae mouled/mouldit*

N.B. These forms are significantly different from the traditional Scots forms which also occur in Ulster-Scots literature – where the 'l' is silent rather than the 'd':
  haud rather than *houl* for 'hold'
  faud rather than *foul* for 'fold'
  taud rather than *toul* for 'told'

Although some of these 'traditional' Scots forms are perhaps spurious, they are common even in relatively recent poetry, for example that of George Savage-Armstrong, 1901:

> "A tau'd ye this wud by yer game"
> "Tae hau'd in mine her han' sae slight"
> "A'll hau'd her last wee luvesome luik"
> "For fau'ded-up mid snaws an' sleet"
> "Puir lad, ye'll fin' it unco cau'd".

Others, such as Herbison, favour the *hauld, tauld* forms, for example *"That tauld me I had wrought enough"*.

Verbs in -*ill*:

kill	kilt ('killed')	hae kilt
bill	bilt	hae bilt
fill	filt	hae filt
mill	milt	hae milt
spill	spilt	hae spilt

Verbs in -*ing*:

sing	sung	hae sung
bring	brung/brocht	hae brung
ring	rung	hae rung

Verbs in -*ynn/-ine*:

bine/bynn ('bind')	boon	hae boon
fine/fynn ('find')	foon	hae foon
mine/mynn ('mind')	mynnit/mindit	hae mynnit/mindit
wine/wynn ('wind')	wun	hae wun
grine/grynn ('grind')	grun	hae grun

Verbs in -*enn*:

lenn or loan ('lend')	lent/lennit*/loant*	hae lent/lennit*/loant*
benn ('bend')	bent/bendit*/bennit*	hae bent/bendit*/bennit*
menn ('mend')	ment/mendit*/mennit*	hae ment/mendit*/mennit*
senn ('send')	sent	hae sent
tenn ('tend')	tendit/tennit*	hae tendit/tennit*

N.B. Some Ulster-Scots speakers 'reinstate' the 'd' in the past tense forms of some of the above verbs, although the final 'd' is invariably 'lost' in the present tense form (eg *mine/mindit, menn/mendit** – the verbs 'mind' for 'remember' and 'mend' for 'improve in health' respectively).

Verbs in -*owe*:

glowe ('glow')	glowed	hae glowed
flowe ('flow')	flawt/flowed	hae flowed
growe ('grow')	growed	hae growed
thowe ('thaw')	thowed	hae thowed

N.B. In all the above verbs the -owe spellings indicate a pronunciation in Ulster-Scots which rhymes with English 'now', 'how' etc.

Verbs in -up:

	past tense:	past participle:
grup ('grip')	grupt	hae grupt
rup ('rip')	rupt	hae rupt
drup ('drip')	drupt	hae drupt
sup ('sip')	supt	hae supt
trup ('trip')	trupt	hae trupt

Verbs in -aa:

blaa ('blow')	blaad	hae blaad
snaa ('snow')	snaad	hae snaad

The English verbs 'lose' (the opposite of 'find') and 'loose' (the opposite of 'tighten') are *loass* and *slakken* in Ulster-Scots. Their past tense forms are *loast* and *slakkent* respectively (rather than 'lost' and 'loosened'). *Climm* ('climb') – and its alternative with the same meaning, *speel* – have the past tense forms *climmed* and *speeled*.

7.6 The 'concord' or agreement between subject and verb ending

In English, as we have seen, the '-s' ending verb form usually occurs only with third person singular subjects (although the 'historical present' or narrative verb forms with -s endings are also common in colloquial English). Consider the way in which the English verbs 'take', 'run', 'be' and 'have' are normally modified:

1st Person Singular:	I take, I run, I am, I have
2nd Person Singular:	you take, you run, you are, you have
3rd Person Singular:	he, she, it takes, runs, is, has
1st Person Plural:	we take, we run, we are, we have
2nd Person Plural:	you take, you run, you are, you have
3rd Person Plural:	they take, they run, they are, they have.

In Ulster-Scots, not only are -s ending verb forms used in for all persons and numbers when narrative or habitual senses are being expressed, but in other senses too Ulster-Scots verbs are not restricted to this singular 'concord' use of -s forms with 3rd person singular subjects, eg: *Aa thae cats is black* (All those cats are black) – here the number of the subject (cats) is plural. This is the so-called 'northern present-tense rule' where verbs are inflected in the present indicative in all persons and numbers except when the personal pronoun subject is immediately adjacent to the verb, in which case only the 2nd and 3rd person singular are inflected.

The use of -s ending verb forms for singular and plural subjects (and for 1st and 2nd person as well as 3rd person subjects), has been a characteristic of Scots writing for centuries. In the early 1600s, letters written in Ulster-Scots display it regularly, for example:

"... quhairin thair is ('are') not gud numbers of our nation".
(Letter from Earl of Abercorn, Strabane, 1614).

"I be thir presents <u>grants</u> ('grant') *me ..."*

"I Sir Robert McClellane ... be thir presentis <u>dois</u> ('do') *faithfully promeiss..."*
"I the said Sir Robert <u>binds</u> ('bind') *me ..."*
"... as utheris his freyndis and coppyholderis <u>dois</u> ('do') *..."*
                    (Indentures, Sir Robert McClelland, near Coleraine, 1614-1617).

"Ye shall wit that their <u>hes</u> ('have') *bin servants of my Lord Cheichesters heir".*
"I take leve and still <u>remains</u> ('remain'), *your loving brother".*
                              (Letter from Robert Adair, Ballymena, 1627).

"Quhat neuis I sall have you sall heir frome me as occasionis <u>fallis</u> ('fall') *out".*
                              (Letter from John Hamilton of Bangor, c.1630).

"... for the mellors <u>vas</u> ('were') *gresting stons"*
                              (Letter from Galgorm to Edmonstone of Ballycarry, 1629).

"And giff my outward actions <u>hes</u> ('have') *nocht bein ansuerable ..."*
"... and it is far by the opinioun many <u>hes</u> ('have') *had of me, young and auld".*
                              (Letter from Isobel Haldane, Ballycarry, c.1630).

The Ulster-Scots poets, writing almost 200 years later, mostly avoided this feature, presumably as it was considered 'bad' grammar. Indeed this is still how it is regarded, although in speech *-s* verb forms with plural subjects are still used frequently. Nevertheless, some examples do occur in the traditional poetry:

> *"Ower a' the ills <u>haes</u>* ('have') *come between"* (Huddleston)
> *"Quoth she – tho' strangers are we twa,*
>   *An' ne'er <u>before's</u>* ('have') *been cheersome"* (Huddleston)
> *"Aft neeborin', towerin' hills <u>is</u>* ('are') *seen"* (Boyle)
> *"<u>There's</u>* ('there are') *money taxes ilka year"* (Boyle)
> *"Or else the markets <u>gangs na</u>* ('do not go') *right"* (Boyle)
> *"Then twa auld men <u>gaes</u>* ('go') *on before"* (Gilmore)
> *"We merch till oor buddies <u>is</u>* ('are') *nimb"* (Savage-Armstrong)
> *"The twa bit threads <u>that's</u>* ('are') *set for you"* (Herbison).

The use of the *-s* form in Ulster-Scots is particularly common on verbs having 3rd person <u>plural</u> subjects, except where the personal pronoun *the* (they) comes immediately adjacent to the verb. It would be strange, for example, to hear someone say **they is daft*, but we can have *thaimuns is daft*. So the *-s* verb form can be used with every person and number in Ulster-Scots, although the alternative forms which equate to English are, of course, also used (eg: *Aa thae cats <u>ir</u> black*). The circumstances where the *-s* verb form is most likely to occur are:

(a) when the subject is not a personal pronoun used by itself (I, you, we etc).

> eg: *Me an ma faithèr is for cumin*
> ('My father and I <u>are</u> going to come' but <u>not</u> **we is for cumin*).
Usually, the weak form of *is* is used eg: *Mae da an <u>me's</u> for cumin*.

Me an hìm daes aa tha reddin oot
('He and I <u>do</u> all the cleaning', but <u>not</u> *we daes aa tha reddin oot*).

The *-s* verb form can, however, be used adjacent to *thaimuns (is)* and *yous'uns (is)*, although not with *the* ('they') and rarely with *yous* ('you') except, for example, in constructions like *yous is tae cum hame noo.*

(b) when the subject is separated from the verb by other words (even if the subject is a personal pronoun).

eg: *We, nae mattèr quhit ye hae in mynn for themorra, <u>is</u> for cumin tae*
         ('We, no matter what you intend doing tomorrow, <u>are</u> going to come too'.)

        You, for aa yer big taak an buiks, <u>disnae</u> unnèrstaun ava ('You, for all you say, and read, <u>don't</u> understand at all'.)

Obviously, if the subject is in the 3rd person plural <u>and</u> removed from the verb, the use of the *-s* form verb becomes almost universal in Ulster-Scots:
        Thon wee lad an hìs da, nae mattèr quhit the dae, <u>isnae</u> for gettin in owre tha duir.
        ('That wee boy and his father, no matter what they do, <u>aren't</u> going to get in through the door'.)

If an 'existential' sentence construction (ie stating the existence of something) such as 'There are ....' is used, the *-s* form also becomes more likely: eg 'there <u>are</u> four hundred people coming', this would usually be *thar'<u>s</u> fower hunner fowk cumin* in Ulster-Scots.

<u>Note</u>: The greeting 'How are you?' can be rendered *Hoo's aboot ye?** (*Bout-ye* is characteristic of Belfast speech) or even *Hoo's thìngs?* [How <u>is</u> things?]

7.7 <u>The *-s* ending on Ulster-Scots verbs</u>

The *-s* ending on verbs is used in a number of other circumstances in Ulster-Scots. In the past tense (eg Gilmore: *"Then hame I goes"*), it is sometimes used for all persons and numbers if the story-telling or '<u>narrative</u>' mood is used. (Colloquial English also uses the '-s' ending in 3rd person singular verbs in narrative mood).

Athoot a coch yer mon <u>taems</u> the wattèr oot, an sae we <u>raxes</u> for oor däsch-cloots an <u>rins</u> fair for hìm. A <u>goes</u> "Ye pauchle ye! A aye <u>taks</u> tent o that.". Hè's nae uise wi hìs hanns. D'ye no mynn quättin-tim yestrae? You <u>cries</u> hìm bak in an <u>taks</u> hìm doon tae redd thà cleeks fae aff o thà buik-kìsts. He cudnae jee thaim ava. You <u>sinthers</u> thaim bot an hè <u>maks</u> oot hè daen it aa hissel!

'Without hesitation he <u>emptied</u> out the water, and so we <u>reached</u> for our tea-towels and <u>ran</u> straight for him. I said "You clumsy fool! I'm always careful with that." He is no good with his hands. Do you remember finishing-time yesterday. You <u>called</u> him back in and <u>took</u> him down to release the catches off the book-chests. He couldn't shift them at all. You pulled them apart, however, and he pretended he had done it himself!'

In the 'habitual' sense, that is, where something occurs on a regular or frequent basis, as a habit, the -s ending can also be used, on occasion, for all persons and numbers (eg Campbell: *"Ye Scotchmen true that wears the blue"*):

> *James an thà wife aye caylzies* in oor hoose, an we bis weel in wi tha sister tae. We niver wants for company. Ilka nicht jist quhan A gets thà weans tae bed, lippen ma wurd, in tha waaks.*

'James and his wife visit our house regularly, and we are on friendly terms with his sister too. We're never short of company. Every night when I have just got the children to bed, depend upon it, in they walk.'

A number of verbs are formed in Ulster-Scots from adverbs of place, and -s endings are particularly common with them, perhaps as a means of indicating their verbal function:

> *He aye awas hame quhan hè shudnae, sae A ootsides an eftèrs him*
> *Sae hè oots wi tha cattèr.*
> 'He always goes home when he shouldn't, so I went outside and chased after him'.
> So he came out with the money.

In summary, the rules for when the -s ending can be applied to Ulster-Scots verbs in the present tense (when a permanent or 'habitual' sense is not intended), involve the use of subjects other than personal pronouns, or the separation of the subject (including personal pronouns) from the verb:

> *James an thà wife bis at thà duir*, agane. A hopes ye, lang afore this noo, haes thà weans pit tae bed? The niver tha yinst haes thocht tae let us know afore the cum owre an visits iz. I – spaikin* for masel noo, – isnae for tholin it nae mair.*

7.8 Making nouns out of verbs

One of the most striking characteristics of Ulster-Scots grammar is a preference for using nouns that are derived from verbs rather than the full verb form. This is a matter of degree, when compared to Standard English, rather than an absolute:

> I must dry my hair – *A maun gie ma hair a wee dry.*
> He has gone swimming – *Hè's awa for a sweem.*
> I think I'll walk into town – *I hae a mynn tae tak a waak in til thà toon.*

> I can't attend/appear at the meeting, so could you apologise for me please
> – *A cannae pit in an appearance at the maetin*, sae ye wudnae pit in an apologie for me, wud ye.*

The effect of this process is to make even greater use of a relatively small number of 'core' verbs such as *tak* ('take'), *get, pit* ('put'), *let, mak* ('make'), *gie* ('give') etc in Ulster-Scots. Obviously then, the behaviour of these core verbs is particularly significant in terms of their past tense forms, -s endings and so on. For example, if we rarely use the verb 'dry', it is more important to know the past tense forms for the core verb such as *gie* in: *A gien ma hair a dry* ('I dried my hair'), than it is to know of any rarer past tense of 'dry'. So also with the habitual sense, for although we might use the *-s* ending with *A dries ma hair ilka nicht*, we would be more likely to say *A gies ma hair a dry ivery nicht*.

With verbs that occur in Ulster-Scots but do not have a counterpart in English, such as *gunk* ('dumbfound') or *dannèr* ('amble, stroll'), the same process of creating verbal nouns applies. Rather than *be gunked* or *dannèr doon thà roád*, we would *get* or *gie a gunk*, and *tak a dannèr*.

Many Standard English verb words are not used as such in Ulster-Scots, although the alternative, preferred verb forms in Ulster-Scots may be shared with English. Take, for example, the verb 'approach' with its literal meaning such as in, 'The man approached the house.' This would not be used in Ulster-Scots. Instead we would find:

> *Tha man cum up tae* ... or *Tha man went up til* ...

However, it would be misleading to suggest that the word 'approach' was always avoided in Ulster-Scots. It is often used as a noun when the sense is 'to approach (a subject)'. 'Have you approached the principal yet?' might be: *Hae ye made an approach tae the heid-maistèr yit?*

The distinctive Ulster-Scots feature here is the tendency to use more formal, literary English verb words as nouns in an Ulster-Scots phrase. Similarly we would *tak a wee taste o* something, meaning 'to take a small amount', but also *hae a taste o that*; or *try a taste o that*, rather than 'taste that'. Other examples include:

advise	- *gie advice tae/gie ye advice*
accuse, blame	- *pit thà blame on*
adhere to, follow	- *be a follyer o*
bribe	- *gie a backhaunner* (also, *square* as a verb, or *creesh tha loof*)
ban	- *pit a bar on*
beckon	- *gie tha nod tae*
beguile	- *hae a houl owre*
bellow	- *gie a guldèr* (also, *guldèr* as a verb)
besiege	- *mak a siege*
bite	- *tak a bite at*
annoy, bother	- *gie ye bothèr*
blast	- *gie a blast*
boiling	- *on thà boil* (also, *aboil*)

It is sometimes observed that a typical 'Ulsterism' is to say *thon fluir needs cleaned*, rather than 'that floor needs cleaning'. However, in Ulster-Scots the more usual expression of this would be *thon fluir cud dae wi a clean*. Here the floor needs a *clean* rather than **cleaned, *clennit*, or **clainin*. We see that the verbal phrase *cud dae wi* is also preferred to 'need'. This introduces another characteristic of Ulster-Scots grammar:

7.9 Making verb phrases out of single verb words

This process again involves the use of a small number of 'core' verbs, and suggests that an enormous range of different verbs in English is replaced by a smaller core of more frequently used verbs in Ulster-Scots. The fact that we, for example, prefer to say *cut doon* for 'abbreviate', *fa intae* for 'inherit', or be *cut aff* or *aa cut* rather than 'embarrassed', might be taken to indicate that Ulster-Scots speakers have a restricted vocabulary. In fact (while this may be true in a sense), the intensified use of a small range of core verbs requires subtleties of expression and intonation that are most difficult for non-speakers to master. Take the core verb *let* (past tense form *lut*) as an example. With compound verb phrases such as *let on, let aff, let in, let oot, let up, let doon* etc, there can be an enormous range of meanings (only some of which are shared with colloquial and Standard English):

> *Tha wynn didnae <u>let up</u> aa nicht* ('The wind didn't <u>abate</u> all night')
> *Quhan dae ye get <u>lut oot</u>?* ('released' eg from prison, or finish school, work, etc).
> *Dinnae <u>let on</u> A'm here* ('Don't <u>tell</u> that I've arrived').
> *A <u>lut on</u> A haed a sair heid* ('I <u>pretended</u> I had a headache').
> *Daes yer boát <u>let in</u>?* ('leak').
> *Cud ye no <u>let</u> thae hingins <u>doon</u>* ('lengthen').
> *The <u>lut</u> a bomb <u>aff</u> in toon theday* ('exploded').

Some (although not all) of these verb compounds are also used in Standard English and here no attempt is made to identify uses that are distinctively (ie exclusive to) Ulster-Scots. However, it is likely that even those Ulster-Scots verbal forms that are shared with Standard English are more frequently used by Ulster-Scots speakers (when compared to literary English).

A small range of Ulster-Scots verbal phrases involving such core verbs as *cum, gie, get, gae, tak* and *pit* include the following. (Phrases with well-established equivalents in colloquial or Standard English are identified by square brackets):

cum aff	-	to happen, take place
cum in (it'll cum in dry shuin)	-	to change (weather)
cum in on (it'll cum in on ye quhan ye're ouler)	-	to affect later on
cum on (quhit cum on ye ye wurnae at thà maetin?)	-	to happen to
cum oot wi (whiles hè cums oot wi a quaer cliver yin)	-	to say, express
cum roon	-	to recover
cum tae (it'll cum tae me in a minute)	-	to remember
[gie owre]	-	to stop doing
gie in tae	-	to admit, confess
[gie in]	-	to submit, surrender
[gie up]	-	to abandon, abdicate
gie aff	-	to scold
[gie it a miss]	-	to avoid
[gie thànks]	-	to say Grace

[gie oot]	- to announce
[gie a haun]	- to help, assist (give a hand)
[get doon]	- to alight, descend
get intae (quhit's gat intae him?)	- to possess one's mind
get ye gan	- to annoy
get the sin	- to sunbathe
get on (quhit wye's at tae get on?)	- to behave
get on (thae weans disnae get on)	- to agree, be friendly
get on for	- to be promoted
get on ye	- to dress, clothe yourself
get it ticht	- to find it hard going
get aa up	- to dress up
get thegither	- to gather, assemble
[get aff wi] (daed ye no get aff wi onieboadie at thà daunce)	- to strike up a courtship
[get aff]	- to finish (work, school etc) for holidays
[get aff]	- to finish (work, school etc) for the day
get tae (thaim weans wud get tae ye)	- to annoy
get tae (A cannae get tae maetin themorra)	- to attend
[get on yer goát]	- to annoy
[get owre]	- to recover
get goin	- to rile
[get throo]	- to spend
gae agin	- to argue
gae wrang	- to lose one's way
[gae (or gang) up til]	- to approach
[gae alang wi]	- to accompany, agree
gae on aboot	- to bemoan, complain
[gae doon wi]	- to take sick
[gae in til]	- to investigate
gae eftèr	- to chase
tak tent	- to pay attention
tak eftèr	- to resemble
tak yer en at	- to be amused by
tak aff (hè taks thon aff his faithèr)	- to inherit (a characteristic)
tak for	- to mistake for
tak it oot o	- to provoke
[tak in]	- to absorb, accommodate
[tak up wi]	- to befriend
[tak owre]	- to assume control
[tak up]	- to accept (an offer)
[tak oot]	- to date, court
[tak oot]	- to arrange (an insurance policy, etc)
[tak doon]	- to dismantle
[tak it up wi]	- to challenge, question, inquire
[tak up wi]	- to co-habit

[pit up wi]	- to tolerate
[pit doon]	- to degrade, belittle
pit doon for	- to register, include (a person)
pit frae (A'll pit him fae cumin)	- to stop (from doing something)
pit tae shore	- to land, beach (a boat)
pit in	- to call at (a ship)
[pit up]	- to give shelter, accommodation
[pit aff]	- to delay, adjourn
pit oot	- to advertise
[pit oot]	- to inconvenience (someone)
[pit in for]	- to apply for (a job etc)
[pit it owre]	- to explain, teach (in general)
pit ye owre it	- to explain, teach (in particular)
[pit on]	- to pretend

This is by no means an exhaustive list of the core verbs that are used in this way, nor indeed is it even anything more than a sample of the way in which these particular core verbs are used in Ulster-Scots.

7.10 The subjunctive and conditional moods

We have already observed that the 'habitual' sense (or 'mood', as it might be called), as well as the 'narrative mood', can alter the verb form in Ulster-Scots. There are a number of other 'moods' which also affect verbs. When a statement expresses doubt, a hypothetical condition, or a lack of certainty, the verb can be described as being in the SUBJUNCTIVE MOOD. Subjunctives occur chiefly in adverbial clauses.

A phrase such as: *A'm for wark themorra* is not in the Subjunctive mood, but when some sort of doubt, hope, or similar qualification is introduced: eg *Gif A be for wark themorra*, not only is the verb conditioned in meaning by this subjunctive mood, but its form can change (in this case from *am* to *be*).

The subjunctive mood is most often introduced in English by 'if' or 'whether', the historic Ulster-Scots forms for both being either *gif* or *gin*. *Gif* and *gin* are thought by some to be altered forms of 'give' (*gif*) and *gien* or 'given' (*gin*) and it is true that we might say *given* (or *gien*) *ye're no owre late, we can baith get* ('providing/if you're not too late, we can both go'). However, the use of *gin* in Ulster-Scots is not restricted to those situations where 'given' could be substituted, but is used as an equivalent for English 'whether'. Another 'mood' called the CONDITIONAL MOOD can be introduced by 'if', 'whether', 'should', 'providing', 'before', 'although' etc. The subjunctive and conditional moods can be difficult to distinguish, but as they affect verb forms in the same way in Ulster-Scots, they are considered here together under the single description of 'Subjunctive'.

In modern spoken English, verbs are rarely affected by the subjunctive mood, although in literary English it is still possible to use 'if .... be' forms, eg 'If the days be long ...'. In colloquial English speech this has all but disappeared so that the verb remains unchanged by the subjunctive eg 'If the days are long ...'. In Ulster-Scots, however, *be* is still widely used to emphasise the subjunctive and conditional mood (*bis*, or *bees* in 3rd person). Historically, as in English, *be* forms were common for the subjunctive mood in Ulster-Scots in the early 1600s (eg *"Quhatever I be ..."*, *"and giff myne be best"* (Letter from Isobel Haldane, Ballycarry, c.1630), and in the traditional poetry several centuries later, eg *"But gin ye be a holy brither"* (Thomson), *"Gin fame or learnin' be a bliss"*, *"But gin they be, I canna men' it"* (Porter), *"If there be ony"* (Boyle), *"But if she be a stoukard chick"*, *"Quoth he – gain ye be for the fair"* (Huddleston), *"If I be there, they'll watch me well"* (Bleakley).

Other conjunctions, besides *gif* ('if'), can introduce the subjunctive, such as *either* (pronounced [eether]) 'either', *less* 'unless', etc:

eg: *gif it <u>bis</u> in thà hoose, A'll bring it*
        let hèr sit tae A <u>be</u> ready
        gif ye <u>be</u> cum hame
        less it <u>bis</u> worth tha seein
        either A <u>be</u> for cumin or no
        gif it <u>bis</u> tae be had in Bilfawst, get it
        gin hìs wine <u>bees</u> bettèr nor mine.

The negative forms *binnae* and *bisnae* are frequently used in the subjunctive mood (again for strong emphasis only):

eg: *gif Mr Broon <u>bisnae</u> here ...*
        gif it <u>bisnae</u> daen aareadie ...
        gin A <u>binnae</u> tha ae yin here

In the examples given above where the subject is in the 3rd person, the *-s* form of the verb is used (*bis, bees,* and *bisnae*). So it is with other Ulster-Scots verbs in this mood:

eg: *if hè <u>daes</u> it richt*
        gif it <u>disnae</u> cum tae themorra
        less hè <u>haes</u> it weel hid
        gif Mr M'Cullough <u>gaes</u> tae Dublin nix month
        gif hè <u>gies</u> ye nae ithèr task
        gif it <u>daes</u> cum tae that
        gif it <u>cums</u> tae that

However, the use of the present tense verb form (including *be, bisnae* etc) is becoming increasingly rare in Ulster-Scots speech. In English, either the past tense or present tense verb form can be used with the subjunctive even if the sense is future.

eg: 'if I <u>were</u> (or <u>was</u>) to go to town ...'
        'if I <u>do</u> (or <u>did</u>) that, would you ...'
        'if he <u>goes</u> (or <u>went</u>) to town, he might not ...'
        'if I <u>go</u> (or <u>went</u>) tomorrow ...'

Today, Ulster-Scots speakers prefer the past-tense verb forms for such future senses of the subjunctive:

        gif A <u>wuz</u> tae gan tae toon ...
        gif A <u>daen</u> that, wud ye ...
        gif he <u>went</u> tae toon, he michtnae ...
        gif A <u>went</u> themorra ...

When the subjunctive sense is in the past tense, however, (eg 'if he <u>were</u> in town yesterday'), this is expressed using *wuz, wud a bin*, or *haed a bin*:

> *gif hìs wine <u>wud a bin</u> bettèr nor mine*
> *gif hìs wine <u>wuz</u> bettèr nor mine.*

Note: *Haed a...*, is an unusual verb form in Ulster-Scots. In a statement such as *if A haed a thocht*, it seems to be a shortened form of 'had have', and is sometimes pronounced [had of]. In English the past participles are formed with 'had', eg 'had been', 'had gone', 'had run' etc. Although in neither English nor Ulster-Scots is the full form 'had have' used, the *haed a* construction is formed possibly by analogy with *wud a* ('would have'). In chapter 10 and in section 8.4 there are further discussions of the *haed a...* construction.

7.11 <u>Present and past participles</u>

(a) Past participles:
In English the <u>past participle</u> form of the verb is that which is used after 'have ...' eg 'I have <u>seen</u> the book', 'I have <u>run</u> the race' etc. As we have seen above, the verb form of the past participle in Ulster-Scots usually provides the past tense form also. In any case these two forms are almost always the same.

> eg: *A <u>saen</u> thà wee lad. A <u>hae saen</u> hìm.*
> *A <u>run</u> thà race. A <u>hae run</u> thà race.*
> *A <u>went</u> tae toon. A <u>hae went</u> tae toon.*

The past participle suggests a past action, but one which bears on the present. *A <u>hae daen</u> thà task* is a completed, past activity, as is *A <u>haed daen</u> thà reddin oot*. However, *haed daen* indicates the activity was completed before something else happened (see section 7.13). These differences of meaning are articulated more clearly in speech when a typical Ulster-Scots word-order is applied (see chapter 10):

> *A <u>hae</u> tha race <u>run</u>*
> *A <u>hae</u> tha reddin oot <u>daen</u>,*

(and)   *A <u>haed</u> thà reddin oot <u>daen</u>.*

Obviously there is a different meaning to 'I have finished the cleaning', compared to 'I had finished the cleaning'. The past participle form of the verb 'be' is *bin* ('been'): *A hae bin loast* and *A haed bin loast*. Here the general rule breaks down, for the past tense form of the verb *be* is *wuz*, and this is different to the past participle form *bin*. *Bin* can be used as a past tense form, however, providing the past tense sense does not imply a completed action.

> eg: *A <u>bin</u> oot aa day*
> *A <u>bin</u> hit in thà leg,* (and it still hurts), but
> *A <u>wuz</u> oot aa day afore A saen hìm* (not *bin*)
> *A <u>wuz</u> hit in thà leg last week*

In the above examples with *bin*, the 'missing' word *hae* might be understood, but in any case, the alternative meanings of *hae bin* and *wuz* are dealt with more fully in section 7.13 and the auxiliary verbs *hae* and *be* are discussed in detail in chapter 8.

(b) Present Participles:
The Present Participle in English is the form of the verb with an '-ing' ending (I am

<u>running</u> the race), and in Ulster-Scots the equivalent form has an *-in* ending *(A saen* hìm <u>coupin</u> thà boát)*.

In addition to forming part of a verb phrase, present participles can be used in English as adjectives, eg the <u>running</u> tap, the <u>spinning</u> wheel (Ulster-Scots: *tha rinnin tap, tha birlin wheel*). Of course, past participles are commonly used as adjectives as well (eg 'the <u>broken</u> bowl' *tha broke boul*). Verbal nouns share the ending '-ing' or *-in* with present participles. They are particularly common in Ulster-Scots, and with verbal nouns the full *-ing* ending was often (but not always) maintained in traditional literature:

eg: *he wrocht at the farming*
        he lowes the fishing
        he's pouerfu guid at the dauncing

As mentioned in chapter 2, in Old Ulster-Scots and Scots documents the endings were clearly distinguished as *-ing* for verbal nouns and *-and* for present participles. *(The wee lads is <u>gaitherand</u> at the bak o the <u>gaithering</u>.)*

In the spoken language, however, the final 'g' and 'd' is (and, presumably, was) generally silent with both forms, so that by the 18th and 19th centuries writers only occasionally made distinction between *-ing* and *-and* endings, preferring instead to use *-in* for verbal nouns and *-an* for present participles or, more often, *-in* for both forms as both sounded alike. It is possible, however, that the continued reluctance by some writers to drop the final 'g' with the *-ing* ending on verbal nouns is a legacy of its historical form.

As with Standard English, the present participle form can be used in either a present time sense *(A'm <u>waakin</u> intae toon)*, or future tense *(A'll be <u>waakin</u> intae toon, A'm <u>waakin</u> intae toon themorra*, or *A'm for <u>waakin</u> intae toon)*, or in the past tense *(A wuz waakin intae toon*, or, *A'm <u>waakin</u> intae toon fae tha motòr wuz stole)*. In all these examples it should be observed that the present participle is used after some form of the verb <u>be</u>.

eg: *dinnae be <u>daein</u> that*
        wha's <u>rinnin</u> ye hame?
        tha day's <u>fairin</u> noo
        ay, scho's <u>houlin</u> up
        A wudnae be <u>lukin</u> ocht mair
        hè haes bin <u>atein</u>* hìs mait*

The present participle form of any verb suggests a sense of ongoing action. *A guldèr* ('I shout' – present tense) could mean that 'I can shout', 'I sometimes shout', or 'I usually shout' (although this 'habitual' mood can sometimes be signalled by using the *-s* ending: *A guldèrs*). *A guldèr*, however, does not necessarily mean 'I am in the process of shouting'. There is no such ambiguity with *'A'm <u>guldèrin</u>'*.

With the verb *be*, the verbal noun is *being* or *bein* and is often used to mean 'a person'. eg: *Quhit soart o a <u>being</u> wud bring thon in*. Of course, *being* is pronounced [bee-in] in Ulster-Scots, and the verbal noun form will be encountered in Ulster-Scots literature with both spellings *being* and *bein*.

As a present participle, the form is *bein*:
> eg: *Quha's bein akward noo?*
> *He's jist bein hissel.*

The word *bein* is also used sometimes in Ulster-Scots in place of 'since', 'seeing that', 'it being the case' etc in English, although *seein* would be the usual form:
> *A gat nae answer bein hè wuz oot.*
> *Bein ye're sae clever, ye can dae it yersel.*

The word *bien* is an adjective in Ulster-Scots meaning, 'cosy, comfortable, well-to-do'. (Note the spelling difference with *bein* although both spellings are found in poetry; eg *"Nearhand there lives a farmer rich and bein"* (Anon-Laggan))
> eg: *Thon's a bien hoose ye'r in noo.*
> *Quhit wye ir ye? Ach, bien eneuch.*

In general the present participle verb form is preferred in Ulster-Scots to the combined use of participles and infinitives in such statements as: 'are you going to eat your food?' *(Ir ye for atein* yer mait?*)* 'he is planning to go out' *(hè's for gan oot)*, 'I was hoping to get it tomorrow' *(A wuz lukin on gettin it themorra)* (see section 7.1).

7.12 The infinitive

The infinitive form of the verb expresses its general meaning without reference to time or person. It is usually accompanied in English by 'to' – eg 'to walk', 'to have' etc. 'Splitting the infinitive' in English (a common 'error') means inserting another word between the 'to' and the verb – eg 'to boldly go'.

In Ulster-Scots the infinitive occasionally is formed by prefixing the words *for tae* or *for til*, and so we find:
> *A'm waitin on ye for til ait yer prittas.*
> ('I'm waiting for you to eat your potatoes').

> *Hè cum for tae see tha picter.*
> ('He came to see the film').

The *for til* usage (rather than *for tae*) is shared with Belfast Ulster-English, and is less common in the core Ulster-Scots areas. Historically, the infinitive had been written as a single word (*forto*, etc), but this is now regarded as an archaic form. Splitting the infinitive in Ulster-Scots is an 'error' only if the additional word is inserted between the *for* and the *tae/til*.
> eg: *A hae cum for tae jist sit an tak tent* ('I have come just to sit and pay attention') is acceptable, but **A hae cum for jist tae sit an tuk tent* is not.

The use of *for tae* and *for til* is particularly common when the meaning is 'in order to': *He maun fynn thà key for til get oot.* ('He must find the key in order to get out'). Examples from Ulster-Scots poetry include: *"His blessing for to gie us"* (Porter), *"Their humble bards for to inspire"* (Boyle), *"That gar't poor Doddery for tae frown"*, *"And the poor heart for to alarm"*, *"this cauld nicht forgets for tae show"*, *"easy it is for to wot"* (Huddleston); *"Nor nae tobacco for to smoke"*, *"Those wee bit comforts for to get"* (Bleakley).

7.13 The 'perfect' and 'progressive' tenses

The 'perfect' tense is used in English in two ways: the 'present perfect' and the 'past perfect'.

(a) The 'present perfect' tense shows that an action is complete at the time of speaking and refers to events which are relevant to the present, but that happened in the past. In English this tense is formed using 'have', but the same senses can be achieved in Ulster-Scots without *hae*:

> 'Yes, I've looked at the book'.
> *Ay, A luk't at thà buik.*

> 'I haven't looked at the book yet'.
> *A hinnae tha buik luk't at yit,* or *A hinnae luk't at thà buik yit.*

> 'I've just heard the news'.
> *A jist heerd thà wittens there.*

> 'I have finished'.
> *A'm daen.*

> 'I haven't finished'.
> *A'm no daen.*

(b) The 'past perfect' tense shows that an action was complete at the time referred to, and deals with actions or statements that are finished or completed. In English this tense is formed using 'had', but the same senses can also be achieved in Ulster-Scots differently:

> 'I had looked at the book'
> *A haed a luk at thà buik,* or
> *A luk't at thà buik* (as well as *A'd luk't at thà buik*).

> 'I hadn't looked at the book yesterday'
> *A niver luk't at thà buik yestreen,* or
> *A haednae gien thà buik a luk yestreen* (as well as *A hadnae luk't ...*)

> 'I had just heard the news'
> *A jist haed heerd thà wittens,* or
> *A jist heerd thà wittens* (as well as *A'd jist heerd thà wittens*).

> 'I had finished'
> *A wuz daen* (as well as *A haed daen*).

> 'I hadn't finished'
> *A wuznae daen* (as well as *A hadnae daen*).

The 'progressive' tense is formed in English using the verb 'be' + the '-ing' verb form. It is used to show that (a) an action is going on at the time of speaking (the 'present progressive' tense, eg 'I am looking'), or, (b) was going on throughout the time referred to (eg the 'past progressive' tense, 'I was looking'). Indeed, the progressive tense can also be used to show that an action will be going on at a future time – by use of a time adverb such as 'next week' in a sentence like 'I <u>am leaving</u> next week' (see section 7.1).

Progressive and perfect tenses can be combined in English to give the compound 'present perfect progressive' and the 'past perfect progressive tenses':
(a) The <u>present perfect progressive tense</u> is formed in English by using 'have been' + the '-ing' verb form (ie the present participle). For example, 'I <u>have been looking</u> ....'. This indicates a past, ongoing situation that continues to the present.

In Ulster-Scots, sentence constructions such as *A hae bin lukin...* are not always used to convey the same meaning. Instead, the present tense form of the verb *be* can be used + -*in* (verb present participle), <u>or</u> *be* + verb past tense form. Usually, a time adverb is required to make the sense clear.

> eg: *Thon cat <u>is scrabbin</u> thà fluir aa week.*
> *<u>A'm lukin</u> thon buik aa day.*
> *Thae fowks <u>is staunin</u> thar this twonnie* minutes.*
> *Quhit lentht* o time <u>ir ye leevin</u> in Ulstèr?* ('How long <u>have you been living</u> in Ulster?')
> *<u>Ir ye raidin</u>* thon buik lang?* ('Have you been reading that book for long?')
> *Thon wee fella <u>is sut</u>* thar wi a sair heid fae tha morn.*
> *Ach, <u>A'm waitin</u> on hìm cumin this thrie yeir an mair.* ('<u>I've been waiting</u> for him to come for three years or more').

Note the use of *this* to emphasise the 'have been and still am' meaning of *A'm waitin* (see section 4.3). It is because of a similarity with *A'm waitin* in the 'just now' sense, that the distinctive Ulster-Scots construction of the present perfect requires a time adverb or qualifying phrase to show the meaning:

> *A'm waitin <u>this twa hòors</u>.*
> *A'm waitin <u>fae last nicht</u>.*
> *Hè's stuid thar <u>aa tha time</u>.*

In fact, exactly the same sort of qualifying phrase is required to distinguish a future tense meaning of *be* + participle (see section 7.1).

> eg: *A'm waitin thar <u>themorra nicht</u>.*
> ('I'll be waiting there tomorrow night'.)
>
> *A'm lukin thon buik <u>for themorra</u>.*
> ('I'll be wanting that book tomorrow'.)
>
> *Thaim yins is flittin tae Inglann <u>nix yeir</u>.*
> ('Those people will be moving to England next year'.)

Very occasionally, the word *bin* ('been') can be moved to the end of a sentence to emphasise that a continuous and continuing past time sense is intended:

> 'He has been very hungry'.
> *Hè's gye hung'rie bin.*
>
> 'She has been very lonely'.
> *Scho's desperit lonesome bin.*

(b) The <u>past perfect progressive</u> tense is formed in English by using 'had been' + '-ing', eg 'I <u>had been looking</u>...', and indicates a past, ongoing situation that does <u>not</u> continue to the present. Again, in Ulster-Scots, a word-for-word translation such as *A'd bin lukin* is not always used. Rather, the past tense of the verb *be* can also be used with the main verb behaving in much the same way as in the constructions outlined above for the 'present perfect' progressive senses.

> *Thon cat <u>wuz scrabbin</u> thà fluir aa week.*
> ('That cat <u>had been scratching</u> the floor all week'.)

> *A <u>wuz lukin</u> thon buik yesterae aa day.*
> ('I <u>had been looking</u> for that book all day yesterday'.)

> *Thae fowks* <u>wuz stuid</u>* thair for twonnie minutes.*
> ('Those people <u>had been standing</u> there for twenty minutes'.)

> *We <u>wur foondèrt</u> here quhaniver thà wunns cum.*
> ('We <u>had been freezing</u> here when the winds came'.)

In some cases, when the present perfect progressive tense is used in English (although the action or situation described is obviously completed), the Ulster-Scots equivalent of the <u>past</u> perfect progressive can also be used:

> '<u>I've been doing</u> all sorts of things'.
> *A <u>wuz daein</u> aa soarts o things,* (also, *A <u>bin daein</u> aa soarts o things*).

> 'Where <u>have you been</u>?'
> *Quhar <u>wur ye</u>?* (also, *Quhar ye <u>bin</u>?*).

In summary, a whole range of time or tense senses can sometimes be achieved in Ulster-Scots by qualifying the sense through adding an adverbial phrase (rather than altering the verb form). The following examples illustrate the range of senses frequently used in speech but where a similar verb phrase construction is used:

(a) 'I <u>have waited</u> for him long enough'.
   A'm waitin on hìm lang eneuch.

(b) 'I <u>had waited</u> for him all day'.
   A <u>waitit</u> on hìm aa day.

(c) 'I <u>am waiting</u> for him right now'.
   A'<u>m waitin</u> on hìm jist noo.

(d) 'I <u>have been waiting</u> for him for two days'.
   A'<u>m waitin</u> on hìm this twa days.

(e) 'I <u>had been waiting</u> for him all last year'.
   A <u>wuz waitin</u> on hìm aa last yeir.

(f) 'I <u>will be waiting</u> for him again tonight'.
   A'<u>m waitin</u> on hìm thenicht agane.

7.14 Verbs 'a-prefixing'

In modern dialects of southern British English and southern American English the present participles of verbs are often prefixed by 'a-' when the verb describes an action being done by the subject: eg 'The wind is a-blowing the trees' (ie the 'Active Voice' – see section 10.9).

In current Ulster-Scots speech, the present participles of verbs are more often prefixed by 'a-' when the verb is in the 'Passive Voice': eg *Tha trèes is a-blawin wi tha wunn* (ie the 'being'+ past participle form of the verb: 'The trees are being blown by the wind'). Other examples include:

> A'm *a-calin* for ma tay
> 'I'm being called for my tea'

> *Thon oul fella's a-killin wi tha drìnk* (more usually *killin hissel*)
> 'That old boy's being killed by drink'

Some particular 'a-' prefixed present participles are used idiomatically:
> *Thon coo's a-bullin*
> 'That cow's 'ready' (ie in oestrus) for a bull'

> *Hè's hònest eneuch, bot hè's worth a-watchin*
> 'He's honest enough, but needs to be watched.'
[Note: things can be *worth a-haein* or *worth a-seein*.]

> *Ma maither's a-waitin on this last sax month*
> 'My mother has been dying (being waited for) for the last six months'.

> *Ye'r a-wantin for yer tay*
> 'You are needed for your tea' ('You're being wanted')

However, in Ulster-Scots poetry, a- prefixed verbs occur most frequently in the Active Voice, for example:
> "A wanton whiteret she espy'd,
>   A sportin' at a cairn" (Thomson)
> "And tells how happy she has been
>   A-burning nits on Hallowe'en" (Thomson)
> "Of hapless prodigals a choakin" (Huddleston)
> "And bleezin' mortal a' a weepin" (Huddleston)
> "Or sets sic plagues a gangin" (Huddleston)
> "A-huntin' a' your life" (Kerr)
> "Wee Jimmie lies a-deein" (Kerr)
> "My heart is a-tearing" (Beggs)
> "An' tae the pad he's aff a-whis'lin" (Huddleston)
> "Some leuker-on begins a sneerin" (Porter)
> "Frae singin' then he fa's a swearin" (Porter)
> "Another woman fa's a screechin" (Boyle)
> "A messenger arrives a' sweatin" (Boyle) [perhaps 'all sweating']
> "Wee shawlie, pressin saft an' werm

> *roon' my breast a-glowin"* (Savage-Armstrong)
> *"A mock the squalls a-blowin"* (Savage-Armstrong)
> *"A sez tae yer fayther a-coortin"* (Savage-Armstrong)
> *"Auld John o' Ralloo went a-huntin' the hare"* (Savage-Armstrong)
> *"Then Grant began a laughin, O"* (Herbison)
> *"Which set them a' a laughin, O"* (Herbison).

These '*a*'s are derived historically from an earlier *on-* prefix (rather than *ge-*). However, when we attempt to trace this feature in the earliest Ulster documents of the medieval period, we find frequent use of the Germanic prefix *ge-* in front of verb past participles in the form *I-* or *y-*: eg *sen ze to hym on lettre y-send* ('since you, to him, a letter, a-sent'). Today, with the exceptions of the usages *haed a toul ..., haed a knowed ...* etc (ie following 'had') which are discussed in sections 8.4 and chapter 10, the 'a-' prefixing of verbs in modern Ulster-Scots appears to occur only with present participle verb forms, and not with past participles. However, it may be significant that the past participle forms (eg 'wanted', 'called' etc) are part and parcel of the Passive Voice forms in the 'English' versions of the above examples (eg *a-wanting* = 'being wanted').

Note: In English, certain adverbs have assimilated an 'a-' prefix, perhaps from their related verbs, such as 'asleep' and 'awake', but in Ulster-Scots the forms *sleepin* and *wakkin* or *woke** are used. On the other hand, *aboil* is used for 'boiling', and either *alow, lichtit* or *lowin* for 'alight' (as in a fire). 'Awry' is *athraw*, derived from *a-* + *thraw* ('twist'), eg *"My hoes she'll able spy a-thra"* (Thomson).

CHAPTER 8:
THE PRIMARY AUXILIARY VERBS

8.1 The verb phrase

In every sentence there must be at least one word acting as the main verb, for example, *A taks coffee* ('I (always) take coffee'). However, the verb form can often consist of a group of words rather than a single verb word. These 'compound' verb forms still contain at least one verb word, for example, *let* in the compound verb form *let on* ('pretended'): *A lut on A wuz oot* ('I pretended I was out'). Indeed, the verb phrase may contain other additional (auxiliary) verb words as well, eg *A cud dae wi a bite for dinnèr.* ('I need some dinner'), where *cud* ('could') is an auxiliary verb to the main verb *dae* ('do').

As we have seen, Ulster-Scots speakers also prefer to make nouns out of verbs (eg *he gien thà duir a dunt*, rather than **he duntit thà duir*. Clearly *gien a dunt* is the total verb form, even though a noun *(a dunt)* is included.

Essential to any description of the behaviour of verbs in Ulster-Scots, therefore, is an understanding of how the complex structures which underlly verb phrases operate, as well as of the behaviour of single verb words.

Any verb phrase must contain a main verb to which any other verb words in the phrase will be auxiliary. In the phrase *A hae bin daein it*, the main verb is *dae* ('do'), and the verbs *hae* ('have') and *bin* ('been') are acting as auxiliaries.

Some verbs are used only as main verbs, such as *girn, shuit, tak, waak, pit, let* etc. So it is that we can *tak a waak, pit on a girn* or *let aff a shot*, but we cannot combine them in such a way as **tak waak thà doug* or *pit girnin on. In English we can, rarely, combine a few main verbs, such as in 'let go the rope', but in Ulster-Scots even this would be *lee tha raip gae*. However, some verbal phrases can contain lots of verbs: eg: *Mebbe A cud hae bin daein wi pittin up tha money for tha coffee.* ('Perhaps I needed to/should have paid for the coffee'). Here we have, in a single verbal phrase, the auxiliary verbs *cud* ('could'), *hae* ('have') and *bin* ('been' – past participle of 'be'). *Daein* ('doing' – present participle of *dae*) acts as the main verb, and *pittin* ('putting' – present participle of 'put') also acts as a full or main verb, although in the latter case the verb phrase *pittin up tha money* functions *in toto* in an equivalent way to the English verb 'paying'.

8.2 Auxiliary or 'additional' verbs

The simplest way of distinguishing auxiliary verbs from full verbs is to learn which verbs in Ulster-Scots can operate as auxiliaries. There are only 15:

BE (be)
DAE (do)
HAE (have)
WULL (will)
WUD (would)
CAN (can)
CUD (could)
MAUN (must)
SHUD (should)
NEED/NAED* (need)
MICHT (might)
DAR (dare)
USE TAE (used to)
MAY (ought)
BETTÈR (ought)

Some of the 'secondary' auxiliary verbs (such as *bettèr* and *use tae*) are of question-able status as auxiliaries since they do not display all the appropriate characteristics (see Chapter 9).

The 'primary' auxiliary verbs *be*, *dae* and *hae*, however, have each got a range of forms (*be*, *bees*, *am*, *is*, *ir*, *wuz*, *bin*, *wur*, and *bein* are the variant forms of *BE*; as *hae*, *haes*, *haed*, *haen* and *haein* are for *HAE*, and *dae*, *div*, *daed*, *daes*, *daen* and *daein* are for *DAE*). These three verbs might also be described as the most frequently used verbs in both English and Ulster-Scots, although they are not used in identical ways in the two languages. They are also distinguished by the fact that they sometimes act alone (as full verbs) and sometimes as auxiliaries. The remainder of the other auxil-iary verbs are not really inflected into different forms in Ulster-Scots, although in English 'could', 'would', 'should' and 'might' can be regarded in one sense as inflected forms of 'can', 'will', 'shall' and 'may'. In Ulster-Scots, as we shall see, *can*, *cud*, *wull* and *wud* operate in quite distinct ways, 'shall' is not used, and 'may' is used only with a different meaning to that in English.

Although auxiliary verbs operate differently in Ulster-Scots than in English (mostly because they are used with slightly different meanings), the two languages share the characteristic of depending heavily on combinations of auxiliary verbs (in phrases) for all the subtleties of meaning and tense that are provided by complex single verb inflections in other languages:

eg: 'I may have been making some tea when he came home yesterday'
         A cud hae bin wattin thà tay quhaniver hè cum hame yestreen

Note that only one 'main' verb ('making' or *wattin*) occurs in the first verbal phrase here. The other verbs ('may', 'have' and 'been' in English and *cud*, *hae* and *bin* in Ulster-Scots) are auxiliaries, ie they assist, and are added on to, the main verb. Note also that the auxiliary verbs occur in a particular word order. It would not be possi-ble to say *'I been might have', or **A wettin cud hae bin*. At a later stage we will deal with the internal structure of the verbal phrase.

The main purpose of the auxiliary verb is to carry implied or coded information about the whole context of the sentence, but within the verbal phrase. It is important to remember, however, that some of the 15 auxiliary verbs can also operate by themselves as full verbs, eg *BE* can be used as an auxiliary *(hè is daein weel theday)* or as a full verb *(tha wee lad is fae Newry)*. Even this is not as simple as it might seem, for in Ulster-Scots there is a tendency to use *wud be* rather than *is* as a full verb. *(Tha wee lad'd be fae Newry)*. This feature carries with it slight changes of meaning (compared to Standard English usage) which are discussed in Chapter 9.

Auxiliaries have a number of characteristics in English and Ulster-Scots usage that not only tell us about how they behave but also help us to identify them:

(a) negative inflections:

Apart from the verb *be*, which has the negative forms *isnae, binnae, wurnae* etc, when it acts as a main verb (eg *Hè isnae here*) as well as an auxiliary, only auxiliary verbs have negative forms -

> *binnae, bisnae, isnae, wuznae, wurnae*, etc
> *dinnae, disnae, divnae, didnae*
> *hinnae, hadnae, haesnae*
> *winnae*
> *wudnae*
> *cannae*
> *cudnae*
> *maunnae*
> *shudnae*
> *naednae, needednae*
> *michtnae*
> *darnae, durstnae*
> *(usenae)* – rare form
> *(maynae)* – rare form

So although we might say *tha wee lad winnae girn gif hè disnae get hit*, the verbs *girn* and *get* don't have the negative forms **girnae* or **getnae*, and we can't say **tha wee lad girnae gif he getsnae hit*. Therefore, by this criterion alone, *girn* and *get* are main verbs and not auxiliaries.

In Old Scots and Ulster-Scots, negative forms of other verbs were used, such as *i ken nocht*, or *A kenna* (I know not) but although sometimes still used in modern Scots writing, they appear archaic. Certainly, there is little evidence for such negative 'full' verb forms in Ulster-Scots speech today. When Ulster-Scots poetry is examined, however, this feature is surprisingly common:
> *"By chance or fate, it maks na whether"* (Thomson)
> *"I kenna how, aneath the sin"* (Thomson)
> *"A'm vexed, A kennae why"* (Savage-Armstrong)
> *"An' risenae high aboon the airth"* (Savage-Armstrong)
> *"Ye kenna how to wear your claes"* (Huddleston)
> *"We pleadna boys, for rich ragout"* (Huddleston)
> *"He kensna how"* (Huddleston)
> *"I carna tho' I face the priest"* (Huddleston)

> *"But Doddery ken'dna what tae ca' them"* (Huddleston)
> *"I wish'dna tae see sic a squad"* (Huddleston)
> *"That weepsna whare woe is, and smilesna wi glee"* (Orr)
> *"He kentna when to stap"* (Orr)
> *"They meantna to partake in"* (Orr)
> *"For death, or fate, it maksna whether"* (Anon-Laggan)
> *"I makena this rhyming report"* (Porter)
> *"Ye knowna how to use it"* (Porter)
> *"He caredna meikle what he saw"* (Boyle)
> *"He gaed na far for them I 'tweel'"* (Boyle)
> *"Or else the markets gangs na right"* (Boyle)
> *"I carena then how markets stan"* (Boyle)

One common term which is used to form a negative auxiliary is *niver*. Ulster-Scots speakers often prefer *A niver seen hìm yestrae* to *A didnae see hìm yestrae* or *A niver got til thà meetin theday*. Obviously 'never' (which is historically derived from 'not ever') does not mean 'didn't ever', but is a general negative term. For example, we might also say *Hè's niver yin o thon crood, is hè?* ('He isn't one of that crowd, is he?') or *A niver mindit yer claes* ('I didn't remember your clothes'). The important point to note here is that *niver*, like *nae* ('not') comes after an auxiliary verb *(wud niver ...)*, and in front of a full verb (*A niver saen ...., A niver gat ...* etc). However, *niver* can also, occasionally, occur after a full verb. In the example *Hè's niver yin o thon crood, is hè?*, the verb *is* is acting as a full verb, and not as an auxiliary. In other contexts such as *A sa niver a yin*, or *He said niver a wurd*, the word *niver* may be regarded as acting as an adverb, or as an equivalent to 'not': 'He said not ...', 'I saw not ...' etc.

(b) inversion:

The second characteristic of auxiliary verbs, and a good test to identify them, is that they can come <u>before</u> the subject in a simple question:

eg: *Is thà wee lad cumin hame?* (inverted from *Tha wee lad is cumin hame*)

         Hae ye pit a licht tae tha fire? (inverted from *Ye hae pit ...*)
         Wull thà weans be oot? (inverted from *Tha weans wull be ...*)

This inversion cannot occur with full verbs (except with *be, dae* and *hae* when they operate as full verbs), and so we don't ask **pit ye a licht til thà fire?*. Instead, as with negatives, we introduce an auxiliary in front (usually *DAE*).
         Dae ye like it? (not **like ye it?*)
         Hae A a likin for it? (not **like A it?*)

(c) tagging, eg *(..., sae A daed)*:

One characteristic of auxiliary verbs that is peculiar to Ulster-Scots is the repetition at the end of a sentence of a 'tag' in the manner: *A gien hìm a guid dig on thà bake, sae A daed*. The verb *DAE* is always used with full verbs when there is no other auxiliary to repeat, but if we do have an auxiliary, then that is used: *A'd gie hìm a guid whalin, sae A wud!*

This feature, as all Ulster-Scots speakers will recognise, is particularly common in speech, but rarely used in writing. Indeed, it is so widespread and firmly established, that many speakers don't articulate the auxiliary at all except at the end.

> *See thon dug, blak, sae it is*
> *foundèrt, sae A am*
> *Awa tae hèr mìthèrs, sae scho wuz.*
> *For oot thenicht, sae A am.*

In these tags, although the 'Standard Scots' spelling of *sae* for 'so' is used, the pronunciation can be [so], [s'] or [sa] – rarely [say]. With the tag *sae A am*, the pronunciation in Belfast and adjacent Ulster-Scots areas is [so ee-yam].

Again, a full verb cannot be used in this way: **pit thà licht on, sae A pit*, but rather .... *sae A daed*.

The tag may be introduced by *sure...*, rather than *sae...*:
> *Tha ithèrs wudnae a left thon mess, sure the wudnae*

Tagging can occur with negative auxiliaries:
> *Scho wuznae awa, sae scho wuznae*
or by substituting *neether* for *sae* (and retaining the tag auxiliary in positive form):
> *Scho wuznae awa, neether scho wuz*
> *Thon dug's no et hìs dinnèr, neether hè haes.*

The use of *nether* or *neether* to introduce a negative tag is usually limited to contexts where confirmation or agreement with a previous statement is understood. It can also be used to introduce a 'stand alone' confirmatory phrase, rather than a tag, eg *Neether hè haes*. Tagging is one of the most striking peculiarities of Ulster-Scots grammar, and may be connected to a much more fundamental and significant principle – that of placing the verb at the <u>end</u> of the sentence. The word order and sentence construction of Ulster-Scots will be considered again in more detail in chapter 10.

(d) emphatic assertion:

The last characteristic of auxiliary verbs to be considered here is their use in emphasising, asserting or stressing a statement such as *Ye'll get it themorra*, or *Ye can dae it richtlie*. In speech, these two examples might be expressed:
> *Wull ye no get it themorra, ach, ye <u>wull so</u>*
> *Dinnae tell me ye cannae dae it, ye <u>can so</u>*, with emphasis on the <u>so</u> at the end. It would be impossible to use full verbs in this way: **A gat a wee bit, A gat so*. Once again the full verb would most often be replaced by *dae (... A daed so)*. The 'tag' might, for emphasis, start with '*sure*':

> *Ye <u>can so</u> dae it, <u>sure</u> ye can.*
> *Ye <u>wull so</u> get it, <u>sure</u> ye wull.*
or
> *Ach sure ye wull so get it themorra.*
> *Sure so A daed dae it, sae A daed.*

Notes: As with Standard English, most auxiliaries have no -*s* form for 3rd person singular (except the primary auxiliaries *dae, hae* and *be*, where we have *daes, haes* and *wuz, bees, bis* or *is*) – so we have *he cud, wud, wull, shud*, etc.

Some auxiliaries have unstressed forms – the 'weak' or contracted forms eg: *A'd, A'm, A'll* for *A wud, A am, A wull* etc.

8.3 The auxiliary verb *BE*

The verb *BE* behaves in completely idiosyncratic ways (as it does in English).

BE has five 'strong forms' in the present tense (that is, emphatic and not contracted spellings and pronunciations): *am, is, ir, be* and *bees*.

> *A am* (contracted form *A'm*)
> *ye ir* (contracted form *ye'r*)
> *hè, scho, hit is* (contracted form *hè's* etc.)
> *we ir* (contracted form *we'r*)
> *youse ir (yous'r/yis'r)*
> *the ir (the'r)*

There is no contracted form for *be*, while the contracted form of *bees* is *bis*.

Apart from the circumstances in which *is* is used with plural subjects other than the personal pronouns, the above are all roughly equivalent to the English present tense forms of the same verb. However, in Ulster-Scots they are not used as frequently (particularly in the strong form), as another auxiliary is often added to the verb *be* in Ulster-Scots.

> *Thon motòr wud be owre echt yeir oul noo.* ('That car is over eight years old now'.)

> *Tha wee fella daes be in oor motòr ilka day.* ('The boy is in our car every day'.)

Ulster-Scots also avoids the strong *is, am* and *ir* forms when there is any sense of continuity, permanence or habit intended. So, rather than 'I am sick in the mornings', or even 'I get sick in the mornings', we would say:

> *A wud be* (or *dae be*) *seek o a moarnin.*
or   *A wud* (or *dae*) *tak bad o a moarnin.*

With the *dae be* form, we can find:
A dae be seek, sae A be (or, even more rarely, *A dae be seek, sae A bees*).

This introduces some highly unusual uses of *BE* in Ulster-Scots:

> *A bees bad ilka morn sae A am.*
> *He aye bees bad quhan hè rises.*

Bees (contracted form *bis*) can be used to concord with any person (I, you, we etc) or number (singular or plural). This is because the *-s* form of verbs in Ulster-Scots can be used to indicate a 'habitual' or ongoing condition. Nevertheless, *be* is also used with the same meaning. *(A be in thà hoose ivery nicht.)* It is not usual to find *be* or *bees* used immediately after a personal pronoun (**A be, ye be, he bees* etc). It is, however, very common when a subject 'phrase' is used, or where the personal pronoun is removed from the verb (*A aye be ..* etc). In all probability the complex rules surrounding the sentence constructions when *be* and *bees* can be used are similar to those where *is* (rather than *ir*) can be found. We do not find, for example, **They's niver gan oot thenicht* ('They are surely not going out tonight') but we will hear *Thaim yins is niver gan oot thenicht* (see section 7.6).

'Be' as the full verb *for tae be*

The verb *BE* can be used as a main verb (eg The cat <u>is</u> black), or as an 'auxiliary' to another (eg The cat <u>is getting</u> fed.) With *be* as a main verb, we can chart the range of different ways in which a simple statement like 'We are country folk' can be changed in meaning by the use of alternative forms of *be*:

We ir kintra fowk or *We'r kintra fowk* (weak form). Here the usage is the same as in English and is undoubtedly the most common usage in Ulster-Scots also. The following variants, however, are mostly shared with Ulster-English dialect, and some (marked *) are not found in the core Ulster-Scots areas. Indeed, some of the forms are attested properly only in Ulster-Scots literature. In any case, they are rare (or at least occasional) forms.

We wud be kintra fowk or *We'd be kintra fowk*. The use of the auxiliary *wud* and *be* where a Standard English speaker might more often use the verb 'are' by itself is another universal characteristic of Ulster speech, eg: *Wud ye be in, John?* for 'Are you in, John?' The *wud be* form, however, implies 'we are (and always have been) country folk'. It also emphasises politely that the listener is being told a fact.

*We be** kintra fowk*. Here, the speaker is stating a 'perpetual' fact in an even more assertive way.

Note: In contrast to usages such as *"I canna tell how be't"* (Huddleston), the negative form *binnae* can equate to 'don't be' or 'be not', and does not necessarily indicate an habitual mood, for example *"Now gies a laugh and bena swear"* (Huddleston); *"Sae be na frighted"* (Boyle).

We bees (or *bis**) *kintra fowk*. This use of *bees* rather than *be* has a softening effect, and would be regarded as less aggressive.

We dae be there whiles, bot no affen. Particularly if the *dae* is stressed, this suggests that the listener might doubt the speaker, and so is arguing rather than argumentative.

We div be kintra fowk. By using *div* as the emphatic form of *dae* a writer (for this form is rarely heard in speech now) employs the most assertive alternative.

**We is kintra fowk*. This is not heard in Ulster-Scots, as the personal pronoun immediately precedes the verb 'be'. However, *We fowks is fae tha kintra* is acceptable Ulster-Scots.

Although it is now becoming archaic in English, the use of *be* in sentences beginning with 'if', 'whether', etc ('<u>If</u> we <u>be</u> country folk, then ...') is still common in Ulster-Scots speech (see section 7.10 on Subjunctive or Conditional Mood). *If we <u>be</u> toon yins, sae ...* would often be preferred to **If we <u>ir</u> toon yins, sae ...*, regardless of intended subtlety of meaning.

Counting strong and weak forms together as single forms, this still provides the Ulster-Scots speaker with eight different ways of expressing the English senses of the verb 'be' in the simple examples given: (*ir, is, wud be, dae be, daes be, div be, be,* and *bees.*) *Wud, daes, div* and *dae* are, of course, not forms of *be* at all, but are different auxiliaries in their own right, and so will be considered separately later.

The negative forms of these variations are of interest (*ava,* meaning 'at all' would be a common ending for negated sentences):

We ir kintra fowk.   *We irnae kintra fowk ava.*
We wud be kintra fowk.   *We wudnae be kintra fowk ava.*
We be* kintra fowk.   *We binnae* kintra fowk ava.*
We bees* kintra fowk.   *We bisnae* kintra fowk ava.*
We dae/daes be kintra fowk.   *We dinnae/disnae/niver be/bis kintra fowk ava.*
We div be kintra fowk.   *We divnae be kintra fowk ava.*
We fowk is fae the kintra.   *We fowk isnae fae the kintra ava.*

Before leaving the present tense forms of *be* in Ulster-Scots, we must recognise that the above forms are applied only when the full verb *be* is used in a simple statement of fact – something that is not really a matter of opinion. Consider briefly what the slightly different meanings of the above forms are when a statement might be a subject for debate (such as 'we workers are cold').

Iz warkers <u>is</u> coul.
Iz warkers <u>wud be</u>* coul.

If, in the second example above, the implication was not intended that 'we are always cold' (in an habitual sense), this use of *wud be* might be assertive and argumentative.

Iz warkers daes be coul. In contrast, the *daes be* usage here is more polite than when an undisputed fact is being stated. Here the sense is not one of assertive emphasis, but gently indicates that the situation is ongoing.

Iz warkers be* coul. Here an emphasis is intended about the strength and opinion behind the statement, that it is ongoing, and that we still are cold (it has come to a crunch).

Iz warkers div be coul. This form is most assertive.

Iz warkers bis coul whiles. This form is rarely used in an assertive statement, unless to imply that it is only an opinion and we are not really sure about it.

The past tense forms of the verb *be* (in English 'was' and 'were') are almost as complex as the present tense forms. For the past tense meanings of a simple expression such as 'The Boyds were brought up in the country', we can have:

Tha Boyds bin* raired in tha kintra	('The Boyds were ...')
Tha Boyds wuz aye raired in tha kintra	('The Boyds have always been ...')
Tha Boyds haes bin raired in tha kintra	('The Boyds were ...')
Tha Boyds haed bin raired in tha kintra	('The Boyds were ... [once]')
Tha Boyds is kintra fowk this lang time	('The Boyds have been...')

Wuz or *wur* in Ulster-Scots can often be equivalent in meaning to 'has been' in English.

> *Tha Boyds wuz aye kintra fowk, sae the wur.*
> 'The Boyds have always been country folk'.

Again note that in the past tense forms the plural subject plus the *-s'* verb form is used only when the personal pronoun is not immediately adjacent: the Boyds 'was', but in the tag we find 'so they <u>were</u>'.

> *Tha Boyds wud aye a bin kintra fowk.*

This is almost stating a fact as if it was an opinion – 'to the best of my knowledge', and again is a polite form.

> *Tha Boyds daed be* kintra fowk.* ('The Boyds used to be country folk [all the time]'). This is much more assertive.

> *Tha Boyds (haes) bin kintra fowk.* The *hae* or *haes* is sometimes dropped in such constructions. In almost all Ulster-Scots full verbs, there is no difference between the past time form and the past participle form. So we find *A daen thà dàshes; Hè stunk the hoose oot* (rather than 'did' or 'stank'). Similarly, it is common for Ulster-Scots speakers also to use the past participle *bin* ('been') for the past time of *be*, rather than *wuz* or *wur* eg: *A bin oot theday*, although the possibility of the *hae* being elided (ie lost in sound) remains strong with examples such as these.

If, as we suspect, Ulster-Scots speakers are always careful to indicate whether or not situations are ongoing or temporary, it is surprising that we find inconsistent use made of the past participle forms of *BE (bin)* along with the auxiliary *HAE*. 'Have been' or 'had been' after all do express very clearly that the past time situation is ongoing in English. It is a characteristic of Ulster-Scots that speakers will employ the *hae bin* form in situations where English speakers might prefer 'was' or 'were' (see Section 7.13.)

For example:

> *A wuz waitin twa hòors*, or *A'm waitin this twa hòors.*
> ('I have been waiting two hours'.)

> *A'd bin waitin twa hòors quhaniver sudden-like thà bus cum.*
> ('I was waiting two hours when the bus came suddenly'.)

> *A (hae) bin waitin twa hòors.*
> ('I was waiting two hours'.)

Further nuances of meaning can then be added to the statement by adding other auxiliaries:

> *A wud hae bin waitin near twa hòors*, or *A maun be waitin this twa hòor.*
> ('I reckon I was waiting for nearly two hours'.)

> *A cud/micht hae bin waitin mair nor twa hòors.*
> ('I reckon I might have been waiting for over two hours'.)

There is no future time form of the full verb 'BE' in English (see above section on <u>future tense</u>). Instead there is 'I am going to town tomorrow' (where a present time form is used along with 'going to'), or future time forms of other auxiliaries ('will' and 'shall') are used with 'be': 'I shall be going tomorrow'.

In Ulster-Scots *for* is used in place of 'going to', particularly where there is an intention implied: *A'm for tha toon themorra.* Also, the future sense can be implied even if the present tense form of *be* is used without *for*: *A'm intae toon thenicht again.*

The auxiliary 'shall' is not used in Ulster-Scots but *wull* is (in place of both English 'will' and 'shall'). It is most often used in the weak form: *A'll be oot o tha hoose themorra.*

If there is an urgency in the future action (ie if something must be done), then *be* can be used alone.

> *A be* for toon themorra.* (I must go.)

'Leave him (or 'it') alone' can be either *Let hìm be* or *Lee hìm alane.*

BE + infinitive:

> *Hè bees* tae cum themorra.*
> *Ye be tae be gien thà prize.*

Here the sense of *be* + the infinitive of another verb is close to that of 'must' or 'ought', for example Herbison: *"A wee drap tea they be to gie them"*. Frequently this form is associated with *be tae* in a verbal phrase such as:

> *A be* tae wash thà motòr themorra.*
> ('I have to wash the car tomorrow') (emphatic), or,
> *Hè bees* tae cut thà gress.*
> ('He is, or has, to cut the grass'.)

There is even an idiomatic 'Ulsterism' *be tae be*. This is a common expression which in a sentence like *A be tae be guid* means 'I have to be/must be/am beholden to be good'. An archaic form of this is *boost*, as found in Orr's poetry:

> *"Boost houghel on"*
> *"They boost to forage like the fox"*
> *"Thy quart boost ay hae half a pint"*
> *"Then, sick neist day, poor Mary boost disburse"*.

BE and DAE:

In English 'Be' and 'Do' do not occur together in a verbal phrase if 'do' is operating as the auxiliary and 'be' as the main verb. In Ulster-Scots, however, the following occur:

> *Hè disnae be caul.*
> *Daes hè be caul?*
> *A aye bees* caul an sae daes hè.*
> *Hè daes be coul.*
> *Hè disnae haaf be caul theday.*
> *Hè daes be* tae cum themorra.*

Here *be* is operating as a main verb, but with *dae* as the auxiliary.

The equivalent form of the imperative *dinnae be* occurs in English as with 'don't be too sure' and in the 'if ...', 'whether ...' negatives, such as 'If you don't be quick ...'. Furthermore, in the positive forms of these, 'be' can be used both in English and in Ulster-Scots.

| 'Be sure'. | *Be sartain.* |
| 'If you be quick'. | *Gif ye be quäck.* |

The present participle of the verb *be* is *bein* ('being'). This form is used mostly when *be* is an auxiliary verb. The *bein* ('being') forms must not be confused with the *bin* ('been') form or past participle.

As well as *Hè's bein taen* ('He <u>is being</u> taken' – not *'He <u>has been</u> taken'), and *Hè wuz bein tuk** or *Hè wuz bein a bad wee tòrie*, we can find:

> *Hè cud be bein tuk.*
> *Hè shud be bein tuk.*
> *Hè wud be bein tuk.*
> *Hè micht be bein tuk.*
> *Hè's mebbe bein tuk.*
> *Hè'll mebbe be bein tuk* etc.

Note: Although *taen* is the usual past tense form of 'take', the alternative form *tuk*, which is probably borrowed from Ulster-English, is more easily said after *bein* : *bein tuk* rather than *bein taen*.

8.4 The auxiliary verb *HAE* ('HAVE')

As with *BE*, the verb *HAE* can be a full verb – *A <u>hae</u> twa pun left*, *A wud <u>hae</u> naethin left*, or an auxiliary *A <u>hae</u> bin oot aa nicht.*

There are only two forms of the full verb *hae* in the present tense – *hae* ('have') and the *-s* form *haes* ('has') – and two in the past tense – *haen* and *haed*. As with *be*, and *dae*, the *-s* form can be used with some types of plural subject, and if a habitual sense is intended.

> *A aye haes* a wheen o buiks roon thà hoose.*

The past time form *haen* is also used for the past participle *We hae haen eneuch o yis thenicht*. A fifth form of the verb (the present participle) is *haein* ('having'): *A wuz haein ma tay.*

As noted earlier (section 7.13), *hae* as an auxiliary is often used with *bin* as a pre-ferred alternative to 'was':

> *A hae bin doon thà toon for tae dae tha messages. Weel, A wuz doon thà toon aa day* ('I was in town to shop. In fact, I have been in town all day'.)

When *hae* is used as a main verb, it usually has the meaning of 'being in possession of'. This is often a statement or question of fact, like 'How many cattle do you have?', (or '... have you?'): *Hoo monie kye hae ye?* or *Quhit nummer o kye dae ye hae?* While there is nothing wrong grammatically (in Ulster-Scots) with these forms, this might be regarded as a 'bold' or overly direct question, and so a different auxil-iary would be added:

> *Quhit nummer o kye wud ye hae?*, or
> *Quhit nummer o kye micht ye hae?*

When answering such a question, if there is no reason for 'politeness', and if there is no uncertainty in the answer, the auxiliary may be dropped. So, rather than **A wud hae echtie heid*, we might say *A hae echtie heid*, *A hae got echtie heid* or *A got echtie heid*.

Got in the last example is often used to mean 'possess', or have certain characteris-tics, and not simply to obtain. It is possible that in answering, the speaker might wish to introduce some qualification of meaning:

> *A wud hae echtie heid.* ('I have 80 cattle usually'.)
> *A wud hae (roon) echtie heid.* ('I have about 80 cattle'.)
> *A cud hae (near) echtie heid.* ('I might have as many as about 80 cattle'.)

Hae does not have a contracted form, except *'s* for *haes*, and so *hae* is often dropped and *get* (past time form *got*) used by itself.

> *Hè's got a guid hoose.* ('He has a good house'.)
> *The got* naethìn tae dae.* ('They have nothing to do'.)
> *A got à guid mynn tae ...* ('I've got a good mind to ...'.)

The negative forms are *hinnae* (haven't), *haednae* (hadn't) and *hisnae* (hasn't).

> *A hinnae got ocht.* ('I haven't anything'.)
> *Hae ye got a motòr?* ('Have you a car?' or 'Do you have a car?')
> *A got* nae motòr, sae A hinnae.*
> *Haed hè no got a wheen o thaim – Na, hè haednae.*

If the speaker wishes to use *get* to mean 'obtain', then this is followed usually by a pronoun (*masel, yersel, hissel*, etc).

> *A got masel a new motòr.*
> *Hè went doon thà roád an got hissel a sally rod.*

In English, the full verb HAVE is also used with DO to mean 'take', 'receive', 'expe-rience' etc:

> Did you have nice weather?
> Did you have a good time?
> What did she have – a boy or a girl?
> They had dinner at eight and so did we.

In Ulster-Scots we can readily dispense with the *dae*
>*Haed ye guid weathèr?*
>*Haed ye a guid time?*
>*Quhit haed scho – a wee lad or a wee lass?*
>*The haed dinner at echt an sae haed we.*

Note that the *wud ye hae ...?* type of polite question is not necessary when the meaning of *hae* does not involve possession.

HAE TAE

In Ulster-Scots, *got tae* is sometimes used in place of *hae tae* when the sense is 'have to' or 'must'.
>*A got tae gan noo, sae A hae.* ('I have to go now'.)
>*The'd got tae bring it, sae the haed.* ('They had to take it'.)
>*We got tae see thaim, sae we dae.* ('We must see them'.)

However, much the same meaning is often achieved by using *be tae* -
>*A be tae gan noo,*

or   *maun* ('must')
>*A maun gan noo,*

or   *bettèr*
>*A bettèr gan noo,*

or   *may*
>*A may gan noo.*
>*The may bring it for fear naebodie else daes.*

The use of *get* is sometimes preferred as a verb to *hae* in sentences such as:
>('I'm having a new house built'.) *A'm gettin a new hoose biggit.*
>('He has his hair cut once a month'.) *Hè gets hìs hair cut yinst a montht*.*

Hae is of course one of the most important auxiliaries, as well as being a full verb. In English, both types of the 'have' verb occur together in statements like: 'He has had to be told before', although in Ulster-Scots this could also be *Hè'd got tae be toul afore*.

As an auxiliary *hae* is often dropped, or at best present only in a weak form, so we can have:
>*A bin oot thenicht.* ('I have been out all night'.)
>*Hè stunk thà hoose oot.* ('He stank or had stunk ...').
>*Hè wud a saen* it.* ('He would have seen it'.)
>*A bettèr no gan.* ('I had better not go'.)
>*Ye got tae pit thà cat oot.* ('You have got to put the cat out'.)

Examples of dropping *hae* in Ulster-Scots poetry include:
>*"I wad na [hae] ken'd him"* (Bleakley)
>*"You micht as ready [hae] just went on"* (Kerr)
>*"Gif ye had pass'd his door, ye'd either [hae] heard"* (Orr)
>*"How marvellous wad [hae] been their mense an' grace"* (Orr)
>*"Twad [hae] roused the calm, slow puddle"* (Orr)

> *"Yet ye might [hae] said, is sic na ane alive or dead"* (Porter)
> *"Nor and their skill [haed] chang't gif they kent the hale scheme"* (Orr)
> *"I wad [hae] ben makin' scraps o' metre"* (Orr)
> *"To think the burial I wad [hae] haen"* (Orr)
> *"In a stiff case took he could [hae] gi'en a pill"* (Huddleston)

Given the ease with which *hae* is dropped in Ulster-Scots, it seems probable that the *gat tae* forms described above are derived from *hae gat tae*.

Many Ulster-Scots speakers understand the weak auxiliary *a* (as in *wud a saen*) to be 'of', and so it is often written as *a, o* or *of*: *Hè wud of seen it*. There may be some justification for this in a sentence such as *Gif A haed a seen it*, as it is hard to see how this could mean *'If I had have seen it'. However, some dialectologists understand this feature of Ulster-English and Ulster-Scots speech (*had a-seen, had a-knowed* etc) to be derived from the Germanic *ge-* prefix to past participles (see Chapter 10).

One of the most common Ulster-Scots uses of *hae* is in the construction of verbal phrases, especially where a full verb is changed to a noun, eg: *A wuz haein a waak* rather than 'I was walking', and *A hae mynn o tha day* rather than 'I remember the time'.

> *He wuz jist haein a ait* o hìs epple.*
> ('He was just eating his apple'.)

> *Daed ye hae a sleep ava last nicht?*
> ('Did you sleep at all last night?')

Haen is occasionally used for 'had' – *Hoo lang haes he haen it?* and also occurs in the literature, eg Orr: *"To think the burial I wad haen"*, Thomson: *"That she'd haen children to maintain'd"*.

Idiomatic uses of *HAE* (as a main verb)

> *A hae ye noo.*
> ('I understand now'.)

> *A cudnae hae thon wee wuman.*
> ('I don't like that little woman'.)

> *Yer mon can fairly hae tha fiddle.*
> ('He can play/handle the fiddle well'.)

> *Hè's jist haein ye on.*
> ('He's only kidding'.)

> *Hè haes it in for me.*
> ('He intends to punish me'.)

> *A wuz haed.*
> ('I was tricked'.)

> *A hae haed it wi her.*
> ('I have had enough of her'.)
>
> *Yous hae haed it, sae yis hae.*
> ('You are for it/in trouble').

Hae is also used as a 'tag' at the end of a sentence for emphasis. *Ye cannae dae that, hae!*, or as a 'tag' when there is no verb in the sentence: *Ye for oot, hae?* ('Are you going out?'). Indeed, it can also be used after another tag: *A seen hèr, sae A daed, hae!* In this case it may not be simply *hi!* ('hey'), as in *Hi boy!* ('Hey you!') etc, but is perhaps derived from the verb *hae*. In the *Concise Scots Dictionary*, *hae* (with this spelling) is identified as the imperative 'here!' or 'take this', and is there identified as the verbal form 'have'.

8.5 The auxiliary verb *DAE* ('DO')

DAE, like *BE* and *HAE*, can be a full verb as well as an auxiliary. In the sentence *A'll dae ma bit*, *dae* is a main verb and *wull* in its weak form is the auxiliary. Of course, *DAE* can be a full verb without any auxiliary alongside:

> *Thon boy daes some wark.*
> ('That man does a lot of work'.)
>
> *A daes* it ilka day.* (The habitual sense allows the *-s* form to be used for any person or number subject.)

The past participle form *(hae) daen* is used generally for the past time form as well as *daed* (pronounced [dad]), but only in the main clause, not in the tag!
> *A daen it yesterae, sae A daed.*
> ('I did it yesterday'.)
>
> *Quhasomiver daen ma schune, hisnae thaim daen richt.*
> ('Whoever did my shoes didn't do them right'.)

It must be remembered, however, that in Ulster-Scots the word 'done' or *daen* is also used in place of English 'finished', eg: *Hae ye yer darg daen?* ('Have you finished your work?').

Note that the negative forms *didnae* or *daednae* (didn't), *disnae* (doesn't) etc cannot be used when *dae* is a full verb. For example, we can have *He disnae dae muckle darg.* ('He doesn't do much work'), but not **Hè disnae muckle darg*. The negative forms are used only when *dae* is an auxiliary.

Dae as a full verb is often used in Ulster-Scots to substitute for a more explicit full verb.

> *Hae ye daen yer teeth?*
> ('Have you cleaned your teeth?')
>
> *Is thà beds daen yit?*
> ('Are the beds made yet'.)

Quhit time wud it tak for tae dae a egg?
('How long does it take to boil an egg?')

Dae is used very often, as in English, to make short verbal phrases:

dae up – restore, repair, redecorate, dress up.
dae ye doon – belittle you.
dae wi – tolerate *(A cannae dae wi aa this fechtin.)*
dae in – exhaust *(A'm daen in.)*
dae oot – clean out.
dae awa wi – wipe out.
dae wantin – go without *(Its aa richt, A can dae wantin)*

Dae also acts as a full verb with other meanings:

scho haes little tae dae
('She is very small-minded.')

Wull thon dae?
('Will that be enough'?)

It'll dae gran
('It'll suit very well.')

Hè's no gonnae dae.
('He isn't going to survive/live'.)

Quhit wye's scho daein fae scho flittit?
('What is her situation/material condition since she moved?')

Scho daes for thà minístèr.
('She keeps house for the minister'.)

Tha schap* daes breid.
('The shop keeps bread'.)

A'll dae ye, wee lad.
A'll gie ye a guid daein, wee lad.
('I'll thrash you ...')

DIV, DIVNAE and *NIVER·*

Ulster-Scots has *div* as a literary and probably archaic alternative form of *dae*, which is used in the present tense to give emphasis or to ask a question. The negative form is *divnae* (ie *divnae* is the emphatic form of *dinnae* 'don't').

<u>*Div*</u> *ye daunce?*
'<u>Do</u> you dance?' (emphatic)
<u>*Div*</u> *ye aye dae that?*
'<u>Do</u> you always do that?' (interrogative)

Div ye hae mynn o it?
'Do you (really) remember it?' (interrogative and emphatic)

A divnae ken
'I don't know' (emphatic)

Ye div mak guid pritta farls
'You do make good potato bread' (emphatic).

Niver is used in everyday Ulster-Scots speech as an emphatic, negative past tense form of *dae*. It substitutes regularly for *daednae* ('didn't') and its use extends into Ulster-English colloquial speech.

A statement such as *A niver saen hìm* should not (necessarily) be intepreted as 'I haven't ever seen him' or 'I (have) never seen him', but can (with equal probability) mean 'I didn't see him'. The use of 'never' to imply 'didn't ever' or 'haven't ever' is used in Ulster-Scots and English ('well I never!'). However, in Ulster-Scots, *niver* is used much more frequently when the 'didn't' event being described is a 'one-off':

A niver got ma dännèr theday
'I didn't get my dinner today'

Ye niver gien thà motòr a wasch quhan A telt ye
'You didn't wash the car when I told you'

Tha poastie niver brung ocht yestrae
'The postman didn't bring anything yesterday'

A niver neuk't yer oul pen
'I didn't steal your silly pen'.

This use of *niver* for both 'one-off' and 'not ever' situations is similar to that of *quhaniver* ('whenever') in Ulster-Scots (see section 5.5). In traditional poetry, *niver* often occurs as *ne'er*:

"*Christy ne'er strave to cross their leves*" (Orr)
"*An' ne'er befores been cheersome*" (Huddleston)
"*Your evil tricks you ne'er gave o'er*" (Herbison)

As in English, *dae* has a special function as an auxiliary, as it can take the place of any other main verb, and can enable questions and negatives to be formed independently of the main verb:

A seen him, sae A daed.
(not *... sae A saen).

Daes he ait* epples?
(not *aits he epples).

A dinnae ait* epples.
(not *A aitnae epples.)

The negative forms *dinnae, divnae, disnae*, and *daednae/niver* are used only when *dae* is an auxiliary.

> *Hè daednae see iz,* or *Hè niver saen* me*
> ('He didn't see me'.)

> *A divnae ken* (*divnae* is an emphatic form of *dinnae*)
> ('I don't know')

> *A dinnae hae onie mair.*
> ('I don't have any more'.)

> *Hè niver (daednae) saen (see) me*
> ('He didn't see me')

As an auxiliary *dae* is often used to introduce an 'ongoing' sense or 'habitual' mood (and then is also often in the -*s* form).

> *The dae ait gye an earlie, sae the dae.*
> ('They (do) eat very early'.)

> *Baith o thaim daes get coul.*
> ('Both of them tend to get cold'.)

> *Hè daes be earlie an aa.*
> ('He is (always) early too'.)

It is also used widely to stress a point.
> *A dae smell thà reek fae tha bonefire.*
> ('I do smell smoke from the bonfire'.)

> *Dae ye no yersel? Ach, ye dae so.*
> ('Don't you yourself? You must')

Tags of the *sae A dae* or *sae scho daed* variety are used frequently by many Ulster-Scots speakers, even when *dae* is not necessary in the full sentence.
> *A cum oot boggin*, sae A daed.*
> ('I came out filthy'.)

In speech, the verb in the tag is emphasised more than the words at the start of the sentence (which indeed are often omitted altogether).

> *Gien hèr a dunt, sae he daed.*
> ('He gave her a nudge'.)

The following examples illustrate many of the different ways in which the different forms of *dae* can be used in association with other verbs in 'verbal phrases'.

> *dinnae tak ocht oot*
> *dinnae be takin ocht oot*

> *dinnae be tuk* in wi hìm
> *dinnae be bein tuk* for daft
> hè *cud niver hae bin seen daein* wark, sae hè *cudnae*
> hè *niver's bin seen daein* wark, sae hè *haesnae*
> hè *niver bees seen daein* wark, sae hè *daesnae*
> hè's *niver seen daein* wark, sae hè *isnae*
> hè's *niver seen me workin*, sae hè's *niver*
> hè's *niver bin daein* wark, sae hè *haesnae*
> hè's *niver daein* wark, sae hè's *niver*
> hè *niver daes* wark, sae hè *disnae*
> hè *disnae wark*

8.6 The primary auxiliaries *be*, *hae*, and *dae*

Verb phrases can contain full verbs along with auxiliary verbs. In both English and Ulster-Scots the auxiliaries *BE*, *HAE* and *DAE* are so central to the construction of verbal patterns that they stand apart as PRIMARY AUXILIARIES. They operate in a different way to the other ordinary auxiliaries such as *cud, can, maun, wud*, etc, in that they combine regularly with each other and ordinary auxiliaries in verb phrases, and they have a variety of inflected forms.

In the list of verb phrases at the end of section 8.5, only the fifth example contains an 'ordinary' (secondary) auxiliary *(cud)*, while the others contain only the full verbs *see, tak* and *wark*, along with various combinations and forms of the primary auxiliaries *BE*, *HAE* and *DAE*.

Simple verb phrases: primary pattern:

Verb phrases of the primary pattern consist of a single full verb form, either alone, or with primary auxiliaries only. The following examples involve the full verb *see*, with or without the primary auxiliaries *be*, *dae* or *hae*.

> A *saen** hìm yestreen.
> A *daed see* hìm yestreen.
> A *hae saen* hìm theday.
> A *'m seein* hìm themorra.
> A *haed bin seein* hìm.
> A *bin* seein* hìm.
> A *dae be** seein* hìm.
> A *hae bin seein* naethin ava.

The primary auxiliaries *BE*, *HAE* and *DAE*, therefore, have a variety of forms and can be combined in various ways. However, the other auxiliary verbs (also known as 'modal' or 'secondary auxiliary' verbs) do not have the same wide range of functions as the primary auxiliaries, nor do they have the same variety of forms: there are no other forms of *can* such as **canin, *can'd* or **cans*.

CHAPTER 9:
THE SECONDARY AUXILIARY VERBS

Auxiliary verbs (including the primary auxiliaries *be, dae* and *hae*), are verbs which can combine with the main verb in a compound verb phrase, thereby helping to convey sometimes complex meanings. As explained in section 8.2, only a limited number of verbs can act in this way. The verbs *be, dae* and *hae*, as primary auxiliaries, have a range of special functions that have been outlined in the previous chapter. The remainder of the auxiliaries are known as 'secondary auxiliary' or 'modal' verbs. Consider how a simple sentence such as 'The cat <u>eats</u> mice' (where '<u>eats</u>' is the main verb) can be modified in English by the addition of auxiliary verbs:

(a) <u>Primary Auxiliaries</u>:

> The cat <u>is</u> eating mice
> The cat <u>does</u> eat mice
> The cat <u>has</u> eaten mice
> The cat <u>has been</u> eating mice

(b) <u>Secondary Auxiliaries</u>:

> The cat <u>will</u> eat mice
> The cat <u>shall</u> eat mice
> The cat <u>would</u> eat mice
> The cat <u>should</u> eat mice
> The cat <u>can</u> eat mice
> The cat <u>could</u> eat mice
> The cat <u>must</u> eat mice
> The cat <u>might</u> eat mice
> The cat <u>may</u> eat mice
> The cat <u>used to</u> eat mice
> The cat <u>dares</u> eat mice
> The cat <u>needn't</u> eat mice
> The cat <u>ought to</u> eat mice

Main verbs cannot be used in this way. Sentences such as *'The cat <u>let</u> eat mice' or *'The cat <u>got</u> eat mice', do not make sense. However, primary and secondary auxiliaries can be combined:

> The cat <u>needn't have been</u> eating mice
> The cat <u>may have</u> eaten mice
> The cat <u>could be</u> eating mice

In Ulster-Scots the auxiliary verbs behave and combine, sometimes, in a way similar to their English equivalents, while on other occasions their meaning and usage can be quite different. An understanding of the different nuances of meaning implied by the use of different auxiliaries in Ulster-Scots is made more difficult (not less) by the similarities and close relationship between the two languages. When someone says "you <u>may</u> leave now", how can we tell if the speaker means 'you are permitted to leave', or 'you ought to leave'? Even when such usages are quite distinct between Ulster-Scots and English, many people switch unselfconsciously to the English usage in the presence of an 'educated' listener (or any 'outsider'). When usages are apparently similar in the two languages, these aspects are easily understood, if indeed the intended meanings are, in fact, shared. When the usages have superficial similarities in English and Ulster-Scots, leading to ambiguous constructions, it is easier to misunderstand and misinterpret than it is to detect the nuances of different usage and meaning.

9.1 'WILL'

Wull is used in Ulster-Scots, as in English, as one way to indicate future action, usually in the contracted -*'ll* form, and either as a single auxiliary or in combination with *be, hae* or *dae*:

Tha cat'll ait* mice	'The cat'll eat mice'
Tha cat'll be aitin* mice	'The cat will be eating mice'
Tha cat'll hae mate*	'The cat will have food'
A'll dae it themorra	'I'll do it tomorrow'

With the exception of the combination of *wull* + *be*, these forms can all occur with a present tense meaning 'be ready to'.

A'll dae it noo	'I'll do it now'
A'll hae it noo	'I'll have it now'
A'll ait* it noo	'I'll eat it now' ('I'm ready to eat it now').

'Shall' and 'will':

In Ulster-Scots there is no problem (as there is in English) in distinguishing when 'will' and 'shall' should be used, as 'shall' is not used in Ulster-Scots, and *wull* is always used in its stead.

'Will' as a full verb:

The full verb 'will' is not very well attested in Ulster-Scots.

'I willed it to happen' would be rendered in some other way, such as *A wantit it tae happen*, or *It happen't thà wye A wud a haed it oniehoo*.

Volition:

In English 'will' can be used as a marker of future tense but also can suggest willingness or agreement (volition). ('You will come tomorrow, won't you?'). This would be rendered more plausibly *ye'll be cumin themorra noo?* in Ulster-Scots.

In addition, *wud* can be used with a similar meaning. For example, 'If he will come tomorrow' might be *Gif hè wud cum themorra*, although *Gif hè wuz cumin themorra* or *Gif hè's for cumin themorra* are also possible.

Conditional:
In English, 'If he would come tomorrow ...' would be understood as indicating a conditional rather than volitional mood. Volition implies an intention, desire or agreement. If this 'volition' is not implied, then in Ulster-Scots we would <u>not</u> say:
> **Yer mate themorra's for bein late again.*
> ('Your meal tomorrow will be late again'.)

> **Tha boord'll be for takin hìs wecht aisie*.*
> ('The board will easily bear his weight'.)

> **The wee fella at cums themorra's for bein Scotch.*
> (The boy who comes tomorrow will be Scottish.)

In these cases we would say:
> *Yer mate themorra'll be late again*, or *Yer mate themorra'd be late again*
> *Tha boord'd tak hìs wecht aisie** or *Tha wee fella at cums themorra'd be Scotch.*

Note:
When a contracted form such as *'ll* is used in a sentence, it is the strong, 'full' form such as *wull* that is used in any 'tag' at the end:

> *Hè'd be Scotch, sae hè wud.*
> *It'll be late again, sae it wull.*

'Will' used for induction:

In English 'will' is used for sayings and general truths, eg: 'Pigs'll eat anything' (as well as 'Pigs eat anything'). In Ulster-Scots, *wud* is used: *Pigs wud eat ocht.*

> *Muckle rain'd mak lang strae, sae it wud.*
> ('Much rain makes/or will make, long straw'.)

'Will' as an expression of characteristic behaviour or action:

Again, and similarly, in Ulster-Scots *wud* is often used in place of English 'will': 'She'll sit there for hours doing nothing', would be *Scho'd sit thonner for hòors daein naethin.* Also, *Hè'd tell ye oniethin, sae hè wud*, rather than 'He'll tell you anything'.

'Will' to indicate probability:

In English 'will' is used to indicate that something is probably going to happen, or is probably happening just now.

'That'll be the post now'.

'He'll be at home today'.

Once again Ulster-Scots also (and often preferably) uses *wud* instead of 'will'.

Thon'd be tha poast noo.

Hè'd be in thà hoose theday aa richt'.

Similarly, *wud hae bin* is often used rather than 'will have been':

Thon wud hae bin thà poastie jist noo.

(That'll have been the postman.)

This sense can be progressive, that is, it might be continuing up to the present, as with: 'She'll sit there for hours and will be sitting there now'. Even here, again, Ulster-Scots speakers use *wud*: *Scho'd sit thonner for hòors an wud be sittin on thar yit.*

'Will' for insistence:

The English use of 'will' or 'shall' as an imperative, to insist on something, is always *wull* in Ulster-Scots. For 'You will do as I say' we might say *Ye'll dae quhit ye're toul* or with stress: *Ye wull so.*

'Will' for Promise: (In place of English 'shall')

For example, 'You shall have it tomorrow' is rendered *Ye'll get it themorra* or *Ye can hae it themorra* (obligational).

'Shall we go?'

Wull we gan? (or, *shud we gan?*).

'Will' substituted for 'had' + better:

Instead of a construction such as: 'I <u>had</u> better go home now', an Ulster-Scots speaker is often likely to use *wull* rather than *haed*: *A'll bettèr awa hame noo.*

Negative form:

The negative forms of *wull* are *winnae* ('won't'), and *wull no*:

A winnae get themorra.

A'll no can get themorra.

'I won't be able to go tomorrow'.

9.2 'WOULD'

Wud is perhaps the most used modal auxiliary in Ulster-Scots speech. Its frequency of use in conversation is not only higher in Scots than in English, but it also appears to be even more frequently used in Ulster-Scots than in Scots.

We have already seen that *wud be* can often be used instead of *am, is, ir,* etc in sentences such as *Thon wud be yin o thae new motòrs* ('That's one of those new cars'.)

It is also often used in the form *wud hae* in preference to 'have' or *haes* – eg: *Hè wud hae mair nor that* ('He has more than that'.) In fact, Ulster-Scots prefers *wud* to *wull* in virtually every sense except that indicating simple future time or for insistence.

As in English, *wud* can carry with it a sense of implied doubt or uncertainty.
> *A wud gang, bot ....*
> *A wud say thon's owre lang.*

It is often used as a form of politeness, particularly in questions.
> *Wud ye cum themorra?*

This is of course taken to extremes when asking a favour -
> *Ye wudnae hae tha time on ye, wud ye?* ('Could you tell me the time, please').

Here the negative form is used to stress politeness, and it is also used when giving a polite refusal – *A wudnae be fit tae get* ('I won't be able to go') is regarded as less of a 'let down' than *A winnae be fit tae get.*
> *Wud ye pit a licht til thà fire? A wull surelie.*
> ('Will you light the fire? Certainly I will'.)

9.3 'SHOULD'

Unlike English, where 'should' can also be a past time and 'reported speech' form of SHALL, in Ulster-Scots *shud* is used only in place of 'ought to', or with a sense of obligation. There is no usage whatsoever of 'shall' in Ulster-Scots speech, and so usages of *shud* do not observe the rules of English grammar. *Shud*, however, is widely used in Ulster-Scots to mean 'ought to':
> *Shud A gang themorra or no?*
> ('Ought I to go tomorrow or not?')
> *Ye shud kaep* yer bake shut.*
> ('You should keep your mouth shut')
> *Ye shud a seen tha luk on his faice*

Negative forms *shudnae* and *shud no*:
> *Ye shudnae say that.*
> *Shud ye no get thar earlie?*

Shud a ('should have') can, however, sometimes be used to mean 'was alleged or reported to have': *Scho shud a cum, so the say.*

The idiom 'I should say so' is usually *A wud think sae* in Ulster-Scots.
Note: *Haed bettèr* or *bettèr* is often used in place of *shud*: *Ye'd bettèr get thar earlie*, and even more commonly in speech: *Ye bettèr get thar earlie.*

9.4 'CAN'

'Can' meaning 'have the ability to', or 'be able to':

This is the basic use of the auxiliary verb *can* in English and Ulster-Scots.

> *Hè can ride a bike.*
> 'He can ride a bike'.

Similarly in the past tense, the form *cud* (English 'could') is used:
> *Hè cud ride a bike.*

and future:
> *Hè'll be able tae ride a bike shuin,* or *He cud ride a bike themorra.*

fit tae is also used to mean 'able to' in Ulster-Scots: *Hè's fit tae ride a bike.*
Note: this use of *fit* does not mean physically 'fit' as in English.

'Can' indicating a characteristic:
> *Scho can be gye cattie quhiles.*
> ('She can be very catty at times'.)

However, Ulster-Scots speakers could just as easily substitute *cud*, saying: *scho cud be gye cattie quhiles*, while not necessarily indicating past time.
> *Quhit guid cud/can that dae?*

'Can' indicating permission:

Many Ulster-Scots speakers have witnessed the teacher's 'put down' in school when the child asks: *'Please miss, can A lee the room?'* and the teacher replies: 'I don't know if you <u>can</u> or not, but you <u>may</u>'.

'May' is not used in Ulster-Scots in this sense, but *can* (or the more tentative form *cud*) is used instead. As a child, I remember one teacher demanding: 'It's not "<u>can</u> I leave the room" – what ought it to be?' The innocent's reply was: *'Shud it be "<u>cud</u> a laive the room", Miss?'* This anecdote reveals the type of attitude to Ulster-Scots often found in formal education – 'can' and 'may' are both perfectly good English usages, but only *can* or *cud* is used (for permission) in Ulster-Scots.

'Can' indicating willingness:

Cud is prefered to *can* in Ulster-Scots:

> *Ye cudnae gie tha fire a licht, cud ye?.*
> 'Can you light the fire please?'

> *A cud dae that for ye aa richt.*

9.5 '<u>COULD</u>'

Many of the Ulster-Scots usages of *cud* are described in the above section on *can*. *Cud* in Ulster-Scots is often used interchangeably with *can*, just as *wud* is often used for *wull*. However, in the same way as *wud* can also be used in Ulster-Scots as a separate auxiliary to *wull*, so *cud* is used in distinctive ways in Ulster-Scots. It stands apart from CAN therefore, although (as in English) it is also a past time form of *can*:
> *Ye <u>can</u> hae it noo, but ye <u>cudnae</u> a haed it yesterae*.*

The idioms *A cudnae say* or *A cudnae tell ye* are common substitutes for 'I don't know'.

Another idiomatic use is *cud see ... far eneuch* meaning 'be fed up with':
> *A cud see her far eneuch.*
> 'I'm fed up with her'.

Cud dae wi is usually found in place of 'need'.
> *A cud a daen wi a wheen mair.*
> 'I needed some more'.

Cud is also used to express possibility.
> *Cud be*
> 'possibly'
> *The cud be cumin thenicht*
> 'They might be coming tonight'.

9.6 'MAY'

Neither of the two English usages is possible in Ulster-Scots.

(a)   permission: As we have already seen, *can* or *cud* is always used.

(b)   possibility: With statements such as 'He may come', Ulster-Scots would use:
> *mebbe (Hè'll mebbe cum)*
> *cud (Hè cud cum),* or
> *micht* ('might') – *Hè micht cum.*

In fact the only Ulster-Scots usage of *may* is one not shared with Standard English – that of meaning 'ought' or 'had better':

> *A may gan afore it gets dairk*.*
> *Ye may pit yer coát* on for its gonnae* rain.*

Although clearly an auxiliary, it is rare (if it occurs at all) to use this Ulster-Scots meaning of *may* in the negative *maynae or in the inverted question **maynae ye ...?* forms.

9.7 'MIGHT'

In Ulster-Scots, *micht* is sometimes used for the possibility sense of English 'may', although *cud* is often preferred.
> *It cud/micht rain thenicht.*

However *michtnae* is the only appropriate negative form: *It michtnae rain thenicht.* **It cudnae rain thenicht* means there is no possibility of rain tonight. Another idiomatic sense of *micht* occurs in sentences like: *Ye micht/cud a axt afore ye daen it.* ('You ought to/should have asked before you did it'.)

9.8 'MUST'

The word *maun* (often pronounced [man]) is the usual Ulster-Scots equivalent of the English verb 'must'. *Mote* is an archaic form, restricted to early literary sources, and to the phrase *Sae mote hit be* ('Amen').

Maun indicating obligation

> *A maun awa noo.*
> ('I must go now'.)

> *Ye maunae houl thon raip.*
> ('You mustn't hold that rope'.)

> *Maun hè dae hìs schune in thà hoose?*
> ('Must he clean his shoes in the house?')

Maunae is, however, not in everyday use in Ulster-Scots for some of the above senses. *Dinnae* and *darnae* are often preferred as an imperative or command -
> *Dinnae houl thon raip, nae mattèr quhit ye dae.*
> *Ye darnae houl thon raip.*

To negate the sense of obligation in order to express: 'You are not obliged to hold the rope', it is necessary to say:
> *Ye dinnae hae tae houl ...,* or
> *Ye hinnae got tae houl ...,* or
> *Ye're no gart tae houl ...,* or
> *Ye dinnae need tae ...*

Neednae, in the English sense of 'needn't', does not apply in Ulster-Scots as an alternative to 'mustn't', for *ye neednae houl thon raip* means either 'you had better not hold' or 'don't bother holding'. In most statements *haed bettèr* or 'better' is preferred to convey the sense of obligation.

> *A bettèr get a stairt* made.*
> ('I must get started'.)

> *Ye bettèr be bak, sae ye haed.*
> ('You must come back'.)

'Maun' indicating an estimate:

> *Thar maun be a hunner fowks thar.*
> ('There must be a hundred people there'.)

For past time *maun hae bin* is used. Although *cud* and *cud hae bin* are also used in this way, *maun* implies that the estimate is correct and is not imprecise.

In negative form *wudnae a bin* is preferred to 'can't have been' if there is uncertainty. *Cudnae a bin* is the form used for 'can't have been' when there is a degree of certainty.

Maunae + hae:

The equivalent of 'he can't have seen me' (meaning 'I expect he didn't see me') is, in Ulster-Scots, *hè maunae a saen me.*

9.9 'OUGHT'

The English auxiliary 'ought', expressing obligation or duty: 'I ought to see my mother', is not used in Ulster-Scots. *Shud* is generally used, although *may* can also be used if the sense is more 'I had better' than 'I am obliged to'. There is, however, a full verb *aucht* in Ulster-Scots which means 'to owe'. *Aucht* is used in Ulster-Scots only for the literal sense of 'owing': *A aucht her ten pun.* Probably because of the similarity of these verbs, the idiom *owe it tae* (him etc) is often used in place of the English main verb 'ought'.

> *A owe it tae ma mithèr* for tae see her theday.*

9.10 'DARE'

The full verb *dar* ('dare') is roughly equivalent to 'challenge'.
> *A dar ye tae ait* hìs epple afore hè gets bak.*

As an auxiliary *dar* is rarely used in the positive form, except perhaps for the idiom *A dar say ye're richt.* This idiom's meaning is mild – not 'I make bold to say' but more 'I reckon'. *Dar* is not used with other primary auxiliaries, for example *A dar hae bin* is meaningless, or in inversion the English question 'Dare you go?' would in Ulster-Scots use *dar* as a full verb *Wud ye dar go?*

However, *darnae*, the negative form, is used.
> *Ye darnae dae that.*
> *Hè darnae go near thà dug for fear o gettin bit.*

The past tense forms *durst* (negative *durstnae*) are also in current use, and found in the literature, eg *"But we durst na speak"* (Anon-Laggan).

The meaning here is again 'weak' or metaphorical: 'you had better not' or 'it would be better if you didn't'.

Dar sometimes functions as a main verb in association with other auxiliaries:
> *He daednae dar tae dae it.*

Similarly, *need* and *use tae* can occur as:
> *He daednae need tae cum*
> *He daednae use tae dae that.*

9.11 'NEED'

In Ulster-Scots, *need* or *naed** also has a dubious status as an auxiliary. Like *dar*, it operates as a full verb only in positive sentences (although *cud dae wi* is preferred), or as an auxiliary in negative *(naednae)* form.
> *Hè naednae cum tae A hae hìs room daen.*

An alternative negative form is *need harly* – *ye need harly bother/ye neednae bother*. Occasionally, *naenae* and *neenae* occur as variants of *naednae*. *Wudnae naed tae* is frequently used to mean 'had better not'.

Examples from Ulster-Scots poetry include *needednae* past tense forms:
>
> *"But neededna desired"* (Thomson)
> *"Ye neededna a fash'd man"* (Thomson)
> *"And then I needna muckle fear ye"* (Thomson)
> *"She neednae try sic yarns tae spin"* (Kerr)

9.12 'USED TO'

Another auxiliary of doubtful status in Ulster-Scots is *use, uise* or *yuise*. It can be used in an inverted question and in tags.
>
> *Yuise ye tae cum here?**
> 'Did you use to come here?'.
> *A yuise tae come here, sae A yuist*, aa tha time.*

It also occurs widely in its negative form:
>
> *Hè usen't/yuisnae tae come here ava.*

The doubt about its status as an auxiliary emerges because of the frequency with which *dae* is used with *yuise* for inversion, in a tag, and in negative form:
>
> *Daed ye yuise tae cum here?*
> *A yuise tae, sae A daed.*
> *A niver/didnae yuise tae cum.*

However, *yuise tae* can be used in verbal phrases with primary auxiliaries:
>
> *A yuise tae hae a motòr.*
> *A yuise tae dae it.*

Note: 'Used to' in the sense of 'I have got used to the food now', is *used* or *uist* wi*:
>
> *A'm uist wi tha mait noo.*

9.13 'BETTER'

Ye bettèr gang noo. Here *bettèr* appears to operate as an auxiliary with the sense of 'need to'. It has some characteristics of an adverb too. Although in negation we cannot have **betternae*, we would use *bettèr no*. There is no *-s* form for the 3rd person singular (*hè bettèr cum*, not **hè bettèrs come*). It can also operate as a tag: *Hè bettèr hae bin thar, sae hè bettèr.*
It is difficult to see how *better* operates in this phrase any differently to other modal auxiliaries (such as *wud*): *Hè wud hae bin thar, sae hè wud*, and so the case for considering *bettèr* as an auxiliary verb in Ulster-Scots is a strong one.

9.14 'GET'

> *He cud get stairtit themorra*
> 'He could start tomorrow'

The only auxiliary verb characteristic which applies to the verb *get* is that it can occur directly before the participle of another verb: *get goin, get shiftit, get lit*, etc. It cannot be used in the negative form **getnae*; in inversion **got-hè...?*; or in a 'tag'; **sae A got*; and it <u>does</u> carry an *-s* form in the present tense (*gets*), like main verbs.

Get, therefore, does not behave as other auxiliaries do, although it is a unique verb which can occur in a verb phrase along with a different main verb. Usually such sentences are in the 'passive' voice (section 10.9) and the main verb is a past (occasionally, present) participle:

> *A <u>got huntit</u> oot o tha offíce*
> 'I was chased out of the office'

> *Hè's for <u>gettin kilt</u> quhaniver hè gets hame*
> 'He's going to be killed when he gets home'

> *Quhilk hooses <u>got paintit</u>?*
> 'Which houses were painted?'

> *Daed yis <u>get met up</u> on holyday?*
> 'Did you meet up on holiday?'

> *Daed yis <u>get sut doon</u> ava?*
> 'Were you able to sit down at all?'

> *Hè <u>gets goin</u> tae maetin* tha odd Sabbath*
> 'He is able to get occasionally to church on Sundays'

As we have seen in section 8.4, the verb *get* is often used as a main verb meaning to 'have', 'possess' or 'obtain' in Ulster-Scots, with or without the auxiliary *hae*:

> *A <u>hae got</u> mair nor eneuch*
> 'I have more than enough'

> *A <u>got</u> nane theday, sae A hinnae*
> 'I haven't any today'

Get also operates as a main verb meaning 'become' where it often occurs at the end of the sentence (section 10.11):

> *Tha heid-yins is gye thran <u>got</u>*
> 'The bosses have become very difficult'

Note: When *get* does operate as an 'auxiliary' to a main verb, the main verb form is almost always a past participle:

> *A jist <u>got stuck</u> intae hìm*
> *Haes tha hoose <u>got biggit</u> yit?*
> *Wull ye <u>get soartit oot</u> themorra?*

It is interesting that it is these same past participle verb forms which in other Germanic languages (and in Old English) carry the *ge-* prefix: eg *keke* ('look') *gekeken* ('looked') in Dutch. However, it would be wrong to regard *get* in its quasi-auxiliary role as a 'prefix' form for main verb participles (see section 8.4 and Chapter 10).

9.15 Combined auxiliaries and 'double modals'

As we have seen in section 8.6, primary auxiliaries can be combined in certain patterns such as *A hae bin daein naethìn ava* ('I have been doing nothing at all'). Secondary auxiliaries can be added to the front of these complex verb phrases in much the same way in both Ulster-Scots and English:

> *A wud a bin daein naethìn ava*
> *A maun a bin daein naethìn ava*
> *A micht a bin daein naethìn ava*
> *A shudnae a bin daein naethìn ava*
> *A cud be daein naethìn ava*

[Note that when a secondary auxiliary is followed by the primary auxiliary *hae*, the weak form *a* is used.]

Double modals

The combination of secondary auxiliaries in constructions such as *A'll can dae it* ('I will be able to do it') or *A micht cud see him themorra* ('I may be able to see him tomorrow') are not possible in Standard English, although this feature is well known in Scots and throughout the American South. 'Double modals', as this feature is termed by linguists, are present in Ulster-Scots, but not so clearly evident in Ulster-Scots literature as in Scottish-Scots writings, and not as predominant in Ulster-Scots speech as in American-English.

In Ulster-Scots, double modals can be used for future time reference, the most common combinations being (a) *wull* and *can*; and, (b) *micht* and *cud*.

(a)   *Mebbe we'll can quät earlie thenicht*
        ('Maybe we'll be able to stop early tonight')

        A'll can dae that themorra
        ('I'll be able to do that tomorrow')

        The'll no can cum wi tha snaa
        ('They'll not be able to come because of the snow')

(b)   *Quhan we get, we micht cud hae a wee drink forbye*
        ('When we arrive we may be able to have a drink as well')
        A micht cud soart her oot themorra
        ('Maybe I could fix it tomorrow')

In Ulster-Scots speech, *micht cud* in such senses as in the above examples would more commonly be expressed as *mebbe cud*. However, this would not be regarded as a 'double modal' since *mebbe* is an adverb and not an auxiliary verb.

> *A mebbe cud soart her oot themorra*
> *We mebbe cud hae a wee drink ...*

Yuist tae wud a ('used to would have', or 'would once have') is in common use in Ulster-Scots and might also be regarded as a 'double modal'.

Modals can be combined with past time reference, but usually with the weak form of *hae (a)*, added as a suffix:

> A *micht a cud a* daen it
> ('I might have been able to do it')

> A *shud a cud a*
> ('I ought to have been able to')

In the same way that *haed a daen* is used as if it was understood to operate, as 'had of'... rather than 'had have ...' (section 8.4), so we can have constructions involving modals + *a* + *hae*:

> A *wud a hae* daen it
> ('I would have done it')

> Hè *cud a hae* tuk her
> ('He could have taken her')

CHAPTER 10:
SENTENCE CONSTRUCTION AND WORD-ORDER (SYNTAX)

Some features of Ulster-Scots syntax (or more specifically, of sentence construction) will not be familiar to non-speakers. This is because these constructions are rarely used in the 'self-consciously' written Ulster-Scots of recent times, and so they remain largely undocumented. Perhaps the most distinctive characteristics are concerned with verb position, but others are quite striking too. For example, *aa* ('all') can be placed after pronouns in Ulster-Scots (section 4.4), a position not acceptable in Standard English except after 'they' in some circumstances (such as *They aa taak Scotch roon Ballyalbanagh*):

>*Quha aa is cumin themorra?*
>*Are yis aa for toon?*

Conjunctions such as *bot* ('but') can be sometimes used as adverbs and are often placed at the end rather than the beginning of the appropriate phrase (section 6.4):

>*A'm for toon thenicht, scho's no cumin bot*
>('I'm going into town tonight, <u>but</u> she isn't coming')

Similarly, *an* ('and') is often used at the beginning of a sentence, rather than between two phrases:

>*Ach fair fa ye John! An hoo's thängs wi you?*

Such changes in word position can obviously affect how we might define the 'part of speech' appropriate to a particular word. Ulster-Scots syntax, however, is more easily understood in terms of how groups of words function together rather than how individual words operate as parts of speech. For example, *thon gye bäg mon wi tha bue motòr* might operate (*in toto*) as the 'subject' or the 'object' of a sentence – as it might in English. Similarly, compound verb phrases (including all the associated auxiliary verbs and adverbial phrases) can function (*in toto*) as the 'verb' of a sentence: <u>*micht a bin cumin whalin doon*</u> *thà brae*.

The most distinctive characteristic of Ulster-Scots sentence construction relates to the position and distribution of those words fulfilling the 'verb' function. In Ulster-Scots speech the general tendency is that the verb, or at least part of the verb phrase, can sometimes occur at the <u>end</u> of the sentence. In some cases this feature is distinctive to Ulster-Scots, and in others it is an 'option' within the range of possible Standard English constructions. Often the actual verb end-word is only a single word or a small part of a verb phrase, but it fulfils an essential function in completing the sense of the verb. It 'resolves' the precise meaning, as in the 'resolution' of progressive harmonies in the final chord of a piece of music.

The 'gradual triumph' since Medieval times of the Subject-Verb-Object word order in English is regarded by Bruce Mitchell in *A Guide To Old English* (Oxford, 1964) as one of the most important syntactical developments to differentiate English from the other Germanic languages.

Old English (Anglo-Saxon) had several characteristics not found in modern Standard English, but relevant perhaps to Ulster-Scots:

(a) a pronoun 'object' could be placed between the subject and the verb (S-O-V):
     we hie ondredon
     ('we them feared')

(b) an infinitive verb form could have a final position:
     he ne meahte ongemong o(th)rum monnum bion
     ('he could not among other men be')

(c) an S... V word order where other elements of the sentence could come between the subject and the verb:
     se micla here (th)e we gefyrn ymbe spræcon
     ('the great army, which we before about spoke')
     gif hie ænige feld secan wolden
     ('if they any open country to seek wished')
     ac hi haefdon (th)a heora stemn geseteene and hiora mete genotudne
     ('but they then had their term of service finished and their food used up')

In modern English, one of the most common basic sentence constructions now involves a Subject-Verb-Object order such as:

'That floor (subject) needs (verb) a new carpet (object)'.

A word-for-word translation into Ulster-Scots might result in this being rendered as:
     Thon flair cud dae wi a new cairpet.

Here, of course, the Subject-Verb-Object structure remains intact. However, as we shall see, some Ulster-Scots speakers, sometimes, prefer an Object-Subject-Verb construction such as: *New cairpet thon flair cud dae wi* (although this could be considered equivalent to an acceptable – if clumsy – English construction such as 'It's a new carpet that that floor needs.')

Other constructions also involving a final verb 'resolution' are possible:
     Dae wi a new cairpet, thon flair, sae it cud

Anyone familiar with written transcripts of conversational speech understands that the sentences of a written language are constructed differently from its spoken counterpart. However, the literary conventions of English sentence construction have characterised most Ulster-Scots literature, even when Ulster-Scots 'dialogue' is being represented.

The syntax of an Ulster-Scots poet such as James Orr, the 'Bard of Ballycarry' (1770-1816), follows an 'English' literary model. Even where a Subject-Object-Verb construction is introduced in a line such as *Waeworth the proud prelatic pack, wha point an' prataoes downa tak!* ('Curse the proud Episcopalians, who don't eat potatoes'), it is not clear if this is an acceptable 'English' literary device to effect the rhyme, or if it is an expression of Ulster-Scots syntax. Consider, for example, Orr's poem 'The Wanderer' (which in terms of its vocabulary is a good example of broken Scotch with English and Scots words being used interchangeably). The 'verbs' (including in some cases adverbial clauses) are underlined:

is	*"Wha's there?" she ax't. The wan'rers rap*	asked
	Against the pane the lassie scaur'd:	frightened
	The blast that bray'd on Slimmis tap	heaved
	Wad hardly let a haet be heard.	
	"A frien'," he cried, "for common crimes	
	"Tost thro' the country fore and aft" –	
said	*"Mair lown,' quo' she – thir's woefu' times!*	(these) are
	"The herd's aboon me on the laft."	is (above me in the loft)
	"I call'd," he whisper'd, "wi' a wight	
	"Wham aft I've help'd wi' han' an' purse;	
	"He wadna let me stay a' night -	
	"Weel! sic a heart's a greater curse:	
	"But Leezie's gentler. Hark that hail!	
	"This piercin' night is rougher far" -	
	"Come roun'," she said, "an' shun the gale,	
	"I'm gaun to slip aside the bar."	
is	*Waes me! how wat ye're? Gie's your hat,*	are Give (me)
	An' dry your face wi' something – hae.	have ('go on!')
	In sic a takin', weel I wat;	understand
	I wad preserve my greatest fae:	
	We'll mak' nae fire; the picquet bauld	
	Might see the light, an' may be stap:	might call
	But I'll sit up: my bed's no cauld,	
go to (it)	*Gae till't awee an' tak' a nap.*	have (a sleep)

The Subject-Object-Verb construction in the opening lines: *The wan'rers rap against the pane* (subject) *the lassie* (object) *scaur'd* (verb), which occurs at the beginning of the poem, appears 'archaic', or 'poetic', or both. Indeed, if the adverbial phrase *thro' the country fore and aft* is considered as part of the verb phrase (modifying *tost*), then lines such as *A friend, for common crimes tost thro' the country fore and aft* also display 'old-fashioned' constructions, but again with the verb and adverbial phrase placed at the end of sentence.

The Scottish metrical Psalms, although written in the 'English' of the 17th century, display the same characteristics of verb positioning at the end of lines with such frequency that it would be difficult to argue that this was simply caused by the need to achieve rhyming metre. In the 23rd Psalm lines such as 'My table (object) thou (sub-

ject) hast furnished (verb)' – rather than 'thou hast furnished my table' – do provide regular iambic metre, but they also suggest a much greater acceptance of this
type of final verb positioning in earlier times. Consider Psalm 26, a fairly typical
Psalm in this respect (verbs and verb phrases to be noted are underlined):

Psalm 26

(1)   *Judge me O Lord, for I have walked*
                  In mine integrity:
          I trusted also in the Lord,
                  Slide therefore shall not I.

(2)   *Examine me, and <u>do</u> me <u>prove</u>;*
                  Try heart and veins, O God:
(3)   *For thy love is before mine eyes,*
                  Thy truths' paths I <u>have trod</u>.

(4)   *With persons vain I <u>have not sat</u>*
                  Nor with dissemblers <u>gone</u>.
(5)   *The assembly of ill Men I <u>hate</u>;*
                  To <u>sit</u> with such I <u>shun</u>.

(6)   *Mine hands in innocence O Lord*
                  I'<u>ll wash and purify</u>;
          So to thine holy altar <u>go</u>
                  And compass it will I

(7)   *That I with voice of thanksgiving*
                  May <u>publish and declare</u>
          And tell of all thy mighty works,
                  That great and wondrous <u>are</u>

(8)   *The habitation of thy house,*
                  Lord, I <u>have loved well</u>;
          Yea, in that place I <u>do delight</u>
                  Where <u>doth</u> thine honour <u>dwell</u>

(9)   *With sinners gather not my soul,*
                  And such as blood <u>would spill</u>:
(10)   *Whose hands devices mischievous,*
                  Whose right hand bribes <u>do fill</u>

(11)   *But as for me, I <u>will walk on</u>*
                  In mine integrity:
          Do thou redeem me, and, O Lord,
                  Be merciful to me

(12)   *My foot upon an even place*
                  <u>Doth stand with steadfastness</u>:
          Within the congregations I
                  Jehovah's name <u>will bless</u>.

All of the Ulster-Scots poets regularly used constructions with the verb in a final position. These formations cannot simply be dismissed as 'poetic', as even that distinction implies usage of 'archaic' constructions, surviving only in formal literature. Examples include:

> "An' fast the door *bar'd*" (Orr)
> "An' when the spae-wife to the Mill-town in hidlins *slips*" (Orr)
> "The hedge-hauntin' blackbird, on ae fit whyles *restin*" (Orr)
> "An' ilka ane five bairns *did bear*" (Boyle)
> "The reamin' bicker neist *gaed roun*" (Boyle)
> "Sic heats again we'*ll never fin*" (Boyle)
> "Nae pig on earth *wad* that gate *squeel*" (Anon-Laggan)
> "But, lad, neist mirk we'*ll* to the haining *drive*" (Starrat)
> "She *neednae try* sic yarns *tae spin*" (Kerr)
> "The clachans wi glee and wi merriment *rang*" (Beggs)
> "No quo' the goodwife, *dinna* sic thing *say*" (Huddleston)
> "Gif *oot* he *gangs*" (Huddleston)
> "The weazle aff in triumph *walks*" (Thomson)
> "Right monie a hurchin I *hae seen*" (Thomson)
> "When in, I'*ll* out the fire *see*" (Thomson)
> "Till down he *daded*" (Thomson)
> "As at the boord apart she *sat*" (Savage-Armstrong)
> "Whaur tae a' save his kinsmen *tae dig is furbid*" (Savage-Armstrong)
> "While new-fledg'd broods the fields *hae taen*" (Dugall)
> "But there ava you *wadna rest*" (Herbison)
> "A better hat I never *saw*" (Herbison)
> "Nor did you fail my books to *paw*" (Herbison)
> "A place where there *were* nane me *saw*" (Sloan)
> "Wi' butterflys een tae examine't he *goes*" (Sloan)
> "When round her snaw white neck my arms I *fling*" (Sloan).

Stepping back even further in time, the 'English' written in Ulster during the early 1400s provides confirmation of the antiquity of these syntactic features:

bot gode zow <u>have</u> in his <u>kepying</u>	('but God <u>have</u> you in his <u>keeping</u>', or 'but God <u>keep</u> you')
sen ze to hym on lettre <u>y send</u>	('since you <u>sent</u> a letter to him')
unwytting he <u>come</u>	('he <u>came</u> unsuspecting')
in he <u>wente</u>	('he went in')
myche he <u>spake</u> and mych he hym <u>profred</u>	('he <u>spoke</u> a lot and <u>offered</u> him a lot')
so that he <u>wold</u> the lond <u>leve</u>	('so that he <u>would leave</u> the land')
he <u>wold not</u> hym <u>hyr</u>	('but he <u>would not listen</u> to him')
hys thought <u>was</u> al <u>I-turned</u>, the lond <u>for to wyn</u>	('his mind <u>was</u> all "<u>turned</u>" <u>to win</u> the land')

thegh he few <u>wer</u>, natheles thay <u>war</u> al hardy and stalwarth he <u>chose</u>	('although they <u>were</u> few, nevertheless all he chose <u>were</u> hardy and stalwart')
Whare non engelesheman <u>I-wepned</u> to for hym <u>was I-seye</u>	('Where no <u>armed</u> Englishman <u>had been seen</u> before him')
that thys <u>seyd</u>	('that <u>said</u> this')
thegh he harm <u>tholled</u>	('although he <u>endured</u> injury')
that him the grace <u>sent</u>	('that <u>sent</u> him grace')

These examples are all taken from two early 15th century documents (one an account of John de Courcy's conquest of Ulster, and the other a letter to the Archbishop of Armagh). The common Germanic linguistic roots of English and Ulster-Scots are clearly demonstrated in the prefixes *I-* and *y-* used with past participles (although these prefixes are foreign to Older Scots in Scotland). Other examples from the same sources include:

Zo leffyte in a cedle <u>y wrete</u>	('you left in a <u>written</u> schedule')
and bar yn his sheld, ernes <u>I-peynted</u>	('and bore on his shield, <u>painted</u> eagles')

In the poetry of Thomson, archaic words such as *yclept* ('called', or 'a-called') occur, and also *ydelvin*: *"o' cotter snools <u>ydelvin dykes</u>"*, ('<u>a-burrowing</u> fences').

The late Brendan Adams speculated that the *a-* prefix used with past participles after the auxiliary verb *had* (eg *If he had a-done that* ...) may have represented a 'worn-down form of the Old English prefix *ge-* still found in Dutch and German [and] written *y-* in Chaucerian English'. While some have argued that this particular feature may be better explained as a reduced 'have' by analogy with *cud a done* ('could have done' etc, see section 8.4), other West Germanic parallels with Ulster-Scots syntax provide convincing pointers to common origins (see section 7.14). Consider the verb positioning and verb forms in the opening lines from the Lord's Prayer (Our Father, who art in heaven, <u>hallowed be</u> thy name) in different West Germanic tongues at different dates:

Unser Vater, der du bist in Himmel, <u>geheiliget werde</u> dein Name (German, 19th century)
Fater ynser, tu in Hümele, din Name <u>urde geheiliget</u> (German, 13th century)
Unse Vader, in dem hemmel, dyn name <u>werde gehilliget</u> (Low German)
Onze Vader, die in de hemelen zijt, uw naam <u>worde geheiligd</u> (Dutch)
Uhs Fader, der y binne ynne himmelen; jen namme <u>worde heilige</u> (Frisian)
Fæder úre, thú the eart on heofenum, <u>si</u> thín nama <u>gehálgod</u> (Anglo-Saxon)
Oure Fader, that art in hevenes, <u>halewid be</u> thi name (English, 13th century)
Oure Father which arte in heven, <u>halowed be</u> thy name (English, 16th century)

In a modern Ulster-Scots version we have:

Oor Faithèr at bees abain, yer name <u>be tovit</u>

A number of Scottish-Scots versions also exist:

Our Father wha art in heaven, Hallowet be thy name (Henderson, 1862)
Our Faether whilk art in heaeven. Hallowet be thy name (Riddell, 1856)
Faither o' us a', bidin Aboon! Thy name be holie! (Smith, 1901)
Faither o us aa, bidan Abune! Thy name be holie (Borrowman, 1979)
Our Faither in heiven, hallowt be thy name (Lorimer, 1983)

In modern Dutch (perhaps the stereotypical 'West Germanic' language) the past participle of most regular verbs is formed by prefixing *ge-* to the stem and adding either *t* or *n*, eg *gehoopt* ('hoped'), *gekeken* ('looked'). Consider, however, how past participles affect the syntax in Dutch:

> *Wij hebben het gekozen*
> ('We have chosen it', or literally, 'we have it a-chosen')

> *Hebben zij de brief gelezen?*
> ('Have they read the letter?, or literally 'Have they the letter a-read?')

The parallels with Ulster-Scots are self-evident in constructions such as *Haes Marie her new drèss gat?*; *Is yer da lang deid? We hae tha kye bocht*. The following examples allow a simple comparison between some English, Dutch and Ulster-Scots verb patterns:

English	Dutch	Ulster-Scots
The child was born last week	Het kind is verleden week geboren	Tha chile is a sennicht boarn (or, more usually, The chile is boarn a week)
I have been here for ten months	Ik ben hier al tien maanden	A'm here this ten month
We have lived here a year	We wonen hier no een jaar	We're here a yeir noo
His father has been dead for years	Zijn vader is reeds jaren dood	His faither is yeirs deid
I have written a letter	Ik heb een breef geschriven	A hae a lettèr writ
The egg has been boiled	Het ei is gekookt	Tha egg is cook't
The ship has sunk	Het schip is gezonken	Tha schip is sunk
I have fallen	Ik ben gevallen	A'm fell doon

In general terms, Ulster-Scots word order differs from English most significantly in that part of the verb phrase can shift to the end of the sentence (and the object can be brought forward in the sentence). There are a number of ways in which the verb phrase is 'resolved' at the end of a sentence in Ulster-Scots, and these are exemplified in more detail in the following sections.

10.1 Object – Subject – Verb construction

The Object-Subject-Verb construction was common in Old English, and is still possible in Modern English, but looks strange (and archaic) in print. It is, however, surprisingly common in Ulster-Scots speech, although it must be said that the usual Standard English constructions are also used interchangeably in Ulster-Scots:

a new carpet (object) *thon fluir* (subject) *cud dae wi* (verb)
aa tha hail fairm Billy labours ('Billy works the whole farm')
this committee, weel a wheen o weemin gat thegithèr an set it up ('A group of women met and formed a committee')
fäsch, cats aits ('cats eat fish')
twa pair o schune A bocht ('I bought two pairs of shoes')

10.2 Prepositional phrase – Subject – Verb construction

This is similar to the OSV construction, but where a prepositional phrase rather than an object occurs at the start of the sentence:

acause o hìs caul Jack cum in
('Jack came in because of his cold')

doon tha loanen tha twa o thaim cum, whustlin
('the two of them came whistling down the lane')

afore echt Jamie went oot
('James went out before eight')

awa til Inglann scho went
('she went away to England')

This construction is most common in narrative style.

10.3 Predicate Adjective – Subject – Verb construction

This construction is also similar to the OSV structure:

daft thon wee lad is	('That boy is daft')
black aa thae cats is	('Those cats are all black')
95 ma ma wuz	('My mother was 95')
sorry yis'll aa be	('You will all be sorry')
richt ye be	('OK')
foondèrt A am	('I am freezing')
a lock o things scho micht be,	('She may be a lot of things, but she's not shy')
bot burdmooth't scho's no	

In the last example, *'a lock o things'* is a predicate nominative, rather than a predicate adjective. Therefore, sentence structures such as *'Tha miníster's wife scho'd be'* or *'A guid fower hunner hè wud hae'* would probably be considered to have a Predicate Nominative – Subject – Verb construction.

Note: As thematic fronting for emphasis provides similar forms in English, it might be expected from the above patterns that constructions such as 'quickly he came in' (which are acceptable but not common in English) would be found in Ulster-Scots. However, it appears that an Adverb-Subject-Verb construction is not particularly characteristic of Ulster-Scots speech when the adverb is directly related to, and modifies, the verb. Presumably the adverb in this case is considered an integral part of the verb 'phrase':

hè <u>cum in quäck</u>, houlin hìs breeks <u>up ticht</u>
('<u>quickly</u> he <u>came in</u>, <u>tightly holding up</u> his trousers')

10.4 '<u>How many' questions</u>

'How old <u>is</u> Tom?' or, 'What age <u>is</u> Tom?' can be *Quhit age <u>wud</u> Tam <u>be</u>?*, or *Quhit'<u>s</u> the age at Tam <u>is</u>?* Indeed many simple questions of the 'how far...?, 'what length ...?' type can, sometimes, be constructed in Ulster-Scots to provide a final verb:

Quhit's tha far Cowlrain <u>is</u>?
'How far <u>is</u> Coleraine?'

Quhit's tha lenth thae wee screws <u>is</u>?
'How long <u>are</u> those little screws?'

Quhit's tha nummer Billy <u>is</u>?
'What number <u>is</u> Billy?'

10.5 <u>Existential sentences</u>

In English, 'existential' sentences usually begin with 'There is ...', 'There are ...', 'There was ...' etc, as these phrases state the 'existence' of the subject or the object. However, existential constructions do not always result in the main verb shifting to the end of the sentence (as with: 'he <u>broke</u> a new glass' *versus* 'There was a new glass he <u>broke</u>'). For example, 'There <u>was</u> a man in the shop' compared with the non-existential construction 'a man <u>was</u> in the shop' only involves a change in verb position in relation to the subject: 'a man'. However, when the existential construction provides initial sentence focus on the <u>object</u> (rather than the subject), then a final verb positioning can result: 'There <u>was</u> a man I <u>knew</u>' (compared with the non-existential construction 'I <u>knew</u> a man'). Similar existential constructions are common in Ulster-Scots, perhaps especially those which facilitate an Object-Subject-Verb construction similar to that outlined in section 10.1 above.

In Scots and Ulster-Scots, the existential form of English 'there' can sometimes be *the* ('they'), so that 'there is' and 'there are' may occur as *the's* and *the'r*. The potential for confusion between *the'r* (literally translated as 'they are') and English 'there' is reduced in practice by the frequent use of the *-s* verb concord with plural subjects in this situation (see sections 7.6 and 7.7):

The's jist tha twa o thaim <u>cumin</u>
('There <u>are</u> only two of them <u>coming</u>')

The's nane o thae coats ye <u>cud hae</u>
('You <u>can't have</u> any of those coats')

The's gye few jabs <u>goin</u>
('There <u>are</u> very few jobs available')

However, many speakers also occasionally use *the'r* in these situations – even for singular subjects – presumably because the *-s* verb concord rule does not apply after 'they' (*the*):

<u>The'r</u> a big heidin in thà paiper anent it
('<u>There is</u> a big headline in the paper about it')

<u>The wur</u> naeboady aboot
('<u>There was</u> no-one around')

<u>Ir the</u> onie cattèr bot?
('<u>Is there</u> any money, however?')

<u>The wur</u> yin o tha Broons tae cum
('<u>There was</u> one of the Browns expected to come')

<u>The'r</u> nae hairm in buik-larnin
('<u>There is</u> no harm in education')

When existential Ulster-Scots sentences involve a 'fronting' of the object (as in other emphatic situations), the verb *be* is often discarded and *this* added (see section 4.3) to give an initial *The this*:

The this coát A <u>hung up</u> (but, more usually, *The wuz this coát...*)
('I <u>hung up</u> a (particular) coat')

The this wee lad <u>cum in</u> (similarly to above, also *The wuz this wee lad ...*)
('A little boy <u>came in</u>')

The this fairm o laun hè <u>bocht</u>
('He <u>bought</u> a farm')

The this oul buik A <u>suen</u>
('I <u>saw</u> an old book')

This becomes *these* for plural objects and subjects:

The these twa oul boys the <u>niver coontit</u>
('They <u>didn't count</u> two old men')

The these oul schune A <u>hae</u>
('I <u>have</u> these old shoes')

An existential construction involving 'fronting' of the object may also serve to give some degree of emphasis to the object. However, when particular emphasis is intended, *see* or *see this* is used in some areas (*dae ye see* or *d'ye see this* in the core Ulster-Scots areas):

> *See this oul buik A <u>hae</u>*
> ('I <u>have</u> a (particular) book')

> *See thon coát A <u>hung up</u>? It's no mine*
> ('You know that coat I <u>hung up</u>? It's not mine', or, 'I <u>hung up</u> that coat, (but) it's not mine').

Note: *See** or *D'ye see* is used just as frequently in Ulster Scots to provide emphasis to the subject of the sentence, in which case the verb position is not necessarily altered:

> *See him an his oul da? the'<u>r niver</u> here**
> ('His father and he <u>are never</u> here')

10.6 <u>Splitting the verb phrase</u>

> *<u>dae wi</u> a guid clain, thon fluir <u>cud</u>*
> *<u>be</u> bettèr aff, hè <u>wud</u>*

This process occurs frequently with verb phrase forms, and usually involves shifting the 'lead' (ie the first) auxiliary verb in the verb phrase to the end of the sentence as in the above examples. In these cases the subject usually immediately precedes the shifted verb element.

Verb phrases with or without auxiliaries are also extremely common in Ulster-Scots speech (section 7.9), and many of these verb forms can also be 'split', with part moving to the end of the sentence:

A <u>hae</u> ma tasks <u>daen</u> (rather than: *A <u>hae daen</u> ma tasks*)
Hè <u>is</u> verie oul <u>gat</u> (rather than: *Hè <u>is gat</u> verie oul*)
Hè <u>cut</u> thà trèe <u>doon</u> (rather than: *Hè <u>cut doon</u> thà trèe*)
A <u>hae</u> tha hoose <u>rid oot</u> (rather than *A <u>hae rid oot</u> thà hoose*)
A'<u>ll get</u> a wee lodger <u>tuk in mebbe</u>* (rather than *A'<u>ll mebbe tak in</u> a wee lodger*)

10.7 <u>final verb 'tags'</u>

> *thon fluir <u>cud dae wi</u> a clain*, sae it <u>cud</u>.*
> or
> *<u>dae wi</u> a guid clain*, thon fluir, sae it <u>cud</u>.*

As we have seen in section 8.2, a characteristic of most Ulster-Scots auxiliary verbs is that they can be used in 'tag' form at the end of a sentence:
> *..., sae hè wud.*
> *..., sae it is.*
> *..., sae A cud.*

When there is no auxiliary verb used or understood as part of the main verb phrase, a form of the verb *dae* is used as a tag (sections 8.2, and 8.5):

> *saen her yestreen, sae A daed.*
> *gien thà duir* a dunt, sae hè daed.*

The 'tag' device is generally used only when no other part of the verb phrase can be brought to the end of the sentence. For example, with the English sentence 'He <u>drew</u> the curtains', it would be more likely to encounter, in everyday speech, *He pulled the curtains <u>owre</u>* (without any tag), than **He pulled <u>owre</u> the curtains, so he did*. However, we might expect to hear *He <u>drew</u> the curtains, <u>so he did</u>*, rather than the first part only without the tag. Similarly, we can expect: *Hè <u>shut</u> thà duir sae he <u>daed</u>*, or *He <u>pu'ed</u> thà duir <u>til</u>*.

Negated auxiliaries also operate as tags, and the same effect of final verb positioning is achieved:

> *A <u>daednae</u> see her, sae A <u>niver</u> / A <u>niver</u> saen her, sae A <u>daednae</u>*
> *Nae coals left, sae thar'<u>s no</u>*
> *Niver foutie wi me, <u>neether</u>* hè <u>wuz</u>*

10.8 *Hae* as a tag

Hae ('have') is a common interjection used in Ulster-Scots speech at the end of phrases and sentences (see section 8.4). In the poem 'The Wanderer', written by James Orr *c*1798 (and cited at the beginning of this chapter), the second line of the last verse reads:

> *An' dry your face wi' something – <u>hae</u>.*

Although *hae* can be added as an emphasiser at the end of any syntactic construction, it is particularly common in the 'Have you ...?', 'Do you...?' and 'Are you...?' type of direct question to a third person. Indeed, the Ulster-Scots equivalents of such questions involve no auxiliary verb other than the final *hae*:

> *Ye for oot thenicht, <u>hae</u>?*
> ('<u>Are</u> you going out tonight?')

> *Ye <u>daen</u> wi thon buik, <u>hae</u>?*
> ('<u>Are</u> you <u>finished</u> with that book?')

> *Ye <u>saen</u> ma schune, <u>hae</u>?*
> ('<u>Have</u> you <u>seen</u> my shoes?')

> *Ye <u>gat</u> thà messages, <u>hae</u>?*
> ('<u>Did</u> you <u>do</u> your shopping?')

The verb *hae* is not inflected in this usage (see section 8.4 for confirmation that *hae* is the verb 'have'), so that the 'person' and the 'tense' must be understood from other contextual information:

> *Ye oot yestreen, <u>hae</u>?*
> ('<u>Were</u> you out yesterday?')

Ye <u>wur daen</u> wi thon buik, <u>hae</u>?
('<u>Were</u> you <u>finished</u> with that book?')

Ye <u>see</u> ma schune, <u>hae</u>?
('<u>Do</u> you <u>see</u> my shoes?')

Ye <u>gettin</u> thà messages, <u>hae</u>?
('<u>Are</u> you shopping?')

Hae should be understood, in these examples, to mean 'have', or 'take (what I have just said) as a question.'

10.9 <u>Negative auxiliaries used in questions</u>

When the subject of a sentence combined with a negative auxiliary verb, such as: *he wudnae, thon boy winnae, it disnae* etc are inverted to form a question, the construction follows the pattern:

Wud hè no ...?
Wull thon boy no ...?
Daes it no ...?

and <u>not</u>   * *Wudnae he ...?* etc.

In Ulster-Scots it is not possible to say:

* <u>Dinnae</u> ye ken quhit at is?
* <u>Irnae</u> ye readie for oot?

Although *Daen't ye ...*, *Irn't ye ...* etc are also used frequently, these questions would usually be constructed:

Dae ye <u>no</u> ken quhit it is?
Ir ye <u>no</u> readie for oot?

Here the negative auxiliary is effectively 'split', with the negative indicator *no* moved to a position after the subject. When this type of question also involves a tag, that 'negative indicator' part of the verb is effectively moved to a final position in the sentence:

Naw ken quhit thon is, <u>dae</u> ye <u>no</u>?
'<u>Don't</u> you know what that is?'

Similarly, tags such as **dinnae ye?* ('... don't you?') would not be used.

NOTE: The verb *ken* ('know') is not as widely used in current Ulster-Scots as it is in Scotland. Indeed, apart from occasional use of the past tense form (*kent*), it could only be said to be in current use in the construction: *Dae ye no ken ...?* which is found in some districts. Obviously, the alternative of **Dae ye no know...?* would sound very strange.

10.10 Reconstructing sentences in the passive voice

In the 'passive voice' the action of the verb is experienced by the subject (rather than by the object, in which case it is said to be in the 'active voice'). For example, in the sentence 'James felled the tree', it is the object (the tree) which is 'felled', so that this is in the 'active voice'. However, if the sentence is re-ordered to 'the tree was felled by James', then it is the subject (now 'the tree') which suffers the action of the verb (and so the sentence is in the 'passive voice').

The reconstruction of any sentence from active to passive, in effect, gives emphasis to (and 'fronts') what was originally the 'object' of the sentence in its 'active' voice form. It does not necessarily result in a movement of the verb to the end of the sentence (although it does, in a sense, 'reverse' the original verb-object word order). The chief advantage of the passive is that it enables the speaker to avoid specifying the agent of the action. Therefore, if the 'subject' of an English sentence in the active mood is dispensable, a reconstruction in the passive voice can result in a final verb position:

> *Someboadie haes cut doon aa thae trèes*
> 'Someone has felled all those trees' (active voice)

> *Aa thae trèes haes bin cut doon*
> 'All those trees have been felled' (passive voice)

The active and passive 'voices' of a verb are easily distinguished – a verb is passive in both Ulster-Scots and English if the verb phrase contains a form of the verb *be* together with a past participle. Without this combination, all other forms are active. This can be illustrated with the verb form *for tae tak aff* ('to take off'), whose past participle form is *tuk off* ('taken off'). Active verb forms include the following examples:

> *Hè taks thà day aff.*
> *Hè tuk thà day aff.*
> *Hè is takkin thà day aff.*
> *Hè wuz takkin thà day aff.*
> *Hè haes tuk thà day aff.*
> *Hè haed tuk thà day aff.*

When, however, forms of *be* are combined with *tuk*, or *taen* (used as a past participle), the voice is passive:

> *Tha day is tuk aff.*
> *Tha day wuz tuk aff.*
> *Tha day is bein tuk aff.*
> *Tha day wuz bein tuk aff.*
> *Tha day haes bin tuk aff.*
> *Tha day haed bin tuk aff.*

As we have seen, a distinctive characteristic of Ulster-Scots grammar is the positioning of the verb, or part of the verb form, at the end of the sentence. At the same time, it is clear that the 'object' often migrates to the front of the sentence, or at least in front of the verb. In effect, the 'object' of a sentence in the active voice, becomes the 'subject' of the sentence (and is 'fronted') in the passive voice.

10.11 Putting past participles at the end of sentences

> *James haes thà hoose paintit* (rather than 'has painted the house).
> *Hè's desperit shy gat* (rather than 'has got ...').
> *Hè haes thà day tuk aff* (rather than 'has taken off ...').

This device is a particularly well-used one in Ulster-Scots, even to the extent of preferring past-participle verb forms where they might not be expected in English, except with a different nuance of meaning and context:

> *Hè haes thà bane buried.*
> ('He buried the bone'.)

> *A haed thà curtains pu'd owre afore hè cum.*
> ('I drew the curtains before he came')

> *Eftèr aa that hè gat thaim seperatit.*
> ('He separated them after all that.)

> *Scho bides in a hoose doon thà loanen an scho's onlie daen gettin it renovatit. It wus jist tha yin storie high afore scho gat it aa ris up.*
> ('She lives in a house down the lane and she has just finished renovating it. It was just one storey high before she raised it'.)

10.12 Final positioning of main verbs which indicate a changing state

The 'becoming...' or 'getting...' verbs, which indicate a changing state of the subject, are often postponed to the end of the sentence in Ulster-Scots:
> 'He is becoming (or getting) very tall'
> *Hè's verie tal gettin*

This construction can be used in three tenses:

(a)   'That grass is becoming (getting) very tall'
        Thon graiss is gye lang gettin

(b)   'That grass has become (got) very tall'
        Thon graiss is gye lang gat, and

(c)   'That grass had become (got) very tall'
        Thon graiss wuz gye lang gat.

The word 'becoming' does not have much currency in Ulster-Scots. 'Become of' is *cum o*, as in *Quhit's cum o tha Broons?*

When the 'action' or 'change' implied by a small group of main verbs is completed by an adjective (usually complementing the subject), rather than a direct object (eg 'The man turned brown' rather than 'The man turned a stone'), this construction also seems to apply. Verbs such as 'changing...', 'turning...', 'getting...', 'going...', 'growing...', 'shrinking...', 'rising...', 'becoming...', etc, can all be used in Ulster-Scots in this way, remembering of course that words such as *tùrn* ('turn') and *schäft* ('shift') are used commonly in Ulster-Scots in preference to 'change' (and of course *get* rather than 'become').

'All those leaves <u>have changed</u> (or <u>turned</u>) to brown'
Aa thae laifs <u>is</u> broon <u>turnt</u>
(Note: although *got* or *gat* is not used in all these examples, it is otherwise a preferred alternative.)

'The days <u>have become</u> very cold'
Tha days <u>is</u> verie caul <u>gat</u>

'The days <u>are becoming</u> very cold'
Tha days <u>is</u> verie caul <u>gettin</u>

'He <u>has become</u> very difficult'
Hè'<u>s</u> gye thran <u>gat</u>

'The children <u>have grown</u> very tall'
Tha weans <u>is</u> powerfu bäg <u>grew</u> (or ... *got*, etc).

'I'<u>ve become</u> too tired this year to do anything'
A'<u>m</u> owre wabbit <u>cum</u> for tae dae ocht the yeir

'That bush <u>has grown</u> (<u>risen</u>) too high'
Thon bush <u>is</u> owre heich <u>ris</u>

'Sure they'<u>ve</u> all <u>moved</u> to America'
Sure the'<u>r</u> aa awa tae Americae, <u>flittit</u>

'The walls <u>are sliding</u> down the hill'
Tha waas <u>is</u> awa doon thà brae <u>slidin</u>

'He <u>had sunk</u> up to his armpits before they came'
Hè <u>wuz</u> up til hìs oxtèrs <u>sunk</u> afore the cum

'The clouds <u>have moved</u> over to the east'
Tha cloods <u>is</u> across tae tha aist <u>schäftit</u>

'His face <u>had turned</u> bright red when she embarrassed him by laughing'
Hìs bake* <u>wuz</u> bricht rid <u>turnt</u> quhaniver scho affrontit hìm wi lauchin

'It'<u>s going</u> too fast'
Scho'<u>s</u> owre quäck <u>gangin</u>

Note: When the verb *be* acts as the main verb in a similar way to the above, the same principles apply to the positioning of *bein* ('being') and *bin* ('been'), although the following forms are rare:

'The man <u>is being</u> very difficult'
Tha mon <u>is</u> gye thran <u>bein</u>

'The man was being very difficult'
Tha mon wuz gye thran bein

'The man has been very difficult for the past two nights'
Tha mon is gye thran bin this twa nichts past

10.13 Putting the 'object' at the front

Besides using the passive voice as a device to place the object at the beginning of a sentence, other techniques are employed in Ulster-Scots, such as the object indicator *see* or *ye see*:

See thon trèe, Jamie haes it cut doon.
Ye see neist Monday, hè is for takin it aff again.*

Object 'complements' (which tell more about a direct object), along with those adverbs which modify the object rather than the verb, tend to be placed towards the front (along with the object itself).

Monies thà upset nicht we haed.
('We had many upset nights'.)

Abain tha waa-heid tha ruif o tha hoose is aff.
('The house is roofless above the wall-head'.)

An this big stew scho daen.
('And she made a big stew'.)

Yin time ma mithèr toul us.
('My mother told us one time'.)

A wiser boadie tha daeins made Andra.
('The events made Andrew a wiser person'.)

Daft scho caa'd me.
('She called me silly.)

... an a wheen o coppers ye wud a gien her ...
('and you would give her a few coppers')

... for at wuz hoo scho aye gat paid
('as she was always paid that way')

Ae nicht, ma da toul me, thar wuz this storm the wur in an thà boát wuz driv up til Portmuck he sez.
('My father told me they were in a storm one night and he said the boat was driven up to Portmuck'.)

Note that where the verb is 'transitive' (that is, when it requires a direct object to make sense), the completion of the transitive verb meaning will come at the end of a sentence in the active voice:

'He <u>extinguished</u> the candle',

<u>or</u>,   'He <u>blew out</u> the candle',

<u>or</u>,   'He <u>blew</u> the candle <u>out</u>'.

The Ulster-Scots way of expressing this would be *Hè <u>blew</u> tha cannle <u>oot</u>*. Here the object ('the candle') is often quite acceptable at the end of a sentence because it is understood to belong with the verb words themselves, almost as an integral part of the verb phrase. So *blew thà cannle oot* and *wuz driv up til Portmuck* are understood to fulfil the same verb function as an 'intransitive' verb such as *cum doon* ('fell') in a clause like *see last nicht, thon wuz some rain <u>cum doon</u>*.

10.14 '<u>Ulster-Scots' nouns understood as 'English' verb equivalents</u>

We have already seen that Ulster-Scots verb forms differ significantly from English in their pattern of use. In the first place a relatively small number of simple 'core' verbs are used in verb phrases in preference to single-word verbs (eg *<u>cum</u> up tae* for 'approach', *<u>let</u> on* for 'pretend' etc). This signals that the whole verb phrase (which can be quite lengthy and complex in Ulster-Scots) is understood *in toto* to function as the 'verb' element in Ulster-Scots syntax. Indeed, as we have seen, the verb phrase can be (and often is) broken up into elements and distributed throughout the sentence, with only a part of the verb phrase moving towards the end. Adverbial phrases (ie adverbs and phrases modifying the verb) are <u>also</u> treated as an extension of the verb form in Ulster-Scots, and may be placed at the end of sentences. For example, the adverb *quäck* ('quickly') would not be 'fronted' in Ulster-Scots in a sentence such as '<u>quickly</u>, he <u>ran</u> inside the house'; 'he <u>quickly ran</u> inside the house; or even, 'he <u>ran quickly</u> inside the house'. As Ulster-Scots speakers would regard *quäck* as part of the verb phrase, a more likely construction would be: *he <u>run quäck</u> ben thà hoose*, or *he <u>run</u> ben thà hoose <u>quäck</u>*.

The second major verb characteristic of Ulster-Scots is the tendency to translate single word English verbs into 'nouns' (see 7.8). This means that the nouns so created are not regarded as objects of the sentence (as they might be in English), but rather as part of the verb phrase:

> *A <u>tuk</u> masel intae toon <u>a danner</u>*
> ('I <u>took a walk</u>/<u>walked</u> into town')

> *A <u>went awa</u> doon thà raa <u>a waak</u>.*
> ('I <u>walked</u> down the street'.)

> *Hè <u>gien</u> tha dorr <u>a dunt</u>*
> ('He <u>gave a knock on</u>/<u>knocked</u> the door')

> *A cudnae stap, sae A <u>pit in ma apologie</u>.*
> ('I <u>apologised</u> for not being able to stay'.)

> *A <u>gien</u> ma pipe <u>a licht</u>*
> ('I <u>gave a light to</u>/<u>lit</u> my pipe')

In these examples, it might appear that the words 'walk' and 'apology' etc simply act as nouns, when they are understood by Ulster-Scots speakers to act as part of verb phrases such as *tak a dandèr, hae a swim* etc.

10.15 Descriptive verbal phrases

A descriptive verbal phrase describes or elaborates on the 'action' suggested by the verb: *Maistèr Boyd* (subject) *wuz raxed oot* (verbal phrase) *on thà flet o hìs bak* (adverbial phrase). Here, significantly, the final phrase is really a modification of the verb, and describes how Mr Boyd was lying.

In a more complex sentence, where there are 'descriptive verbal phrases' which extend or complete the meaning of the verbs, the same principle applies:

> *The mair tha kintra heirskip oor ain fowk haes is miskent, sae far as luiks is concarnit, an made little o, the jist chughie at wi a no canny lippen at ithèrs taks for want o wut.*

> 'Although our cultural heritage appears to be unacknowledged and belittled by our own people, they just carry on with an extraordinary trust in life that appears naive to outsiders.'

Taking the following more complex sentences from a novel, it is possible to illustrate how the word-order might be changed in Ulster-Scots:

> 'Master Boyd was known by the children as "wee Boydie" at the beginning, and, of course, before long he became "old Scaldie" [a scaldie is a nestling]. He always took a great notion for a drink – he thought of it as a bit of a thirst – when he strolled into town, particularly if he happened on a few old friends. It was understandable that he was not always able to call in the children next morning, although he was supposed to open up the school.
> Wrapped up in a blanket, nursing a head-ache, Master Boyd was stretched out on the flat of his back, frightened to move in case his head separated from his body. "Never again" he said, "I've become too old for all of this."

Very few changes to the construction of these sentences are required to give their Ulster-Scots form:

> *"Wee Boydie" wuz quhit Maistèr Boyd wuz caa'd wi tha weans tae stairt wi, an o coorse it wuznae lang afore it wuz "oul scaldie" he gat. A muckle greenin for tha drink – a wee drooth wuz quhit hè thocht – aye cum on him, speciallie quhan he wud be doon thà toon for a dander an faa in wi qwarthie oul billies. The mair in thà morn tha scuil wuz for him tae apen, ye cud see throu him no aye bein fit tae crie tha weans in.*
> *Hapt in a blanket, wi a sair heid tae thole, Maistèr Boyd wus raxed flet oot on his bak, wi nae thocht o jeein hissel for fear his heid an boadie wud sinther. "Niver agane" qu'he, "A'm owre oul for aa this got."*

— ooo0ooo —

10.16 Conclusion

Ulster-Scots sentence construction is often similar to English. When it differs from English, it is still clearly 'Germanic' in terms of the broad principles under which its words are modified and ordered. However, this chapter does not provide a set of syntactic rules for Ulster-Scots grammar. Its purpose has been to identify which features differ most from English syntax, and, if possible, to identify any broad principles which give pattern to these characteristic features.

In general, there is a tendency towards a word order that occasionally favours moving the object (in comparison with English) towards the front of the sentence, and the verb towards the end. The terms 'object', 'subject' and 'verb' are generalised to include the entire word groups within a sentence that fulfil these broad grammatical purposes – not just single words. Frequently, it is not the whole verb phrase that shifts to the end of the sentence, but just one part, or even one word. This final 'verb' element usually provides a resolution or modification of the meaning of the verb.

Translating English prose into Ulster-Scots requires a knowledge of more than Ulster-Scots vocabulary. Ulster-Scots syntax, including a basic understanding of the idioms, grammar and usage of the tongue must also be applied. Indeed, Ulster-Scots speech is often highly idiomatic and only occasionally do idioms, 'sayings' or proverbs follow the final verb 'rule' (as in *richt ye be, in ye get, on ye go*) ('all right', 'get in', 'go on' etc). Most idioms stand by themselves, and their usages must be learned individually:

a gleed o wut	('a spark of intelligence')	*mair nor middlin*	('better than average')
quhit dae the caa ye	('what is your name?')	*dinnae cruddle yer sook*	('don't upset yourself')
fair fa ye!	('hello, welcome')	*houl yer wheesht*	('keep quiet')
Dear sain ye!	('God bless you')	*mair lown*	('quieten down')
quhit fittle?	('how are you?')	*s'lang noo*	('farewell, so long')
quhit wey ir ye?	('how are you?')	*Ye awa?*	('are you going?')
ye lang swem?	('have you been here long?')	*creesh tha loof*	('grease the palm')
awa abain me	('above my head')	*houl on a wee*	('wait a minute')
amang them be it	('settle it among yourselves')	*eh wha!*	('what about that then!')

Similarly, numerous proverbs *(saws)* decorate Ulster-Scots speech, but these cannot be regarded as 'translations' of English proverbs (although some are similar):

Aboot tha muin thair is a bruch, tha weathèr wull be coul an ruch.

A cock's aye crouse on hìs ain midden
Ye cannae heed aa ye hear
Tha warl's ill divid
They aa complains o want o siller, bot nane o want o sense
Aa cracks maunnae be trew't
Ae scabbit scheep'll smit a hirsel
Eild an poortith's sair tae thole/oul age an poverty's ill tae thole
Thole aye an while poustie/chughie at tae ye'r strang

In Ulster-Scots speech the common pattern of intonation is to raise both pitch and volume towards the end of each utterance, giving the final emphasis to the verb form. Often there is a corresponding lack of emphasis on (or even omission of) the first portion of each sentence. In speech, a sentence such as *A wud rathèr hae jam, sae A wud* would almost always be rendered as *A'd rathèr hae jam, sae A wud* – and often with the initial *A'd* not articulated at all. When all else fails in achieving an element of the verb phrase at the end of the sentence, Ulster-Scots speakers regularly resort to the interjection *hae* ('have'), which, as we have observed, is added to the end of statements in a decidedly emphatic way:

Sonce fa ye, hae
Luk at thon boy in thà schap, hae
Gie'z ma hat bak, hae

When confronted with an English text to translate, the would-be student of Ulster-Scots will have problems to contend with besides differences of vocabulary, syntax, grammar and idiom. English 'formal' literature is peppered with prepositions, conjunctions and other words and phrases such as 'nevertheless...', 'although...', 'however...', 'for some time now...', 'despite...' etc. The Ulster-Scots equivalents for these, drawn as they are from a spoken language, seem informal and colloquial, and can appear to treat scientific or serious subjects in an undignified way. This, however, may be due as much to the low status of the language itself as it is to differences between formal written language and informal speech. As an aid, some Ulster-Scots equivalents for the most common such 'formal English' idioms are provided:

alas!	-	*waesucks!*
although	-	*tha mair*
although it no longer matters	-	*tha mair its aa yin noo*
according to	-	*ownin til*
		accoardin tae
and so on	-	*an that*
because of	-	*owre tha heid o*
		on accoont o
but for	-	*onlie for*
by way of	-	*in tha wye o*

certainly	-	*for certes*
		for sure
		atweel
concerning	-	*anent*
		adae wi
as far as I'm concerned	-	*for me*
considering how little	-	*for aa*
despite	-	*tha mair o*
despite all that	-	*wi aa that*
		yit an wi aa
in every detail	-	*frae enn tae yin*
for some time now	-	*this quhile*
for example, take	-	*luk at tha*
however	-	*bot*
		hooaniver
in order to	-	*for tae*
indeed	-	*so*
		deed
		atweel
nevertheless	-	*aa tha quhile*
		jist tha same
once again	-	*yinst mair*
occasionally	-	*betimes*
		quhiles
or else	-	*or less*
perhaps	-	*aiblins*
the same subject	-	*tha yin thing*
somewhat, rather	-	*a wee bit*
		a weethin
sometimes	-	*quhiles*

undoubtedly	-	*nae mistak bot*
		nae doot
		forouten ween
the very best	-	*owre ocht*

— oo0oo —

This book can provide only an introduction to Ulster-Scots grammar for non-speakers. The interwoven history of English and Scots, the similarities between them, and the influence of each of the two languages on each other, make translation a somewhat subjective exercise. Most Ulster-Scots writers have an 'inner ear' – a real or imaginary speaker who acts in the mind of the writer. The Ulster-Scots forms that such a muse can trigger, in effect, provide a mental process of translation; an 'Uncle Wullie' who is imagined conveying – in Ulster-Scots speech – the English concepts and sentences to be reconstructed. Such instinctive translation attempts are usually fine for humorous stories of country life, because 'Uncle Wullie' can come through loud and clear with those. However, when serious academic (or even scientific) texts are to be translated, then our Ulster-Scots vocabulary, grammar and 'Uncle Wullie' can all be found wanting. Ulster-Scots translations of serious English texts can appear to trivialise, making the translated version appear colloquial. The terms 'High German' and 'Low German', although originally used to describe the varieties of language found in the higher locations of southern Germany and the northern coastal lowlands respectively, refer today to the relative status of the two languages. There is no usage among linguists of the terms 'Low English' or 'High English', similar to those recognised for Low and High German (although 'colloquial' and 'Standard' English appear to approximate). Ulster-Scots is not simply colloquial English, even though some of the grammatical forms involved in translating into Ulster-Scots may also be colloquial English.

Proponents of the Frisian language in the Netherlands consider that if Frisian is not used for serious subjects and scientific texts, then it will "become a dialect" (Frisian has a linguistic relationship with Dutch similar to that of Scots with English). Elsewhere in Europe, the distinction between when a 'dialect' becomes a 'language' is more often made (a) in terms of a tongue's history (did it ever enjoy official status as a state language?), (b) the degree of distinctiveness of its vocabulary, (c) the existence of a literary tradition, (d) the presence of different dialects within the tongue, and (perhaps most importantly), (e) discrete rules of grammar and syntax. Scots, in all of these respects (and Ulster-Scots, in most of them), satisfy the criteria necessary for classification as a language, hence the acceptance of their full linguistic status by the European Bureau for Lesser Used Languages.

The Ulster-Scots grammar presented in this book provides no more than a starting point for the work of the Ulster-Scots Academy. In the fullness of time, Ulster-Scots linguists may (and hopefully will) debate rules of standardisation for spelling, vocabulary and grammar for the modern language.

CHAPTER 11:
A READER OF ULSTER-SCOTS PROSE

The text of the Bible has been used for language learning in many parts of the world. Indeed it was used for the teaching of Gaelic in Ulster schools 150 years ago. It made sense to use a text whose meaning in the reader's first literary language would be already known – especially if religious motivations could be satisfied at the same time. In the Ulster Presbyterian tradition, the high priority given to universal education over the past 300 years was largely due to the desire to ensure that all could read the Bible for themselves.

For any European lesser-used language, the possession of a Bible translation in that tongue is an important symbol of the status of the language. It is unfortunate that a full translation of the complete Bible into Scots was not completed at the time of the Reformation. *The New Testament in Scots* was translated from the original Greek to Scots by W L Lorimer relatively recently, and published by his son in 1985. Ulster-Scots readers can have some difficulty with the Scottish-Scots of Lorimer's work, but it is widely acknowledged as a masterpiece of Scots literary translation, and has had enormous influence in improving the status of Scots.

The Ulster-Scots reader provided here is not an adaption of parts of Lorimer's *New Testament in Scots*, or P H Waddell's *The Psalms: Frae Hebrew intil Scottis* (first published 1871). Instead, it contains 'translations' from the King James English Bible (ie the Authorised Version of 1611), examined in parallel with the Modern English *Good News* Bible.

11.1 Psalms

Psalm 1

1. Hè's ae sonsie mon, him at disnae waak thà gates hè gits toul wi tha wickit, an winnae staun alang wi wrang-daers, an wi jamphers winnae tak a sait
2. Bot hè is hairt-gled wi tha rule-buik o tha Loard an gies muckle thocht on it bi day an nicht.
3. Hè's liken tae a trèe ats forenent wattèr burns plantit an quhit gies her frute cum hairst, an haes laifs at disnae wizen an dee. Nae mattèr quhit hè daes, hè bees til hae guid poustie.
4. No sae wi tha wickit bot! Like shellins the ir, at wi tha wunn gets blaw't awa.
5. An syne thà wickit winnae staun in thà big soartin oot tae cum, an wrang-daers wull no win ben thà maetin o tha guid-leevin.
6. For thà gates o tha guid-leevin tha Lord kens fu weel. Tha roáds o tha wickit's a deid loss bot.

Psalm 2

1. Quhitfor daes aa tha leids o tha warl git ris up an aa the fowks compluthers for naethìn ava?
2. Tha kängs o tha yirth haes tuk a staun, an thà heich-heidyins maets thegithèr agin thà Loard an agin his Anointit Yin.
3. "Cum on an bust thàir chains up" the sez "an th'ow thair lang'ls aff".
4. Tha Yin at sits abune in thà lift lauchs, tha Loard hè scoffs at thàim aa.
5. Than hè barges thàim, an quhan hè gets mad he fair scars thàim, goin:
6. "A hae ma käng pit until ma halie heicht o Zion".
7. A be tae declare quhit the Loard haes set oot. Hè sez til me "Ye be ma ain sinn, for theday A'm becum yer faithèr.
8. Jist ax an A'll gie ye aa tha leids for yer tocher, tha thonder-maist neuks o tha yirth for tae houl as yer ain.
9. Ye can boss thàim aa wi a staff o airn, ye can ding thàim til smithereens like delft".
10. Sae, yous kängs, wise up, an yous heidyins o tha yirth tak tent.
11. Lout ye tae tha Loard an wark afeart unnèr him. Be thankit wi jittèrs an tremmlin.
12. Gie tha sinn a kiss, for fear hè gets mad an ye gets daen in alang yer ain gate for hè haes a lowe at can be kinnl't in nae time ava. Blessit be aa quha lippens til hissel alane.

Psalm 3

1. O Loard, hae, quhit a crood o faes thrangs aboot me, quhit nummers sets thàirsels up agin me.
2. See him, the aa go's "God winnae save him".
3. Bot you bees a bield aboot me, O Loard ma Powerfu Yin, at gies ma heid a heft.
4. A guldèr til thà Loard an he gies answer frae hìs halie heicht
5. A taks a lie doon for tae hae a slaep. A wud wak again afore lang bot for tha Loard uphoudin me.
6. A winnae be ascard o tha thoosans at haes set thàirsels agin me, compassin thàirsels roon me on ilka airt.
7. Get up O Loard, Save us O mine God
   for ye hae gien aa ma foes a guid dig up thà bake
   ye hae bustit thà taeth o tha wickit.
8. Frae tha Loard cums yer safe-kaepin
   Sonse fa yer fowks for aye.

Psalm 4

1. Spaik bak quhan A cries at ye,
   O ma richtious God
   Gie iz a let up fae ma sair vexation
   Gie us yer mercie an tak tent til ma prayers.
2. Hoo lang, boys, is yis for pittin tae schame
   aa ma guids-gree.

Hoo lang is yis for haein fause gods, an yer
    heids fu o nónsense.
3.   Bot mairk yous, tha Loard haes kep seperate thà guid-leevin
    fowks for hissel.
    Tha Loard wull tak tent quhan A crie on hìm.
4.   Dinnae dae wrang quhan yis git mad
    Tak a guid luk at yersels, hairt an soul, quhan yis are in yer beds, an be
whisht.
5.   Aye gie tha richt offerins, an pit aa yer lippen on tha Lord.
6.   Monies thà fowks asts, "Quha's gonnie schaw us ocht guid?"
    Let thà licht o yer face schine on us O Loard.
7.   Ye hae gien ma hairt mair gree nor onie time quhan thàir coarn an wine wuz
in plentie.
8.   A can lay me doon an lie fu lown, for its yer sell, O Loard, at lats me bide safe.

Psalm 5

1.   Give ear til ma sang, O Loard
    tak tent til ma souchs.
2.   Listen ma scraich, ma Käng an mine God
    for its til yersel at A maks ma prayers.
3.   Ilk muin, O Loard, ye hears ma crie
    Ilka morn A asts ye for somethìn
    an than houls on wi haip.
4.   You binnae a God at likes ill-daein, the wickit winnae be let bide alang wi ye.
5.   Tha stuck-up, prood fowks, cannae staun in yer licht,
    ye hates aa thaim at daes wrang.
6.   Liars ye ding doon, bluidthirstie an sleekit men thà Lord cannae thole ava.
7.   Masel bot, A'm for tha ben o yer hoose acause o yer guid grah
    A'll bow doon wi respec facin yer halie temple.
8.   Gie-us thà airt, O Loard, o yer ain richt roáds,
    Mak yer gate straucht afore me.
9.   Ye cudnae gie credit til yin wurd the quo fae oot o thàir mooths
    thàir hairts bis set on ill-daein.
    Thair thrapple is a gapin grave, wi thair tongue the aye taak lees.
10.   Gie it oot at the be in thà wrang, O God
    Let thàim get thàir cum-uppance for bein sae sleekit
    Pit thàim oot for aa thae ill-daeins at the hae daen
    for the hae ris up agin ye.
11.   Bot blythe be aa at luk til yersel for safétie
    the can gie oot hairtsome sangs for aye.
    Luk til thàir care
    an thàim at lo'es yer name'll be fit tae be fain in ye.
12.   For sure, O Loard, ye bis guid til the richt-hairtit,
    Ye put yer help roon aboot thàim like a bield.

Psalm 6

1.   O Loard, dinnae rage me an get mad,
    nor gie it tae me in yer temper.

2.   Let iz aff, Loard, for A haes a dwaam heid,
     O Loard, sairt me oot, for ma banes is wyll sair.
3.   Ma sowl is in a torment
     Hoo lang O Loard maun A thole.
4.   Hereawa an save ma sowl, Loard, tak pitie on us an luk eftèr me, for fear A
     dee.
5.   Nane ats deid haes mynn o ye, thars nae tovin fae tha buryin-grun.
6.   A'm fair daen oot wi ma ain moanin, ilka nicht A hae drookit ma bed wi
     girnin, ma boulstèr bis wrängin wi ma greetin.
7.   A'm near no able tae see ocht, for ma een is baith swoll wi greetin owre the
     heid o thae ill-daers.
8.   Awa fae me, yis bad yins, for tha Loard gies ear til ma sabbin.
9.   Tha Loard haes heerd ma threap, hè is for gien ma prayer a repone.
10. Aa ma faes is gonnae git schameit an be sair fash't. Wi yin big scattèrin the'll
     be driv oot.

11.2 Tha Guid Wittins O Matthew

Chaiptèr 1

1.   Be it kent til aa men. Ane listin o tha forebears o Jesus Christ quha cum doon
        fae Dauvit, at wuz hissel cum doon fae Abraham.
2-6.   Frae Abraham tae Käng Dauvit, thir forebears is listit: Abraham, Isaac, Jacob,
        Judah an hìs brithèrs; then cums Peres an Serah (quhase maithèr wuz Tamar),
        Hesron, Ram, Amminadab, Nahshon, Salmon, Boaz (quhase maithèr wus
        Rahab), Obed (quhase maithèr wus Ruth), Jesse, an Käng Dauvit.
6-11.   Frae Dauvit til thà Cairriein-Awa o tha fowks o Israel intil Babylon thir fore-
        bears is listit: Dauvit, Solomon (quhase maithèr wuz thà wumman at afore
        wuz thà guidwife o Uriah), Rehoboam, Abijah, Asa, Jehosyphit, Jehoran,
        Ussiah, Jotham, Ahes, Hesekiah, Manassah, Amon, Josiah, an Jehoiachin
        alang wi hìs brithèrs.
12-16. Frae eftèr tha Cairriein-Awa til Christ wuz boarn, thir forebears is listit:
        Jehoiachin, Shealtiel, Sarubbabel, Abiud, Eliakim, Asor, Sadok, Achim,
        Eluid, Eleasor, Matthan, Jacob an Joseph, at wuz merriet on Marie, tha
        maithèr o Jesus, at the caa Christ.
17.   Sae thar wud be fowertaen genérations fae Abraham til Dauvit, an fowertaen
        fae Dauvit til thà Cairriein-Awa tae Babylon, an fowertaen fae tha Cairriein-
        Awa til Christ.
18.   Here is quhit-wey tha birth o Jesus Christ cum aboot. Hìs maithèr Marie wuz
        trystit til Joseph. Afore the gat merriet bot, Marie foon oot scho wuz for haein
        ane bairn wi tha Halie Speerit.
19.   Her mon Joseph wuz a dacent boadie at aye daen quhit wus richt. Hè wuznae
        mynnit for tae affront Marie afore tha warl, an sae he ettlet tae bust up thàir
        tryst hidlinwyes.
20-21. Quhan hè wus fixin on this ane angel o tha Loard cum til hìm in a draim an
        qo he "Joseph, sinn o Dauvit, dinnae be afeard for tae tak Marie for yer guid-
        wife. Tha bairn at scho cairries wuz gat wi tha Hailie Speerit. Scho is for haein
        ane sinn, an hit bees Jesus ye maun caa him, for hè is gonnae save hìs fowk
        frae thair sins".
22-23. Noo this aa cum aboot sae as thà wurd spake bi the Lord th'ou the Prophet

micht cum tae be: "Behaud, ane virgin wull get pregnant an hae a sinn, an the'll caa his name Immanual" – at stauns for "God wi us".

24. Sae quhan Joseph haed waukit frae hìs slaep, he tuk Marie an gat merriet on hèr, as tha angel o tha Loard gart hìm dae. Hè didnae dae onie sex wi her bot, tae scho haed haen a sinn; an hè caa'd thà bairn Jesus.

Chaiptèr 2

1-2. Jesus wuz boarn in thà toon o Bethlehem in Judea, in thà day o Käng Herod. It wuz nae time ava eftèr this afore a wheen spaemen fae tha Aist cum til Jerusalem an begoud speirin, "Quhar wud thà bairn be at bees tae be tha Käng o tha Jews? We hae saen hìs starn ris up in thà Aist, an haes cum for tae warschip hìm."

3-4. Käng Herod wuz sair pit oot wi that, alang wi aabodie in thà hail o Jerusalem. He brung aa tha Heid-Priests an Dominies o tha Law thegither an spierit at thaim "Quhar is thà Christ tae be boarn?"

5-6. "Ben thà toon o Bethlehem in Judea" the sez, "jist thà wye tha Prophet screivit:
  'See thee, Bethelem, in thà laun o Judah,
  ye're naegate thà laist amang thà toons o Judah,
  for frae thee wull cum oot ane heich heid-yin
  at wull be ane herd til ma fowk o Israel'."

7. Sae Herod caa'd thà spaemen fae tha Aist til maetin wi hìm in hidlins, an larnt frae thaim thà verie day-an-hòor o tha starn's kythin.

8. Neist hè sends thaim awa til Bethlehem tae dae as hè bid, "Gang an hae a guid luk for tha bairn", qo he, "an quhan yis hae foon hìm gie us tha wittins, sae as A can gang masel an warschip hìm forbye."

9-10. An sae the tuk thà gate at the wur bid, an behaud, yinst mair the saen thà starn afore thaim at the saen in thà Aist. Muckle blythe the aa wuz tae quhan the saen thà starn gangin on afore thaim tae it cum abune thà hoose quhar tha bairn wuz.

11. Syne the gaed ben, an quhan the saen tha bairn wi hìs maithèr Marie, the hunkert forrits on thàir knees an gien hìm warschip. Than the brocht oot thàir hansels o gowd, an frankinsense, an myrrh, an gien thàim til thà bairn.

12. Eftèr aa this, the fuir awa hame bi anaithèr gate nor the haen won, sin the haed gat warnishit in a draim no tae gang bak near Herod.

13. Eftèr tha spaemen haed tuk aff hame, ane angel o the Loard kythed til Joseph in a draim an qo'd "Herod wull be lukin thà wean for tae kill hìm. Sae, ye maun flit wi tha wean an hìs maithèr til Egypp, saicret-like, an stap thonnèr tae A gar yis lave."

14-15. Sae Joseph tuk aff for Egypp in thà nicht wi tha wean an thà maithèr, quhar hè stapt tae Herod wuz deid. For sae it boost tae be, at thà wurd spake wi tha Loard th'oo tha Prophet micht cum tae be: "A cried ma son fae oot o Egypp".

16. Quhan it twigged wi Herod at he wuz haed on bi the spaemen fae tha Aist, hè flew aff tha hannle. Hè gart aa tha wee fellas in Bethlehem be slauchtert, baith in thà toon an in thà kintra roon aboot, gif the wuz twa yeir oul an young'r – bein thà time as he larnt fae tha spaemen o tha kythin o tha starn.

17-18. Hit wuz aa this roád sae as thà wurd spake bi Jeremiah tha Prophet wud cum trùe.

"A soon cud be heerd in Ramah
        tha soon o hairtsome yammerin
Rachael girnin for her weans
        scho winnae hae onie consolin
for the be nae mair."

19-21. Eftèr Herod wuz deid, ane angel o tha Loard kythed in a draim til Joseph in Egypp an qo'd: "Git yersel up, tak thà wean an hìs maithèr, an gang bak til thà laun o Israel, for thàimins at socht thà bairn's life is deid." Sae Joseph gat hissel up wi tha wean an the wean's maithèr an tuk aff awa bak tae Israel.

22. Bot, quhan Joseph heerd at Archelan wuz noo tha neist Käng o Judea eftèr hìs faithèr Herod, he wuz feard tae gang thonner-roads. He wuz telt in a draim for tae fair aff intil Galilee, an settle in a toon caa'd Nasareth, sae as thir wurds spake wi the Prophets micht get daen: "Hè wull git caa'd a Nasarene".

Chaiptèr 3

1. In thaim days John the Baptist wuz gan roon thà Desert o Judea praichin.
2. An sayin, "Yis bettèr chainge, for tha kängrik o haiven is near".
3. This is hìm at wuz spake o bi the prophet Isiah:
    "Tha soon o yin criein in thà desert,
    Redds tha gate for tha Loard,
    an maks straucht pads for hìm".
4. John's claes wuz made fae tha hairs o camels, an roon hìs wame he haed a laither belt. Hìs mait wuz locusts an wyll honie.
5. Fowks gaed oot til him fae Jerusalem an aa Judea an thà hail kintra o tha Jordan.
6. Makin confésion o thair sins, the wur baptisit in thà Jordan Wattèr.
7. Quhan hè saen a wheen o Pharasees an Saducees bot, cumin tae quhar hè wuz baptisin thaim, sez hè til thaim "Yis clatter o coul snakes yis! Quha let on at ye maun flee fae tha bargein ats cumin til yis?"
8. Bring oot frute up tae kaepin wi yer guid leevin.
9. An dinnae think yis can say til yersels "We hae Abraham for wor faithèr," A'm tellin ye that fae oot thir stanes God cud rair childèr for Abraham.
10. Tha hatchet's waitin at thà fit o tha trèes, an ilka trèe at disnae hae guid frute wull get cut doon an buck't intil thà fire.
11. A baptize ye wi wattèr tae mairk yer turnin tae guid-livin. Eftèr me bot, wull cum yin at bis mair powerfu nor me, quhase saunels A binnae fit for tae arrie. Hè wull baptize ye wi tha Hailie Spierit an wi fire.
12. Hìs coarn-graip is in hìs haun, an hè wull redd oot hìs th'ashin fluir, draain hìs whait in til thà barn an burnin thà showes wi a lowe at cannae be pit oot.
13. Than frae oot o Galilee Jesus cum til thà Jordan for tae be baptisit wi John.
14. John made a try tae pit him aff bot, an sez "A'm lukin for tae be baptisit wi yersel, an ye're cumin til me".
15. Jesus repones, "Sae mote hit be noo; this is the richt thing for us tae dae sae as aa guid gates can cum tae be". Than John gaed alang wi it.
16. Richt eftèr Jesus gat baptisit, hè gaed up oot o tha wattèr. Than haiven aped up an hè saen thà speerit o God cumin doon like a doo an lut on hìm.
17. An a voice frae haivin qos "This bis ma Sinn, at A lo'e; an at A'm weel plaisit wi".

Chaiptèr 4

1. Than thà Speerit tuk Jesus aff intil thà desert for tae hae tha deil temp't hìm.
2. Eftèr fastin for fowertie day an fowertie nicht hè gat a hung'r on hìm.
3. Tha temptèr cum til hìm an sez "Gif ye be tha Sinn o God, mak thir stanes tùrn intae breid".
4. Jesus gien hìs repone "It's in thà Buik: 'Mon disnae leev on breid alane, bot on ilka wurd at cums oot o tha mooth o God".
5. Than thà deil tuk hìm til thà Hailie Citie an gart hìm staun at thà verie tap heicht o tha Temple.
6. "Gin ye be tha Sinn o God" qo he "lep aff. For its in thà Buik:
   Hè wull commaun hìs angels
        anent ye
   an the wull gie ye a läft up in thàir hauns
        Sae as ye winnae ding yer fut
        agin a stane".
7. Jesus gien hìm tha repone "Its in thà Buik forbye:
   Dinnae be pittin thà Loard yer God tae tha test".
8. An then, tha deil tuk hìm til a gye heich moontain an schawt hìm aa tha kin-ricks o the warl an thàir fancie daeins.
9. "Aa this A wull gie ye", qo he "gin ye wud mak a bow an gie warschip tae me".
10. Jesus ses til him "Awa or that, Satan, for its in thà Buik: 'Gie warschip til thà Lord yer God, an sarve naebodie bot hìm'."
11. Than tha deil tuk aff fae him, an angels cum tae be wi hìm.
12. Quhan Jesus heerd at John haed bin pit in jail, hè cum bak til Galilee.
13. Laivin Nazareth, hè went an leevd in Capernum, quhilk wuz fornent thà lough in thà kintra o Zebulum an Naphtali.
14. Sae as quhit aa tha prophet Isiah sez wud cum tae be:
15. "Laun o Zebulum an laun o Naphtali,
    tha gate til thà sey, alang thà Jordan,
    Galilee o tha Gentiles -
16. Tha fowks at leevs in thà dairk,
        haes seen ane muckle licht;
    an thae fowks at bides in thà laun
        o the schaida o deein ane licht haes ris".
17. Frae then on Jesus stairtit for tae praich, "Tùrn awa fae yer sins, for thà kän-grick o heiven is nearhaun!"
18. Quhan Jesus wuz takin a dannèr alang thà shore o Lough Galilee, hè saen twa braithèrs at wuz fäschers, Simon (caa'd Pettèr) an hìs braithèr Andra, warkin wi a net at thà fäschin in thà lough.
19. Jesus sez til thàim "Cum wi me, an A'll larn yis for tae fäsch for men".
20. Aa at yinst the drappit thàir nets an gaed wi hìm.
21. On hè went an saen twa ithèr brithèrs, Jamie an Ian, tha sinns o Zebedee, soartin thair nets oot. Jesus cried on thaim an richt awa the left thà boát on thair faithèr, an gaed wi him.
23. Aa aboot Galilee Jesus went, larnin fowks in thà sinygoges, giein oot thà Guid Wittins anent thà kängrick, an makin fowks at haed aa kynn o ills an sairs weel.
24. Tha Wittins anent hìm went oot th'oo tha hail kintra o Syria, sae as fowks

brung til him aa soarts o ailments: fowks wi demons, an epyleptics, an paryl-
itics – an Jesus made thàim aa weel.

25.   Bäg croods fallait hìm frae Galilea an thà Ten Toons, frae Jerusalem, an thà
laun owre tha Jordan Wattèr.

Chaiptèr 5

1.   Jesus saen thà croods an speelit a brae quhare hè tuk a sait. Hìs disciples
gaitherit roonaboot hìm,
2.   an hè beguid for tae larn thàim:
3.   Blythe be thaimins at kens weel at the be puir o speerit; tha kängrick o heiven
belangs thaim.
4.   Blythe be thaimins at is mournsome
God wull gie thaim an aisin o hairt.
5.   Blythe be thaimins at is hummle
the'll get quhat God haes made promyse o.
6.   Blythe be thaimins as luks naethìn mair nor for tae darg wi sic as God haes
naed o: God wull gie thaim full satysfaction.
7.   Blythe be thaimins at is kynn an forgiein
God wull be kynn an forgiein wi thaim.
8.   Blythe be thaimins wi clain hairts
For the'll see God!
9.   Blythe be thaimins at haes wrocht for paice
God wull caa thaim hìs childhèr.
10.   Blythe be thaimins at aye gits a pit doon for daein quhat God wud hae thaim
dae: tha kängrick o heiven belangs til thaim.
11.   Blythe mote yis be quhan fowks miscaa ye an pit ye doon an gie oot lees agin
yis for fallyin me.
12.   Be hairtfu an blythe, for in heiven a bäg hansel is kep for yis. Thir roád is
quhit-wye tha práphets at bade afore yis wuz persycutit.
13.   Yis are like saut for aa monkynn. Gin saut losses hits saut taste, bot, thar binnae nae roád at ye cud mak hit sautie again. Hit haes waeworth gat, sae it is
buck't oot an fowks staun aa owre it.
14.   Yis are like licht for tha hail yirth. Ane citie biggit on a hill cannae be hid.
15.   Naebodie pits licht til a lamp an than pits it ablow a boul, na, he pits her up
abeen, on a staun, quhar scho gies licht for aabodie in thà hoose.
16.   Wi sic a roád yer licht maun be gien oot afore fowks, sae as the can see tha
guid darg at ye daes an tove yer Faithèr in heiven.
17.   Dinnae jalouse at A hae cum for tae dae awa wi tha Rule o Moses an thà larnin
o tha prophets. A hinnae cum tae dae awa wi aa that, mair like for tae mak
thair taichins cum tae be.
18.   Hae mynn o this – at sae lang as heiven an yirth be, no yin wee dot nor haet
o tha Laa is for bein daen awa wi – no til thà enn o aa thìngs.
19.   Sae, quhasomiver gaes agin me wi tha verie laist o thae commanns, an larns
ithèrs for tae dae tha same, wull be tha laist in tha kängrick o hciven. On thà
ithèr haun, thaim at gangs wi tha Laa an larns ithèrs for tae dae tha same, wull
be bäg in thà Kängrick o heiven.
20.   Sae A'm tellin ye, at yis winnae be fit tae gang in til thà kängrick o heiven gif
yis dinnae be mair le'al nor thà dominies o tha Laa, an thà Pharysees, an aye
daes quhat God is lukin yis tae dae.

21. Yis hae heerd at fowks wuz toul lang syne; "Dinnae dae murdìr; oniebodie at daes is for gittin brung tae coort".

22. Noo A'm tellin ye bot; him at gets mad wi hìs brithèr is for gittin brocht tae coort: Him at miscaas hìs brithèr, 'Ye nae-guid pauchle' is for gettin brocht afore tha Cooncil, an hìm at caas hìs brithèr a coof wull hae muckle risk o gangin til tha lowes o hell.

23. Sae, gif ye're jist aboot tae gie yer hansel tae God at thà altàr, an thar ye hae mynn at yer brithèr houls ocht agin ye.

24. Lee yer hansel thar tae tha fore o tha altèr, gang straucht aff an mak a paice wi yer braithèr an cum bák eftèr an haun oot yer hansel tae God.

25. Gin oniebodie gaes tae laa agin ye an taks ye tae coort, mak hit up wi hìm quhan ye yit hae time, afore ye git thà lentht o coort. Yinst ye be thar, hè wull haun ye owre til thà judge, at wull haun ye owre til thà polis, an ye'll git pit intae jail.

26. Thar ye'll stap, A ledge, aye an quhile ye pay tha fine til thà last pennie.

27. Yis hae heerd at it wuz spake; 'Dinnae dae adultèrie'.

28. Noo A'm tellin ye bot, oniebodie at luks near a wumman, an wud hae her, bis in thà wrang for daein adultèrie wi her in hìs hairt.

29. Sae gin yer richt ee gars ye for tae sin, tak her oot an clod her awa. It'll be a brave bit bettèr for ye til loss a pairt o yer bodie as tae hae yer hail bodie th'own intae hell.

30. Gif yer richt haun gars ye for tae sin, cut it aff on clod it awá. It'll be mair guid for ye tae loss yin o yer limbs as yer hail bodie for tae gang til hell.

31. It wuz spake forbye, 'Oniebodie at gies tha wife a divorce maun gie her a screivit line o divorce'.

32. Noo A'm tellin ye bot, gif a mon gies hìs guidwife a divorce for onie cause forbye her no bein faithfu, than hè is in thà wrang for makin her dae adultèrie gif scho gets merriet agane, an thà mon scho merries on daes adultèrie anaa.

33. Yis hae heerd forbye at fowks wuz toul lang syne, 'Dinnae brak yer wurd, bot dae quhit yis hae gien a vow til thà Lord for tae dae'.

34. Noo A'm tellin ye bot, dinnae mak use o onie aith quhan ye mak a promise. Dinnae sweer bi heivin, for hit is God's th'one;

35. nor bi Jerusalem, for hit is tha citie o the big Käng.

36. Dinnae even sweer bi yer heid, for ye cannae mak a ae hair whit or blák.

37. Jist go 'Ay' or 'Nae' – ocht eke ye qo cums fae tha deil.

38. Yis hae heerd at it wuz spake, 'A ee for a ee, an a tuith for a tuith'.

39. Noo A'm tellin ye bot, dinnae get yer ain bák on somebodie at daes ye wrang. Gin onebodie gies ye a dig on thà richt-haun side o the bake, let him hut ye on the left-haun side forbye.

40. An gif somebodie taks ye til thà coort for tae hae yer sark aff o yer bák, let him hae yer coát forbye.

11.3 Tha Guid Wittins O Luke

Chaiptèr 1

1-4 Guid frein Theophilis: Monies thà fowk haes pit thair haun til scrievin ane bit discoorse o aa thae thängs at haes bin brocht tae pass amang us. The hae pit doon quhit wuz telt us wi thaimins at saen thir thängs wi thair ain een frae tha verie stairt, an eftèrhaun the become praicher-men o tha wurd. An sae, ma warthie billie, bein as A hae tuk tent for tae be weel-larnt o tha ins an oots o tha hail storie, A thocht ye cud dae waur nor hae me set it doon in guid an richt ordèr. A daen this task sae as ye can ken hoo siccar an sevendible is aathings quhilk ye hae bin larnt.

5.   In thà days at Herod wuz the Käng o Judea, thar wuz this priest caa'd Sachariah at wuz ae o tha Priestlie Order o Abijah. Hìs guidwife wuz caa'd Elspeth, an scho wuz a dauchter o ane priestlie hoose an aa. Tha baith o thaim wuz guid-livin in thà sicht o God an kepp aa God's biddins an commaunmenns. The hadnae onie weans bot, for Elspeth cudnae hae childhèr an scho an Sachariah wuz baith gye an oul.

Ae day Sachariah wuz in thà Temple daein hìs darg, seein til thà duties o hìs saicred wark. As tha priests aye daen bi custom, lots wuz drew for tae see quhilk yin o thaim wud brunn thà incense on thà altàr. Sachariah gat chuse, an sae hè gaed inbye tha Temple o tha Loard quhaniver tha hail thong o tha fowks wuz stuid mákin prayers ootbye.

11.   Ane angel o tha Loard kythed til Sachariah staunnin on the richt haun side o tha altàr quhar tha insense wuz brunt. Sachariah gat a quare gunk at thà sicht o tha angel, an wuz hairt-scared. Bot thà angel sez til him: "Dinnae be feard, Sachariah. God haes heerd thà prayer ye made, an yer guidwife Elspeth wull bear ane son til ye. He maun be caa'd wi the name o John. Unco happiness ye'll hae o him, an monie fowk'll be blythe owre hìs birth. Hè wull be muckle in thà sicht o tha Loard. He maunnae tak drìnk, an frae leein in his maithèr's wame hè wull be fu o the Haillie Speerit. Monies thà sinn o Israel wull be airtit bak til thair ain Loard God.

17.   Hè wull gang afore tha Loard, strang an michtie like Elijah tha Prophet, sowtherin thà hairts o faithèrs an bairns, an larnin thà fowks at's no bidable tha richt an guid gates o God. Hè wull hae tha Loard's fowks gat guid an reddie for hìm. Sachariah sez til thà angel: "Quhit-wye wud A ken gif it sae be? A'm an oul mon, an thà guidwife is oul forbye."

"A bees Gabriel" wuz thà angel's repone. "A staun in thà licht o God at brung me tae taak wi ye an gie ye thir guid wittins. Ye hinnae tuk ma wuird bot, o quhit wull cum trùe quhan thà time cums. Bein as ye hae misdootit me, ye winnae can taak. An ye'll stap tung-lang'lt or this haes aa cum tae be."

21.   Aa this time, tha fowks wuz waitin on Sachariah an ferliein quhit-for wuz hè takin sic lang hòors in thà Temple. Quhan hè cum oot, hè cudnae spake til thaim ava, an sae the kent hè maun hae haen a vision in thà Temple. No haein thà pouer o taakin, hè jist stuid stannin thar makin signs wi hìs hauns.

23.   Quhan hìs day's darg in thà Temple wuz daen, Sachariah gaed hame. It wisnae owre lang eftèr that quhan hìs guidwife Elspeth gat pregnant an for five montht scho didnae lee tha hoose. "Noo, at lang last, thà Loard haes gien me ane heft," qo scho "Hè haes taen awa tha affront A hae dree'd amang fowk".

26.   Quhan Elspeth wuz in her saxt montht, tha angel Gabriel gat sent bi God tae ane toon in Galilee caa'd Nasareth. Hè wuz daein a message til this lass at wuz trystit til ane mon bi the name o Joseph at haed forebears richt bak til Käng Dauvit. Tha lass wuz caa'd Marie.

28.   Tha angel cum til her an go's: "Guid on ye. Tha Lord bees wi ye an haes gien ye ae muckle blessin."

29.   Marie wuz fair flummoxt wi tha angel's wurd an scho thocht on quhit it aa micht bode.

30.   Tha angel than sez til her: "Dinnae be feard, Marie. Ye hae foon favour wi

God. Ye wull get pregnant an hae a sinn at ye be tae caa Jesus. Hè wull be muckle big wi fowk, an be caa'd the Sinn o tha Maist Heich God. Hè wull be made Käng bi tha Loard God, like hìs forebear Dauvit wuz, an hè wull be käng o tha sinns an dauchters o Jacob for aye: thar winnae be nae enn til hìs rule."

34. Syne Marie sez til the angel "Quhit-wye cud that be? Sure a hinnae kent onie mon".

35. "Tha Haillie Speerit" qo tha angel. "Wull cum owre ye, an tha pouer o God wull lut on ye. Acause o this, tha haillie bairn wull be caa'd tha Sinn o God.

36. Hae mynn o yer sib-freen Elspeth. The aa sez scho cudnae hae childèr, yit scho hersel is sax montht gone, forbye bein owre oul. Nocht thar be at God cannae dae."

38. "A bees tha sarvint o tha Lord" goes Marie "Sae lat it be jist like ye sez." An wi that tha angel quat wi her an gaed hìs gate.

39. No lang eftèr, Marie gat hersel soartit oot an hied aff til a toon in thà Uplanns o Judea quhar Sacariah bade. Scho gaed intae hìs hoose an hailsit Elspeth. Quhan Elspeth heerd Marie's hailsin tha bairn shiftit in her wame. Elspeth wus owre ocht tuk bi the Hallie Speerit, an guldert oot, "Blissit be ye amang weeman, an blissit be tha bairn ye're for haein. Quhit-for sud a hae aa these big daeins on me, wi ma Loard's maithèr cumin for tae see me? For tha verie meenit a heerd yer hailsin, tha bairn lep for joy in ma wame. Blessit atweill is her at disnae misdoot at thà wurd at wuz brung fae the Loard wud een cum tae be."

46. Quo's Mary,
    "Ma hairt lauds at thà Loard
        ma sowl stouns wi joy in God ma saviour,
    for hè haes kep mynn o me, hìs hummle sarvint-lass!
        Frae noo on, aa fowks is gonnae caa me blissit,
    acause o tha big thängs the Michtie God haes daen for me.
        Haillie hìs name aye bees,
    frae age til age his mercie bides wi aa thaim at fears hìm.
        Hìs straing airm haes wrocht michtie thängs;
    skailin thà prood an heich wi aa thair plons.
        Hè hes dung michtie kängs doon fae thair th'ones,
    an gien ane heft til thà laich an hummle;
        Aa thaim ats stairvin hungrie
    hè haes gien thair fu o guid fairin
        an huntit thà gearie an gethert tuim-haunit awa.
    Hè haes kep tha dale hè daen wi oor forebears,
        an haes cum til thà aid o hìs sarvint, Israel.
    Hè wuz mynnfu tae gie mercie til Abraham,
        an syne wi aa hìs saed an braed for aye."

56. Marie stapt owre for near thie montht wi Elspeth, an syne gaed bak til her ain hame.

57. Tha hòor cum for Elspeth tae hae her bairn, an scho haed a sinn.

58. Her neebors an kin heerd quhit-wey tha Loard haed bin pouerfu kynn til her, an the aa wuz real plaised alang wi her.

59. Quhan thà bairn wuz ane sennicht oul, the cum for tae hae him circumcisit, an the wur for caa'in him Sacariah, for his faithèr. Hìs maithèr bot, ses "na! Ye maun caa him John."

60. The sez til her, "bot ye hinnae ocht o yer freens wi thon name!" Neist the daen signs til thà bairn's faithèr, astin tae let thaim ken quhit wuz his mynn anent thà name.

63. Sachariah axed for ane screivin-boord, an pit doon, "His name daes be John." Quhit a gunk the aa gat! At jist that meenit hìs lips wuz unstuck, an hìs tung wuz lowsit, an he begoud tae spake, ruisin God.

65. Tha neebors wuz aa hairt-scared, an thà wittins anent thir daeins wuz tha hail crack aroon thà Uplanns o Judea.

66. Aabodie at heerd o it thocht on it an axed, "Quha is this wean gonnae be?" Aa cud see for certes as tha pouer o tha Lord wuz wi hìm.

67. John's faithèr Sachariah wuz fu up wi tha Haillie Speerit, an hè spake tha wurd o God:

68. "Blessit be tha Lord, tha God o Israel!
Hè haes cum for tae gie ane haun til his ain fowk
an haes set hìm free.

69. Hè haes rearit ane feckfu delivrer,
frae oot thà Hoose o hìs sarvint Dauvit.

70. Hè gien ane promise bi his haillie prophets
in thà langsyne time

71. at hè wud save us frae oor faemen,
frae tha pouer o aa thae at hates us.

72. Hè sez hè wud hannle oor forebears wi mercie,
an aye kaep mynn o hìs saicred covénant.

73-74. Wi tha aith at he swar til oor forefaithèr Abraham,
hè sez hè wud save us frae oor foemen,
an let us gie sarvice wi'oot bein feard

75. sae we can be haillie an richt-gangin
aa oor boarn days.

76. An ye, ma bairn, wull be caa'd a prophet o tha Maist Heich God.
Ye wull gang afore him tae redd hìs gate for him,

77. tae mak kent til his fowk thà road o salvation bi haein thàir sins forgien.

78. Oor God daes be merciefu an kynn.
Hè wull gar tha speelin sun o salvation cast its beams
fae tha lift doon on us,

79. an gie licht til thaim at bides
in thà mirk o tha schadda o daith
an tae airt oor faet in thà gate o paice."

80. Tha bairn raxed up tae monhuid, gettin bäg an strang in baith bodie an speerit. He bade in thà desert or tha day cum for hìs kythin as ane prophet in Israel.

Chaiptèr 2

1. Roon that time, quhan Quirinius wuz Governor o Syria, tha Emperor Augustus gart aa tha fowks in thà warl be coontit. Siccan ane listin haednae bin daen afore, an aabodie gaed for tae get registrate, ilkane til hìs ain toon.

4. Joseph gaed fae tha toon o Nasareth i Galilee til thà toon o Bethlehem i Judea, quhilk toon wuz quhar Käng Dauvit wuz boarn, bein as Joseph belanged thà root an saed o Dauvit.

5. Hè an Marie, at he wuz trystit til, gaed for tae get mairkit up in thà census

thegithèr. Marie wus expectin, an scho wuz due tha time quhan the gat til Bethlehem.

7. Scho gien birth til her first sinn, swealit hìm wi swaddlin-claes, an beddit hìm in a heck, syne thar wuz nae ruim for thaim in thà inn.

8. The wur a wheen herds i thon pairt o tha kintra at wuz stappin aa nicht in thà fiels, lukin eftèr thair yows. Al o a suddent ane angel o tha Loard kythed til thaim, an thà glorie o tha Loard shint its licht roon aboot thaim. Tha herds wuz unco sair frichtit, bot thà angel ses til thaim; "Binnae yis nane ascared! A hae cum wi guid wittins for yis, at wull gie muckle blytheness til aa fowk. Theday, in Dauvitstoon, yer Saviour wuz boarn – Christ thà Loard!

12. An bi this gate ye'll hae tha pruif: ye'll fynn thà bairn swealit wi swaddlin-claes an liggin intil a heck.

13. Syne in a gliff ane muckle thrang o ithèr angels, like thà airmies o heiven, kythed fornent thà ae angel for tae gie laud tae God bi liltin;

        "Glorie tae God in thà heicht o heiven,
        an paice on thà yird til aa thaim at Hè's
        plaised wi!"

15. Quhan thà angels quat thaim an gaed on bak tae heiven, tha herds sez til ithèr, "C'mon an gang owrebye til Bethlehem an hae a luik at thir daeins at thà Loard haes made beknownst til us."

16. Sae the hied aff an foon Marie an Joseph an saen thà bairn liggin intil thà heck. Quhan thà herds saen him, the telt quhat thà angel haed bin sayin anent thà bairn. Aa at heerd it wuz fair gunked bi quhat thà herds telt thaim.

19. Marie haed mynn o aa thir daeins an thocht lang on thaim. Tha herds tuk aff, liltin tae God thair laud for aa the saen an heerd; it wus aa jist like quhat tha angel haed telt thaim.

21. Ae sennicht eftèr, quhan thà bairn boost tae be haein hìs circumcisin, the gien him tha name o Jesus, like quhat tha angel haed gart thaim dae quhan thà bairn wus conceivit.

22. An quhan thà nummer o days requirit bi tha laws o Moses for reddin-oot onie new maithèr wuz up, the brung him til Jerusalem; for tae preesint him til thà Loard.

23. (For its writ in thà laas o tha Loard, ilka male bairn at apens up a wame wull be caa'd Haillie til thà Loard.)

24. An the cum for tae gie in ane offerin o twa doos, the wye it sez in thà laas o the Loard.

25. An, behoul, thar cum ane mon in Jerusalem at wuz caa'd Simon; an thà same boy wuz ane guid-leevin, God-fearin mon at jist leeved for tha day quhan Israel wud be sauvit. He haed thà Haillie Spirit bidin wi him.

26. An haed telt him hè wudnae dee afore hìs ain een haed behoult tha Annointit o tha Loard.

27. Sae noo, shiftit bi tha Spirit for tae cum intil thà Temple, Simon gaed thar jist quhan Jesus's maithèr an faithèr haed brung him in for tae dae wi tha bairn aa quhit tha laa an custom gart thaim dae.

28. Simon tuk houl o tha bairn in hìs airms an gien thànks til God.

29.   "Noo, Loard, ye hae kep yer wurd,
        an ye can let yer servint awa wi paice o mynn.

30.   Wi ma ain een A hae saen yer salvation,

31.   quhilk thou haes gat reddie in thà sicht
        o aa tha fowks o tha yird;

32.   Ane licht o yer ain mynn til thà Gentiles,
               an for tae bring glorie til yer fowk Israel."
33.   Tha bairn's faithèr an maithèr ferliet sair at quhit Simon qo'd anent him.
34.   Simon gien thaim baith ane blessin an sez til Marie hìs maithèr, "This bairn o
       yourn haes bin chuse wi God for tae be tha doonfa o monies – an thà heft o
       monies – tha Israelite. Forbye hè's for bein a spae fae God at monie fowk
       wull spake agin.
35.   An sae aa thair dorn thochts wull oot. An sorra, like ane shairp swuird, wull
       brak yer hairt."

Index and English/Ulster-Scots Glossary

The following glossary should be used as an index rather than as an English to Ulster-Scots "dictionary". Chapter and section numbers are given for each word form.

The vocabulary used in this book has been restricted to a basic core in order that the grammatical points are not obscured. Word forms shared between English and Ulster-Scots have not been indexed when their meanings are also shared. Consequently, this grammar should be used in conjunction with James Fenton's *The Hamely Tongue* for current Ulster-Scots vocabulary, and *The Concise Scots Dictionary* for the full historical range of Scots and Ulster-Scots words.

Words which are not in current use by native speakers, particularly as evidenced by *The Hamely Tongue*, are italicised in the index, e.g. *unco*. These archaic words nevertheless form part of the Ulster-Scots literary record.

The different spelling forms of words in this index may represent either archaic spellings or "non-standard" Ulster-Scots pronunciation spellings. These forms are <u>not</u> italicised, as they represent non-standard forms of words in current use. Such variations in form from the "norm" are identified in the text.

chosen chuse, 11.2
church maetin, 7.9, 9.14; Meetin Hoose, 2.6
city citie, 11.2
claim *ledge*, 0.4
claw cla, 7.5
clean clain, 1.3, 6.1, 10.6
clean out dae oot, 8.5
cleaning reddin, 4.3, 7.6
clear redd, 1.6, 5.3, 7.7
clear out redd oot, 7.11
cleared redd oot, 7.5; rid oot, 7.5, 10.6
clever cliver, 7.9
climb climm, 6.1, 7.5; speel, 2.2, 5.3, 5.5, 6.1, 7.5
climbed climmed, 6.1, 7.5; clum, 6.1; speeled, 7.5; speelit, 6.5
climbing speelin, 5.1
clock clack, clawk, 3.1, 3.3
cloth claith, 3.3; dud, 5.1
clothes claes, 4.3, 5.4, 6.3, 6.4, 6.5, 7.1, 8.2
clouds cloods, 3.1, 10.12
clumsy fuitless, haunless, 5.1; pauchle, 7.7
coal coals, 2.2, 2.4, 10.7
coat coát, 1.4, 6.5, 9.6, 10.5
cocky croose, 5.1
cohabit tak up wi, 7.9
coin *babee*, 2.7, 5.5; *bawbee*, 2.7; *plack*, 5.5
cold cau'd, 5.3, 7.5; caul, 5.1, 6.4, 10.2, 10.12; cauld, 1.5, 3.2, 5.1, 7.5, 7.12; coul, 0.0, 6.3, 8.3, 8.5, 10.16; coul', cowl, 1.5; stairvin, 5.1
cold (in nature) caulrife, cauldrife, 5.1
collection clatter, 11.2; hattèral, racherie, 2.2
collude compluther, 11.1
come cum, 6.4, 7.6, 7.9, 9.1, 9.2, 9.15; kim, 1.7
comfortable bien, 7.11
compassionate carefu, 5.1
compelled gar't, 7.12
complain nyitter, 1.6; gae on aboot, 7.9
complaining chirmin, 6.4
completely fairly, 0.4; perfaitlie, 5.6
conceited bäg-heidit, 5.1
concerning aboot, 6.3; adae wi, 6.3, 10.16; anent, 6.3, 10.5, 10.16, 11.2; on, 6.3
constantly *close*, 5.3
content *fain*, 11.1
contentment *gree*, 11.1
corn coarn, 0.0, 11.1
cost coast, 5.3, 5.6
cosy bien, 7.11
coughing hosten, 2.2
could cud, 0.4, 1.3, 8.2, 9.5; cudnae, 8.2
couldn't cudnae, 5.4, 5.8, 6.5, 7.7, 9.5
council cooncil, 1.3
counted coontit, 3.2, 10.5
counter coonter, coontèr, 6.1
country kintra, 1.7, 2.2, 8.3, 10.15
county coontie, 6.1
couple qwarthie, 1.5, 2.7; twa three, 4.3, 7.4; twa-thrie, 2.7; tworthy, 2.7; wheen, 2.2, 8.4, 9.5
court tak oot, 7.9
courting a-coortin, 7.14
covenanter covénenter, 1.4
cover co'er, 1.2
cow coo, 1.1, 1.3, 2.4, 2.6, 5.0, 7.14
cows kye, 2.4, 3.2, 4.3, 5.5
cowshed byre, 6.0
crave craav, 1.2
cried grat, 7.5
crockery delft, 11.1
crouched hunkert, 11.2

crowd crood, 4.3, 8.2; hirsel, 5.1; thrang, 4.3, 11.1
crown croon, 1.3; bap, 2.0
cruel cruyel, 1.6
cry girn, 2.2, 8.0; greet, 7.5; scraich, 11.1
crying girnin, 4.3, 11.1; greetin, 11.1
cum came, 10.2
cunning sleekit, 2.3
cup *bicker*, 4.3, 7.5, 10.0
curiosity ferlie, 2.2
curse *waeworth*, 10.0, 11.2
curtains *hingins*, 0.4, 7.9
daddy daddie, 1.1
dance daunce, 2.1, 6.5, 7.9
dancing dauncing, 7.11
dare dar, durst, 8.2, 9.10; darnae, durstnae, 8.2
daren't darnae, durstnae, 9.10
dark dairk, 9.6
dark (in nature) dairksome, 5.1
darkly *darklins*, 5.1
date tak oot, get aff wi, 7.9
daughter dauchter, 4.3, 5.1
dawn scraich-o-day, peep-o-day, 3.3
daybreak scraich-o-day, paep-o-day, 2.6
dead deid, 1.3, 5.2, 5.3, 10.13
deceive dec'ave, 5.1
December Decemmer, 3.3
decent daicent, 4.3
declare *ledge*, 1.4
defeat defait, 7.5
defeated defaitit, bait, bate, 7.5
degrade pit doon, 7.9
delay pit aff, 7.9
depend on lippen, 7.7
depth deptht, 2.7
derived deriv, 7.5
descend get doon, 7.9
desire *dessing*, 0.4
desperately desperit, 5.3
despicable foutie, 10.7
despite tha mair o, 10.16
despite all that wi aa that, yit an wi aa, 10.16
determination *ment*, 3.2
devil deil, 3.2
did daed, 5.3, 7.3, 10.7; daen, 5.1, 5.3, 6.3, 7.5, 7.7, 7.10, 8.5; done, 7.5
didn't daednae, 8.5; didnae, 7.3, 7.9, 8.2, 8.5; niver, 5.3, 6.4, 7.3, 8.2, 8.5, 10.5
die dee, 7.4, 11.1
died dee'd, 7.4
difficult thran, 2.2, 5.1, 9.14, 10.12; *thrawart*, 5.1
dinner dännèr, 8.5; dinnèr, 1.5, 3.1, 6.5, 7.3, 8.2; dinther, 1.5
direct road, 5.3
direction airt, 11.1; roád, 5.3
dirty mingin, 5.1
disappear *tine*, 2.2
dishes däshes, 8.3
dismantle tak doon, 7.9
dispute tulzie, 1.6; threap, 11.1
distance far, *abeich*, 5.4
ditch sheuch, 1.2, 6.1; shough, 1.0
dived div, dove, 7.5
divided divid, 10.16
do dae, 0.4, 8.2, 8.3, 8.5; daed, 8.2; daein, 8.2; daen, 8.2; daes, 7.6, 7.10, 8.2; didnae, 8.2; dinnae, 8.2; disnae, 8.2; div, 8.2, 8.3, 8.5; divnae, 8.2; dois, 7.6
doctor doctòr, 7.1
does daes, 8.5
doesn't disnae, 7.10, 8.5

firm   sevendible, 11.2
first   färss, 2.7; furst, 1.3, 2.7
fish   fäsch, 1.5, 7.0, 10.1
fishermen   fäschers, 11.2
fist   nieve, 2.0
fistful   nievefu, 1.5, 2.2
fitting   feat, 2.2
fixed   soartit, 7.5
flag   fleg, 1.7
flat   flet, 10.15
flew   flicht, flit, 7.5
flighty   *leesome*, 5.1
flock   hirsel, 10.16
floor   fluir, 1.3, 6.1, 7.8, 7.13; flure, 1.3; flare, 0.4, 1.3
flow   flowe, 7.5
flowed   flawt, flaud, 7.5
flower   flooer, 1.3, 4.3
flown   flaud, flichtit, flitted, flowed, 7.5
flu   flyue, 1.6
flute   flyute, 1.6
fly   flee, 4.3
foe   fae, 1.3, 11.1
fold   *haining*, 10.0
fold   faud, 7.5; fauld, 6.1; foul, 1.5, 7.5
folded   fouldit, fau'ded, 7.5; foulit, 7.4
folk   fowk, 1.1, 1.7, 8.3, 10.15; yins, 8.3
fond   fonn, 3.1
food   mait, 0.0, 1.3, 5.5, 7.11, 9.12; mate, 0.0, 9.1
fool   coof, 11.2
foot   fit, 1.0, 2.0, 2.4, 2.7, 5.1, 5.5
football   fitbaa, 3.1, 5.3
for   fur, 6.2, 6.3, 7.5; tae, 6.3; tha lenth o, 5.6
forbidden   furbid, 10.0
forceful   *feekfu*, 11.2
forehead   broo, 2.0
foretold   foretall, 3.3
fork   graip, 6.1
forked   forket, 7.4
former   *umquhille*, 1.2
fortnight   foartnicht, 3.3
fortunate   sonsie, 11.1
fortune-teller   spae-wife, 10.0
forty   fawrtie, 2.7; fowertie, 2.4
forwards   forrids, 5.3; forrits, 11.2
found   fan, 1.5, 4.3; foon, 1.5, 7.5
four   fivver, 0.4, 1.0, 2.0, 2.7; fower, 0.4, 1.0, 2.0, 2.7, 3.1, 7.6
fourteen   fowertaen, 2.7
fourth   fowertht, 2.7
fox   tod, 5.2
fragments   smithereens, 11.1
freezing   foondert, 10.3; foondèrt, 7.13
friend   *billie*, 11.2; freen, 4.3; frien, 2.2; frien', 5.6
friendly   cheersome, weel in wi, 7.7
friends   *billies*, 5.1, 10.15; freyndis, 7.6
frighten   scaur, 10.0
frightened   frighted, 8.3
frightens   scars, 11.1
from   fae, 1.5, 2.7, 3.1, 4.3, 5.5, 6.1, 7.1, 7.7, 8.3, 8.5; fom, 2.7; fra, 3.2; frae, 0.4, 1.5, 2.2, 2.7, 3.3, 6.1, 7.14, 11.0; on, 6.1; wi, 6.3
front   fore, 11.2
frothy   reamin, 7.5, 10.0; reaming, 4.3
frozen   foundèrt, 8.2
fruit   frute, 11.1
full   fu, 1.5, 5.1, 7.4; fu', 5.4
furnishing   plenishen, 5.4
furthermost   thonder-maist, 11.1
gable   gavel, 1.2

game   gaime, 1.3
garden   gairden, 1.5, 1.6
gather   get thegither, 7.9
gathering   gaitherand, gaithering, 7.11
gave   gied, 1.0, 2.3, 7.5; gien, 2.2, 2.7, 4.2, 4.3, 5.3, 6.0, 6.5, 7.5, 7.8, 8.0, 8.2, 8.5, 10.7, 10.14; gi'en, 7.5; give, 7.5
general   genèral, gentheral, 1.5
get to   win, 11.1
ghosts   ghaists, 4.3
gift   hansel, 11.2
girl   doll, 4.3; hizzie, 4.3, 5.1; lass, 2.2, 2.3, 3.2, 4.3; lassie, 2.2, 2.3; wee doll, wee thing, 4.3
girls   lasses, 5.3
give   gi', 5.3; gie, 2.7, 3.2, 4.3, 5.3, 5.5, 5.8, 6.3, 6.4, 6.5, 7.8, 7.9, 7.12, 8.2, 8.3, 9.4; gies, 7.10
give me   gies, 8.3
given   gien, 7.10, 7.13, 10.13; gi'en, 5.5, 8.4; giffen, 1.2, 3.2; giffin, 0.4
glance   gliff, 11.2
glass   gless, 5.6
gleaming   sklentin, 7.4
glided   glid, 7.5
glow   glowe, 7.5
glowed   glowed, 7.5
glue   glyue, 1.6
go   awa, 5.4, 7.7, 9.8; gae, 7.5, 7.9, 8.0; gaes, 7.6, 7.10; gan, 2.0, 6.3, 6.5, 7.5, 7.10, 8.4, 9.1, 9.6; *gang*, 2.7, 3.1, 3.2, 4.3, 5.0, 5.3, 7.5, 7.6, 9.2, 9.3, 10.0
goat   goát, 1.4
goes   *gangs*, 1.6, 5.4, 10.12
going   *a gangin*, 7.14; gan, 3.1, 5.4, 5.5, 7.1, 7.11, 8.3; *gangin*, 7.1, 10.12; ganin, 7.1; gaun, 7.4
going to   for, 5.3, 5.5, 7.0, 7.1, 7.6, 7.11, 8.3, 9.1; gonnae, 8.5, 9.6
gold   goul, goold, gool, 1.5; gowd, 1.5, 11.2
golden   gowden, 2.2
golf   gowf, 6.1
gone   awa, 6.1, 7.8; gaed, gaen, 7.5; gaun, 2.2; went, 7.5, 7.11
good   brave, 1.2, 5.1, 5.2; braw, 1.2; guid, 1.0, 1.1, 1.3, 2.2, 2.4, 3.1, 4.3, 5.1, 5.2, 5.8, 6.3, 7.11, 8.2, 8.3, 8.4, 9.4, 10.6; gud, 3.2, 7.6; gude, 1.0; quaer, 2.4, 5.2; powerfu, some, 5.2
goose   giss, 1.7
gooseberry   gussgab, 5.1
gorse   whin, 1.3; whun, 1.3, 1.5
gossip   crack, 10.16
got   gat, 2.2, 4.1, 5.1, 5.2, 5.6, 6.2, 7.3, 7.11, 8.3, 9.14, 10.13
grand   gran, 8.5; graun, 7.1
grandmother   grannie, 1.2, 2.3, 4.3; graunie, 4.3
grass   girse, 1.5; graiss, 10.12; gress, 5.1, 7.1, 8.3
grease   creesh, 10.16
great   desperate, 5.2; muckle, 10.15; *unco*, 5.3, 5.4
greedy   graedie, 5.1
green   graen, 5.1
grew   growed, graud, 7.5
grey   greh, 5.1
grind   grynn, grine, 7.5
grip   grup, 7.5
gripped   grupt, 7.5
grissly   greezly, 5.4
ground   grun, 1.5, 7.5; groon, 1.5
grouse   grows, 1.2
groveller   snool, 10.0
grow   growe, 7.5
grown   grew, 3.1, 10.12; growed, 7.5
guide-rope   tow, 3.2

that, 5.3; *'tweel* (I 'tweel = atweel), 8.2
infect   smit, 10.16
infected   smit, 7.5
infectious   smittle, 7.5
influence   inflyuance, 1.6
inherit   fa intae, tak aff, 7.9
inheritance   tocher, 11.1
injury   *skaith*, 2.2
inland   up-kintra, 5.1
innermost   *benmaist*, inmaist, 5.1
inquire   tak it up wi, 7.9
inside   *ben*, 5.3, 5.4, 6.1, 10.13
intelligence   wut, 10.16
interest   intèress, 1.5
into   intae, 2.0, 6.1, 7.11; intil, 6.1, 11.0
investigate   gae in til, 7.9
iron   airn, 11.1
is   are, 7.14; be, 0.4, 7.1; bis, 7.1, 7.7, 8.3; bees, 7.1, 7.10, 8.3; daes be, is, 8.3
island   islann, 1.5
isn't   bisnae, 7.10; isnae, 7.7
it   hit, 4.1, 4.3, 5.1, 5.3, 6.3, 6.5, 7.0, 8.3, 9.8; scho, 5.3
itself   itsel, its lane, 4.2
January   *Jennerwarry*, 3.3
jaws   gowl, 2.0
job   jab, 10.5
joiner   cairpentèr, 6.3
jot   haet, 2.2
jowl   gowl, chollers, 2.0
jowls   chollers, 2.0
joyful   hairt-gled, 11.1
July   Julaai, 3.3
June   Juín, 3.3
just   jist, 1.3, 2.2, 2.7, 4.1, 4.3, 7.1, 7.7, 7.11, 7.12, 7.13, 9.1, 10.5, 10.15; onlie, 10.11
keep   kaep, 9.3
keep quiet   houl yer wheesht, 10.16
kept   keepet, 7.4; keipit, 0.4; kepp, 1.1, 1.5, 1.6
killed   kilt, 1.1, 7.4, 7.5, 9.14
kind   kin, 2.2; kynn, 1.5; kyun, 4.3; soart, 4.3
kindled   kinnl't, 11.1
kingdom   *kängrik*, 11.2
kingdoms   *kinricks*, 11.2
knew   kent, knowed, 5.3
knock   dunt, 10.14, 11.2
knoll   knowe, 1.5
know   ken, 1.5, 3.1, 4.1, 5.1, 5.6, 5.3, 6.4, 8.2, 8.4, 8.5, 10.9; wit, 7.6
know not   kenna, 7.5
known   knowed, 7.14
lack   want, 7.7, 10.16
ladder   lather, 5.4; lether, 6.1
laid-back   aisy-gan, 5.3
land   lann, 1.3, 1.5; laun, 1.1, 1.5, 2.2, 10.5; pit tae shore, 7.9
lane   loanen, 2.3, 2.5, 6.1, 10.2, 10.11; loanie, 2.3; loanin', 5.4; rodden, 5.1
large   muckle, 4.3
largely   gyelie, maistlie, 5.6
lashed   lasht, 5.3
last   hinmaist, hinnèrmaist, 5.1
last night   *yestreen*, 7.3
late (the)   umquhille, *umqu'hile*, 1.2
later   eftèr, latèr, 5.5
laugh   leugh, 1.0
laughed   laucht, 2.2; leugh, 2.2, 5.5
laughing   lauchin, 10.12
laughs   lauchs, 11.1
law   laa, 11.2

lead   laid, 1.3, 2.6; leid, 1.3; leiden, 5.1
leader   heid-yin, 6.3
leaders   heich-heidyins, 11.1
leak   let in, 7.9
leap   lep, 11.2
learn   larn, 2.1
learned   larnit, 7.4
learning   larnin, 3.1; lear, 2.2
lease   leash, 1.5
least   laist, 11.2
leave   lee, 2.5, 5.1, 6.2, 8.0, 8.3, 9.4; leve, 7.6
leaves   laifs, 10.12, 11.1
left-handed   feuggie, 1.6
legs   shanks, 2.0
lend   lenn, 7.5; loan, 7.1, 7.5
lending   loanin, 7.1
length   lenth, 1.5, 2.7, 5.2, 5.5, 10.4; lentht, 2.7, 3.1, 4.3, 5.3, 7.1, 7.13
lengthen   let doon, 7.9
lent   lent, lennit, loant, 7.5
less   no sae, 5.1
lest   less, 1.1, 1.5
let   loot, 1.3; lut, 7.5, 7.9
letter   lettèr, 10.13
levy   lewie, 1.2
liar   le'er, 6.2
lie   lee, 5.1
lies   lees, 2.2
lift   heft, 11.1
light   licht, 1.5, 5.8, 7.5, 8.2, 9.2, 9.4, 10.14
light (in nature)   lightsome, 5.1
lighted   lichtit, lut, 7.5
liking   greenin, 10.15
lit   lut, 7.5
little   awee, 2.2, 10.0; wee, 2.0, 2.2, 5.3, 10.4; wee bit, 7.12
live   bide, 10.11, 11.1; leeve, 6.2; lieve, 0.4
lived   leev'd, 5.1
lives   lees, 2.3
living   leevin, 4.3, 5.3, 7.13
local   locyal, 1.6
loft   laft, 6.0, 6.1
lonely   lonesome, 5.1, 5.3, 7.13
long   lang, 1.3, 2.4, 2.7, 3.1, 3.3, 5.1, 6.3, 6.5, 7.5, 7.7, 7.13, 8.4, 9.2, 10.15
long ago   *lang syne*, langsine, 5.5
longer   lang'r, 5.5
look   leuk, 1.0, 1.3, 1.6; luik, 7.5; luk, 1.3, 3.1, 7.13, 9.3
looked   luk't, 7.13
looker-on   leuker-on, 7.14
loose   loass, slakken, 7.5
loosed   slakkent, 7.5
loosened   lowsit, 11.2
looses   *tynes*, 4.3
Lord   Loard, 11.1
lose   loass, 5.5
lose way   gae wrang, 7.9
lost   loast, 1.1, 6.5, 7.5, 7.11; *tin'd*, 5.5
lot   lock, 2.2, 10.3; some, guid wheen, 2.2
love   grah, 11.1; lo'e, 1.2, 5.3; lowe, 1.2, 5.1, 7.11
lovely   bonnie, 2.2; luvesome, 7.5
low   laich, 5.1; laigh, 1.5, 2.2
lower   laicher, nether, 5.1
lowest   laichest, maist laich, nethermaist, 5.1
loyal   le'al, 11.2
lunge   leenge, 5.3
lying   *liggin*, 11.2
made   gar't, 7.12; gart, 11.2

send senn, 7.5
sent *y-send*, 7.14
separate sinther, 7.7, 10.15
separated seperatit, 10.11
September Sictemmer, 3.3
seriously serious, 5.3
serve serf, 1.2
set on lit on, 7.5
settle redd, 1.6
seven *sen*, seiven, 2.7
seventeen *sentaen*, seiventeen, 2.7; *se'nteen*, 3.3
seventy seiventie, 2.7
several qwathie, 10.15; twa-thie, 10.13
sew shoo, 1.5
shadow schaida, 11.2
shall *sall*, 1.2, 2.7, 7.6; *'se* 2.7; wull, 7.1, 9.1
sharp sherp, shairp, 1.3
she scho, 1.2, 1.7, 2.5, 3.1, 4.1, 4.3, 5.1, 5.3, 6.3, 6.4, 7.0, 7.5, 7.11, 7.13, 8.2, 8.3, 8.5, 9.1; sho, 2.5
shed shade, 2.2
sheep scheep, 10.16
shelter *bield*, 11.1; pit up, 7.9; shilter, 1.7
shilling shillin, schillin, 2.7
ship schip, 2.4; schippe, 1.2
shirt sark, 11.2
shoe shae, 2.4
shoes schune, 1.1, 1.5, 2.4, 5.1, 6.3, 6.4, 8.5, 9.8, 10.1, 10.5, 10.8; shoen, 1.0; shune, 1.5
shook sheuk, 1.6
shoot shuit, 8.0
shop schap, 1.3, 2.6, 4.1, 6.1, 6.2, 7.1, 8.5
short schoart, schairt, 1.5
should bettèr, 9.3; shud, 1.2, 1.3, 8.2, 9.3; shudnae, 8.2; sud, 1.2; suld, 0.4
shoulder shooder, 1.1, 1.5, 2.0; shoodèr, shoodher, 1.5; shooldher, 1.1; shou'der, 2.2; shouldèr, should-hèr, 1.5; shouller, 2.0
shouldn't shudnae, 7.7, 9.3
shout gulder, 7.8, guldèr, 7.11
show schaw, 11.1
shudder grue, 3.2
shy burd mooth't, 10.3; unkit, 5.1
sick seek, tak bad, 8.3
sick with (become) (gae) doon wi, 7.9
sicken scunner, 2.0, 4.3
sided sid, 7.5
sideways sidelin, 4.3; sidelins 5.1, 5.3
sighs souchs, 11.1
sight sicht, 7.5
sighted sichtit, 7.5
sign spae, 11.2
silly daft, 5.1; daftlike, 5.1
since bein, 7.11; fae, 4.3, 5.5, 6.2, 6.5, 7.11, 7.13; frae, 5.5, 6.2, 6.5; sen, 7.14; sin, 5.5, 6.5, 7.3, 7.5
since then *sin syne*, 2.2
sincere *aefauld*, 2.7; *ment*, 5.6
sing lilt, 4.3
singing liltin, 11.2
single ae, yae, 2.7
sip sup, 7.5
sipped supt, 7.5
sister sistèr, 4.3
sited sit, 7.5
six sax, 2.2, 2.7, 3.2, 3.3, 4.3, 6.3, 7.14; säx, 6.2
sixteen saxtaen, 2.7; saxteen, 1.3, 6.2
sixteenth saxtaentht, 2.7
sixty saxtie, 2.7, 3.3
sizeable gye lump, 5.2
skited skit, 7.5

sky lift, 5.1, 5.5, 6.1, 7.5, 11.1
slam dad, 10.0
sleep slaep, 5.3
sleeping slaepin, 1.5
sleepless (in nature) wakrife, wakerife, 5.1
slept slepp, 1.5
slightly *ochtlins, oughtlins*, 5.1
slow drag deedle, 3.1
sly sleekit, 5.1, 11.1
smack dig, 11.1
small wee, 2.2, 5.0, 5.1; sma, 3.3, 5.3; sma', 6.1
smaller wee'r, 5.1
smallest wee'est, 5.1
smart smairt, 1.7
smelly mingin, 5.1
smitten smit, 7.5
smoke reek, 6.5, 8.5
smooth sleekit, 2.3
smote smit, 7.5
snow snaa, 1.3, 6.5, 7.5, 9.15; snaw, 1.3, 2.2, 10.0; snaws, 7.5
snowed snaad, 7.5
so at, 5.6; sa, 0.4, 3.2; sae, 0.4, 2.2, 2.7, 3.2, 3.3, 4.1, 5.5, 5.6, 6.4, 7.3, 7.5, 7.7, 7.8, 7.11, 8.2, 9.8; *syne*, 5.5; that, 5.3, 5.6; thatwye, 5.3
so on (and) an that, 5.3
so-so middlins, 5.3
soaking drookit, 5.6, 6.4
sob sab, 1.3
sold soul, 1.5, 7.5
solitary bare, 2.7
some *antrin*, lock, thing, tha odd, 2.2; wheen, 1.5, 2.2
somehow some-roád(s), some-wey(s), some-gate(s), somehoo, 5.3
someone someboadie, 2.2, 4.3, 6.1, 10.10
something somethin, 2.2
sometimes betimes, 5.5; quhiles, 5.5, 9.4, 10.16; whiles, 7.1, 7.9, 8.3; whyles, 2.7, 5.3, 5.5
somewhat a wee bit, a weethin, 10.16
somewhere someplace, somefer, 5.4
son sinn, 1.3, 2.3, 2.7, 4.3, 11.1; sonnie, 2.3
soon *bedeen*, 5.5; shane, 1.5, 5.5; shuin, 1.1, 1.5, 5.5, 5.6; shune, 1.5
sore sair, 5.1, 6.4, 10.16
sores sairs, 4.3
sort soart, 7.11, 7.13
sorted soartit oot, 9.14
soul sowl, 1.5
sounded soont, 7.4
soup broth, 2.4
sow soo, 6.5
spark gleed, 10.16
spat sput, 7.5
speak spaik, 5.5
speaking spaikin, 7.7
sped *hie'd*, 2.7
speeding whalin, 10.0
spend get throo, 7.9
spilled spilt, 7.5
spinning birlin, 5.1, 7.11
spirit speerit, 11.2
spit speuch, 1.6
spread skail, 1.5
spring spräng, 3.3
stagger staucher, 2.2
stand bide, 6.4; stan, 2.2, 8.2; stann, staun, 1.3; thole, 5.6
standing stannin, 6.1; staunin, 6.0, 7.13; stuid, 7.1
stank stunk, 7.5, 8.3, 8.4

thoughtful thoughtfu, 5.1
thousand thoosan, 2.7, 5.6
thrashing whalin, 4.3
three thie, 1.5, 2.7, 3.2, 7.13; thrie, 2.7
threw cloddit, 6.1; thew, 6.1; throwed, 5.1
thrift had, 2.2
throat craa, gowl, 2.0, thoat, 1.5; thrapple, 2.0
throttle thottle, 2.7
through thoo, 1.5, 2.7, 6.1; *athort*, 5.4, 6.1
throughout *aye an while, aze an quhile*, 5.5
throw clod, 5.4, 11.2; thow, 1.5, 2.7
thud dunt, 10.7
thumb thoom, 2.0
thump dunt, 8.0, 10.7
thunder thunnèr, thunther, 1.5
Thursday Thorsday, 3.3
tidy fait, 5.1
tightly ticht, 10.3
til tae, 6.2, 6.5, 7.10
timid fearsome, 5.1
tip coup, cope, 1.0
tipped coupt, 7.4
tipping coupin, 5.1, 7.11
tired *wabbit*, 10.12
to for tae, 6.0, 7.12; for til, 7.12; on, 6.1; tae, 1.1, 2.1, 3.1, 4.3, 5.1, 5.2, 5.3, 6.1, 6.4, 7.0, 7.6, 7.7, 7.8, 7.10, 7.12, 8.2, 8.4; til, 3.1, 4.1, 4.3, 5.1, 5.2, 5.3, 5.5, 6.1, 6.3, 6.5, 7.5, 7.8, 10.7, 10.13; till, 5.5, 10.0
today theday, 0.4, 2.5, 3.1, 4.1, 4.3, 5.1, 5.2, 5.3, 6.4, 7.1, 7.9, 8.3, 9.1, 9.8, 9.14
together thegither, 3.1, 5.1
told tald, 2.2, 4.3; taud, tau'd, tauld, 7.5; telt, 7.4, 7.5, 8.5; tell't, 4.1, 7.5; toul, 1.5, 5.6, 7.5, 7.14, 8.4, 10.13; tould, 2.5
tolerate can dae wi, 8.5; pit up wi, 7.9; thole, 5.5
tomorrow lemorra, 3.1; themarra, 3.1, 4.1; the moarn, 3.3; themorra, 1.5, 3.1, 3.3, 6.3, 7.1, 7.6, 7.9, 7.10, 7.11, 8.2, 8.3, 9.1, 9.2, 9.3, 9.14, 9.15
tonight thenicht, 2.1, 3.1, 5.3, 5.5, 5.6, 6.0, 7.1, 7.13, 8.2, 8.3, 8.4, 9.5, 9.7, 9.15, 10.8
too an aa, 4.1, 8.5; anaa, 1.4, 4.3; anaw, 1.4; forbye, 7.5; iver, 1.0, 5.6; owre, 0.0, 1.0, 2.2, 3.1, 6.3, 7.10, 9.2, 10.12, 10.15; ow'r, 5.6; tae, 2.2, 3.1, 7.5, 7.6, 7.7
too much owre ocht, 5.6
took taen, 2.3, 5.3, 7.0, 7.3, 7.5, 8.3; ta'en, 7.5; teuk, 1.6; tuk, 1.1, 1.3, 2.2, 3.1, 6.1, 6.4, 7.0, 7.5, 8.3, 10.14
top tap, 3.1
tough teuch, 1.5, 1.6; t'ugh, 1.0, 1.6
towards in bae, 5.4
town toon, 1.3, 2.0, 4.3, 5.3, 6.1, 7.1, 7.5, 7.8, 7.9, 7.10, 7.11, 8.3, 8.4, 10.14; toun, 2.4, 6.1, 7.5; toune, 1.2
tractor tràictèr, 4.3
traditional *hameart*, 5.1
translation *owresettin*, 5.1
tree trèe, 1.5, 2.4, 5.3, 7.14, 10.6, 10.10
trees *treen*, 2.4
trip trup, 7.5
tripped trupt, 7.5
trouble *threap*, 11.1
trousers breeks, 10.3
true trew, 1.2
trust lippen, 10.15
trusts lippens, 11.1
turn tùrn, 5.6
twelfth twalth, twalt, 2.7
twelve qwal, 1.5, 2.7; tuell, 1.2; twal, 2.7, 3.3, 6.3
twentieth twonnietht, 2.7
twenty qwonnie, 1.5, 2.7; twonnie, 2.7, 4.3, 7.13

twerp nyaff, 1.6
twice twyst, 2.7, 3.1
twist quust, 1.5; twust, 1.3, 1.7
twister quuster, 1.5
two qwa, 1.5, 2.7; tua, 1.2; twa, 1.4, 2.2, 2.5, 2.7, 3.2, 4.3, 5.1, 5.3, 5.6, 6.1, 6.3, 7.3, 7.6, 7.13, 8.3, 8.4
udder elder, 2.6
under *aneath*, 6.1; unnèr, 1.5, 6.0, 6.1; unther, 1.5
underneath unnèr, *aneath, ablow*, alow, 6.1
understand unnèrstaun, 5.6, 7.6; wat, 10.0; wot, 7.12
undoubtedly *forouten ween*, 5.4, 10.16; nae doot, nae mistak bot, 10.16
unfairly ill, 7.5
unfamiliar *unco*, 5.3
united unit, pit thegither, 7.5
uniting sowtherin, 11.2
unless less, 7.10
unrecognised misken, 10.15
untidy thooithèr, 5.1; thouithèr, 1.5; throughither, 5.1; throughother, 1.5; throuither, 5.3
until *aye an while*, 6.2, 10.16; tae, 6.2, 10.16; untae, 6.2
up ip, 1.7
uppermost bunermaist, 5.1
upset yourself cruddle yer sook, 10.16
us iz, 0.4, 1.1, 1.7, 6.3, 6.5, 7.1, 7.7, 8.3, 8.5
use uise, 7.7; yuise, 1.6
used not to yuisnae, 9.12
used to uise, uist tae, use, 9.12; usenae, use tae, 8.2; yuise tae, yuist tae, 9.12
useless thraveless, 5.1; uiseless, 5.1
very brave, 5.6; brave an, 5.2; dead, 5.2, 5.3; desperate, 5.2; desperit, 5.3, 7.13; guid an, 5.2; gye, 3.1, 5.2, 5.3, 5.6, 7.3, 7.13, 8.5, 9.4, 9.14, 10.5, 10.12; gye an, 5.2; powerfu, 5.1, 5.2, 5.3, 7.11; quaer, 5.6, 7.9; quaer an, 5.2; rail, 5.2; real, 5.6; terrible, 5.2; unco, 0.4, 5.1, 5.3, 5.6, 7.5; vera, 5.3, 5.6; verie, 1.2, 3.2, 5.3, 5.6, 10.6, 10.12; wile, 5.3; wile guid, 5.2
the very best owre ocht, 10.16
vessel veshel, 1.2; vesshel, 1.5
village clachan, 10.0
visit caylie, caylzie, 1.6, 7.7
void wozd, 1.2
wait houl on, 3.3
wakeful wakerife, 5.1
walk dander, 1.1; dandèr, 1.5; dandhèr, 1.5; danner, 3.2, 10.14; dannèr, 1.1, 1.5, 2.0, 6.1, 7.8; waak, 1.1, 7.7, 7.8, 8.0, 8.4, 10.14
walked waakit, 6.1, 7.4; walk't, walkit, waakt, 7.4
walking waakin, 1.5, 7.11
wall wa, 6.1
wander wannèr, wanthur, 1.5
wandering wan'ring, 2.7
wanting lukin, 7.1, 7.11
wants is lukin, 6.4
warm wairm, 0.0, 6.4; werm, 7.14
warned warnisht, 11.2
was wus, wes, 1.3; wuz, 1.3, 1.7
wash wasch, 8.5
wasn't wuznae, 6.4
water watèr, 1.1, 1.5; wathèr, 1.5; watter, 1.5, 2.2; wattèr, 2.0, 7.7; watthei, 1.5
way gate, 10.0; roád, 5.3, 7.1; wye, 2.7, 5.3, 8.5
ways gates, 5.1, 5.6
we we, 4.1
weak waik, 5.3
wearisome dreekh, 1.5; langsome, 5.1
weather waithèr, 5.3
weaver *wabster*, 4.3

Wednesday Waddnisday, Wensday, 3.3

week *owk*, 2.7, 3.2, 3.3; *sennicht*, 2.7, 3.3, 5.1; waek, 10.13

weight wecht, 4.3, 9.1

welcome *culzie*, 1.6; *fair fa ye*, 10.16

well weel, 2.7, 5.3, 5.4, 5.5, 5.8, 6.4, 7.10, 8.2

well-off bien, 7.11

went gaed, 4.3, 7.5, 8.2; gae'd, 7.5

were wur, 1.1, 1.3, 6.3; vas, 7.6

weren't wurnae, 7.9

west wast, 1.3

western wastren, 1.5

what quhat, 1.2, 7.5, 7.6; quhit, 2.0, 2.7, 3.3, 4.1, 4.3, 5.1, 5.3, 6.4, 7.1, 7.6, 7.9, 7.11, 7.13, 8.5, 9.1; tha, 5.3

whatever quhatever, 0.4, 1.2, 7.10

wheaten whaiten, 5.1

when quhan, 1.1, 1.2, 1.3, 1.5, 3.1, 4.3, 5.5, 6.5, 7.7, 7.9, 8.3, 8.5, 9.15; quhaniver, 5.5, 6.5, 7.1, 7.3, 7.13, 8.3, 8.5, 9.14, 10.12; quhit-time, 5.5; whan, 1.3, 2.3, 5.5, 7.5; whun, 1.3, 6.1; wi, 6.5

whenever quhaniver, quhan, iverytim, 5.5

where quhar, 1.2, 1.5, 4.3, 5.4, 7.13; quhair, 1.2, 5.4; quhaur, 1.1; quhit-place, 5.4; whar, 3.3, 4.3, 5.4; whare, 0.4, 5.1, 8.2; whaur, 1.3, 2.3; whur, 1.3, 5.4

whereas quharas, 1.2

whereby quhorbz, 1.2

wherefore quhairfoir, 1.2

wherein quhairin, 1.2, 3.2, 7.6

whereof quhairof, 1.2, 3.2

whereto quhairto, 1.2

whether whar, 2.7

while as, 5.5; quhan, 5.5, 6.5; quhaniver, 6.5

whilst quhaniver, as, 5.5

whin whun, 1.3

whinge nyirm, 1.6

whisper myowt, 1.6

whistle whussle, 2.6; whustle, 10.2

white quhyt, 1.2

who as, 4.3; at, 4.3, 9.1; quha, 1.1, 1.2, 1.5, 1.7, 4.1, 4.3; that, 4.3; wha, 0.4, 1.2, 2.2, 1.3, 4.1, 4.3, 6.5, 7.5, 7.11

whoever quhasomiver, 8.5, 11.2

whole hale, 1.6, 2.2, 4.3, 5.1, 5.5, 6.1, 8.4

wholesome halsome, 5.3

whom wham, 0.4

whore hoor, 1.5

whose quhais, 1.2; quhas, 4.3

why for why, hoo, hoo-cum, hoo wuz it, 5.6; quhit-for, 4.1, 5.6; quhit-wye, 5.6

wicked wickit, 11.1

wife *goodwife*, 7.5; *guidwife*, 4.3, 10.0; wifie, 2.3

wild wile, 5.2

wildly wild-like, 5.3

wilful wilsome, 5.1

will wull, 7.1, 9.1

willow sally, 8.4

wind wine, 7.5; wunns, 7.13; wynn, 7.5, 7.9

window windae, 5.1; wundee, 6.1

winter wunter, wuntèr, 1.5; wuntèrtim, 3.3

wipe dicht, 4.3, 7.5

wipe out dae awa wi, 8.5

wiped dichtit, 7.5; dighted, 5.5

wise wyse, 3.2

witch wutch, 1.3

with on for, tae, 6.3; wae, 2.2; wi, 0.4, 1.0, 2.2, 3.2, 4.3, 5.1, 5.3, 6.3, 7.1, 7.5, 7.7, 7.13

wither wizen, 11.1

without athoot, 7.7; *forouten*, 5.4; *withouten*, 2.2, 5.4

witness wutness, 1.4

woe wae, 2.2

woman wuman, 8.4; wumman, 10.13

women weemin, 4.3, 5.5; weeminfowk, wifies, 4.3

won't winnae, 5.5, 9.1

wonder wunner, 1.5; wunnèr, 1.5, 6.4

wood plantin, 6.1

wooden wud, wudden, 5.1

word wurd, 7.7, 8.2

work darg, 2.0, 6.0, 8.5; wark, 2.0, 6.5, 7.1, 7.10, 8.5

worked wrocht, 2.0, 6.2, 6.3, 6.5, 7.11; wroght, 5.3; wrought, 7.5

workers warkers, 8.3

working warkin, 5.1

works labours, 10.1; warks, 5.3

world warl, 7.5, 10.16

worldly warldly, 3.2, 5.3

worry fash, 2.0

worse waur, 5.1

worship warschip, 11.2

worst warser, warss, 5.1; warst, 3.2, 5.1; waur, 5.1

worthless *scabbit*, 10.16

worthy wordie, 5.3

would wud, 1.1, 1.3, 5.1, 7.8, 8.2, 9.2; wudnae, 8.2

wouldn't wudnae, 5.8, 6.4, 7.8, 9.2

wound hurt, 5.1; wun, 7.5

wrapped hapt, 10.15

wrapping lappin, 2.6

wrinkled rucklie, 5.1; rucklet, 5.1

wrinkles weeks, 2.0

written writ, 7.5; *screivit*, 11.2

wrong wrang, 0.4, 1.7, 4.3, 5.1, 5.3, 7.5

wrote writ, 7.5; *screivit*, 11.2

year *twalmond*, *towmonn*, twal month, 3.3; yeir, 1.6, 2.5, 3.3, 4.3, 5.1, 6.0, 6.2, 7.3, 7.13, 8.3, 10.13; zeir, 1.2, 1.6

yellow yella, 5.1

yellower yella'er, 5.1

yes ay, 1.7, 7.5, 7.11, 7.13

yesterday yesterae, 7.5, 7.13; yesterie, 9.5; yestrae, 3.3, 7.7, 8.5; *yestreen*, 2.2, 3.3, 5.5, 7.5, 7.13, 10.7, 10.8; yistèrday, 3.3

yet bot, still, 6.4; yit, 3.1, 5.2, 6.4, 7.8, 7.13, 9.14

yolk yock, 3.2

you ye, 1.2, 1.6, 4.1, 9.7; yis, 8.3, 8.4, 9.14; yous, 8.3; youse, 8.3; ze, 1.2, 1.6, 7.14; zou, 1.2; zow, 1.2

you (pl.) yiz, 4.1, 5.3, 5.5, 6.0, 7.1; yous, 4.1, 7.3, 7.6; yous'uns, 4.1, 7.6

youngster wean, 5.3

your yer, 1.1, 1.6, 4.1, 5.1, 6.0, 6.1, 7.5, 7.12, 8.4, 9.3; zour, 1.2

yours *yourn*, 11.2

yourself yer lane, 4.2; yersel, 4.1, 4.2, 5.4, 7.11, 8.4

yourselves yersels, 4.1

youth carle, 2.2; loon, 5.4; *spunkie*, 2.2

zero nocht, nane, ought, 2.7

zoo azoo, 3.2